World War I M

An Annotated Bibliography of Personal Accounts Published in English Since 1919

Edward G. Lengel

Consulting Editor
Martin Gordon

The Scarecrow Press, Inc.
Lanham, Maryland • Toronto • Oxford
2004

SCARECROW PRESS, INC.

Published in the United States of America
by Scarecrow Press, Inc.
A wholly owned subsidiary of
The Rowman & Littlefield Publishing Group, Inc.
4501 Forbes Boulevard, Suite 200, Lanham, Maryland 20706
www.scarecrowpress.com

PO Box 317
Oxford
OX2 9RU, UK

British Library Cataloguing in Publication Information Available

Library of Congress Cataloging-in-Publication Data

Lengel, Edward G.
World War I memories : an annotated bibliography of personal accounts published in English since 1919 / Edward G. Lengel.
p. cm.
Includes bibliographical references and index.
ISBN 0-8108-5008-7 (pbk. : alk. paper)
1. World War, 1914-1918—Personal narratives—Bibliography. 2. English imprints—Bibliography. 3. World War, 1914-1918—Bibliography. I. Title: World
War One memories. II. Title.
Z6207.E8L54 2001
[[D640.A2]]
016.9404'81—dc22

2004003334

™ The paper used in this publication meets the minimum requirements of American National Standard for Information Sciences—Permanence of Paper for Printed Library Materials, ANSI/NISO Z39.48-1992.
Manufactured in the United States of America.

Contents

Preface

This bibliography lists personal accounts of the First World War published in English since 1919. The definition seems simple enough, but what is a personal account? How do I define the First World War? Does it include the Russian intervention or the Central Asian campaign? What does "published" mean? Books? Articles? Desktop publications? One-of-a-kind typescripts? And why have I not included works published between 1914 and 1918? Clearly, some specific guidelines and explanations are in order.

I use the word "personal" to refer to any firsthand description or reminiscence of an author's experience in the First World War. The definition encompasses accounts by men, women, soldiers, and civilians—those who went into the trenches and those who did not—"poor bloody infantry," airmen, sailors, gunners, cavalrymen, clerks, tankers, ambulance drivers, nurses, war correspondents, generals, privates, and others who, one way or another, found their lives changed by the war. I include autobiographies, memoirs, diaries, and letters; but not political memoirs, literary essays, or accounts by civilians who were not seriously affected by the war. I have also omitted anthologies (collected accounts of more than two or three authors), unit histories, works of fiction, biographies, autobiographies that mention the war only in passing, and some religious, spiritualist, and political tracts.

"Published" refers to any printed book or pamphlet that a researcher can find on the used book market or in a major state or international library. I have included many obscure publications, including some held only by the British Library or the Library of Congress; but some extremely rare works—generally original typescripts—available only in one or two private collections or regional libraries have been left out. For reasons of space, I have also omitted accounts published in journal and magazine articles.

This bibliography includes accounts from all the belligerent nations, but only those published in English. Many are translations of works originally published in another language. I have omitted all of the thousands of "personal accounts" published in any country from 1914 to 1918. There are two reasons for this. First, other works, most notably Loleta Irene Dawson's *European War Fiction in English, and Personal Narratives* (1921), have already covered wartime publications reasonably well. Second, the influence of propaganda and censorship makes works published during wartime suspect as sources of evidence for the genuine war experience—if there is such a thing.

The First World War was by definition a global conflict, fought in the trenches of the Western Front, in the foggy Carpathian Mountains, on or under any of the Seven Seas, in Palestine, Mesopotamia, China, Africa, Central Asia, Russia, and just about everywhere else. In some cases, military campaigns spawned by the First World War continued well after Versailles; most notably in territories now encompassed by the former Soviet Union. I have tried to include as many works relating to these campaigns as possible. Thus, this bibliography contains several personal accounts of the Allied intervention in Russia, and of the adventures of the so-called "Dunsterforce" in the Caucasus, even though they occurred in 1919 or 1920. I have omitted, however, any accounts of the Russian Revolution and Civil War.

Each entry begins with publication information, specifying when and where a book was first published (subsequent editions are generally not mentioned unless they contain significant additional material or come under revised titles), its length, and whether it is illustrated. Where possible, the entry continues with a brief summary of the work's contents, whether it consists of reminiscences, diary entries, or letters, the period covered, and the author's war record. Sometimes an entry contains no information on a book's content, for the simple reason that I was unable to find and examine a copy. I have added editorial remarks to some entries, with my own opinion of a book's worth to the collector, enthusiast, or scholar. Of course, not everyone will agree with my standards. I urge interested readers to conduct their own research and form their own conclusions.

Nor will everyone agree with my guidelines for inclusion and omission. Alas, the literature of the First World War is so vast that a more comprehensive bibliography of personal accounts would run at least two volumes and still be incomplete. Keeping this work to a reasonable size has forced me to exclude some truly valuable books. Inevitably, I have also overlooked some works that fall within my guidelines. For these deliberate and inadvertent omissions I apologize—especially to any veterans whose stories might thereby not receive their due share of attention.

Acknowledgments

The debts I have incurred in the preparation of this bibliography have been extensive. Thanks are due first of all to Garth McGowen and John Linneman. Garth has read and reviewed dozens of books in his personal collection and in the library of Cambridge University, providing invaluable information that I would have been unable to acquire on my own. John, with the best collection of World War I personal accounts that I have encountered, has likewise read and reviewed dozens of books. Both gentlemen have carefully checked my bibliography against their own lists, pointed out many of my blunders, and alerted me to books that I would never have considered otherwise. My deepest gratitude to both.

I also could never have completed this bibliography without the generous assistance of the U.S. Army Military History Institute in Carlisle, Pa., which awarded me a General and Mrs. Matthew B. Ridgway Military History Research Grant in the spring of 2003. The Military History Institute holds one of the best public collections of World War I material—published and unpublished—in the world, and its staff displays commensurate professionalism. Specifically, I would like to thank Lieutenant Colonel Thomas L. Hendrix.

Among the many others who have helped me over the past year I must mention Matt Anger, Paul Cora and everyone at the Western Front Association, Tim Read, Chris Baker, Kristen Alexander, John Barry, Gary Mitchell, Sharon Carmack, Andrew Tatham, Tony Glockler, Guy Smith, Royce Morrison, Michele Fry, Neal Sager, Brent Castleberry, and Michael Duffy. I would also like to thank Sue Easun, Karen Gray, and Niki Averill at Scarecrow Press for their prompt, professional, and invaluable assistance in the preparation of this book. Any errors are of course my own.

Last but not least, I thank my wife, Laima, and my children, Mykolas, Laura, and Tomas, for their encouragement and inspiration.

List of Abbreviations

A.D.C.	Aide de Camp
A.D.M.S.	Assistant Director of Medical Services
A.E.F.	American Expeditionary Force
A.F.C.	Australian Flying Corps
A.F.S.	American Field Service
A.I.F.	Australian Imperial Force
ANZAC	Australia and New Zealand Army Corps
A.S.C. (R.A.S.C.)	Army Service Corps
B.E.F.	British Expeditionary Force
C.A.C.	Coast Artillery Corps
C.E.F.	Canadian Expeditionary Force
C.F.A.	Canadian Field Artillery
D.C.M.	Distinguished Conduct Medal
D.S.C.	Distinguished Service Cross
D.S.O.	Distinguished Service Order
ERA	Engine Room Artificer

G.H.Q.	General Headquarters
L.H.F.A.	Light Horse Field Ambulance
M.C.	Military Cross
M.P.	Military Police
M.T.	Motor Transport
N.C.O.	Non-commissioned Officer
N.S.W.	New South Wales
POW	Prisoner of War
R.A.F.	Royal Air Force
R.A.M.C.	Royal Army Medical Corps
R.F.A.	Royal Field Artillery
R.F.C.	Royal Flying Corps
R.N.A.S.	Royal naval Air Service
S.S.U.	Section Sanitaire [Etats-]Unis
U.S.A.A.S.	Unites States Army Ambulance Service
V.A.D.	Voluntary Aid Detachment
V.C.	Victoria Cross
Y.M.C.A.	Young Men's Christian Association

Introduction

The history of personal accounts of the First World War begins with the first diary entry or letter that a soldier penned on his first day of training camp, or after his first moments at the front. Only recently have historians come to fathom the sheer volume of letters and diaries still remaining from that period, most of which never made their way into print. If unpublished accounts of the war have yet to be studied in their full extent, however, so too have published accounts fallen by the wayside.

This fact is somewhat strange. In the United States, not many people aside from a few book collectors have read more than one or two personal accounts. American academics sometimes limit their research to a few well-known works by English poets, and then generalize from them about the "experience" of war. In the United Kingdom, historians like John Keegan, Richard Holmes, Denis Winter, Peter Liddle, and Lynn McDonald have written wonderful books about the personal experience of war. Peter Liddle has established an archive of manuscript diaries and letters at the University of Leeds that has no parallel in the United States. Even British historians, however, tend to rely on well-known authors like Robert Graves and Siegfried Sassoon, and to generalize from their experiences to those of the millions of other soldiers who lived and died in the trenches.

As for the rest of us, we read *All Quiet on the Western Front*, or maybe the fictionalized *Good-bye to All That*, and think we have a pretty good idea of what the soldier's life was like. It seems like a straightforward story of idealism and disillusionment. Young idealists went to war in 1914 or 1917 to fight for king and country, slogged away for years in the mud and blood of the trenches, and—if they survived—returned home bitter and disgusted with patriotism, profiteering, and propaganda. The same story is told again and again in television documentaries, and in popular and academic histories.

Witnesses who contradict this story are generally derided or ignored. In 1930 Douglas Jerrold, a veteran of the Royal Naval Division who was severely wounded on the Somme, published a book that condemned disillusionment as "The Lie About the War," which claimed that he and his fellow veterans were misrepresented in the popular press. His book was ignored, and the one or two modern writers who mention him dismiss Jerrold as a jingoistic fascist.

Charles Carrington, a veteran of the Royal Warwicks who saw years of heavy fighting on the Western Front and won the Military Cross, published a memoir titled *A Subaltern's War* in 1929, and another, *Soldier from the Wars Returning*, in 1965. Carrington slammed *All Quiet on the Western Front* as sensational fiction, and angrily criticized its publishers as shameless publicity-seekers. He claimed that although the war was terrible, it was fought in a good cause; and that although war destroyed the spirit of some soldiers it uplifted others to heights they would otherwise have been unable to reach. But did anybody listen to these veterans? Despite their literary quality and authenticity almost no one reads the works of Carrington or Jerrold today.

Yet they were no cranks. Carrington and Jerrold each saw more fighting than Remarque, who spent no more than two months in or near the trenches. Their attitude toward the war is no less typical, and no less genuine, than that of the disillusioned writers. Most veterans of the English-speaking countries seem to have viewed the war with ambiguity; as, to grossly simplify, a horrible experience that was unavoidable or even necessary. They mourned their friends lost, but remembered with fondness the comradeship of the trenches. They remembered the filth, mud, boredom, lice, and shells; but they also remembered leave in Paris, letters from home, and even moments of hilarity in and out of the trenches. Some, but by no means all, loathed the brass hats of the staff; but they also remembered officers they deeply respected. Some soldiers lost religion, some gained it. They almost never hated the enemy, but few indeed were those who did not continue to believe that their cause had been just.

The most surprising thing about veterans' experiences of the war is their variety. Just as World War I was fought by many means on many fronts, each personality in uniform perceived the war differently. We should generalize only with caution. The disillusion of Siegfried Sassoon and Erich Maria Remarque is genuine and worthy of attention and respect; but so is the ambiguity of Edmund Blunden and Hervey Allen, and (for lack of a better word) the patriotism of Ernst Junger and Charles Carrington.

Almost no veterans of the First World War are alive today. Those of us who remember them continue to memorialize them in meetings or in ceremonies like the Last Post that is still called every evening at the Menin Gate in Belgium. But we can do more. In attics, in archives, in used book stores, and in libraries, are stored the experiences of thousands of soldiers, nurses, and civilians who lived through the terrible years from 1914 to 1918. The majority of them have been read rarely if at all in the past 50 years. What better act of remembrance could we make than to open a few of these books and read the experiences recorded therein?

Cyril Falls—himself a veteran of World War I—made the first significant attempt to catalog these books in 1930, when he published *War Books*. This book, containing a selective bibliography of memoirs published before 1930, and Falls's own biased and brilliant commentary, is still a standard in the field of World War I studies. Since it was first published, however, no attempt has been made to catalog a significant portion of personal accounts of the war. This book is an attempt—admittedly an incomplete one—to fill the gap, bringing Falls up to date by incorporating the hundreds of works published in English through the beginning of the twenty-first century.

Personal accounts are a mixture of diaries, letters, and memoirs. When well-written, diaries are often the most useful of the three types; but frequently they are sketchy and incomplete. Letters are in my opinion the least useful to scholars, because although they have a certain spontaneity, they can also be quite artificial—partly no doubt because they were heavily censored and written with an eye to cheering the folks at home. Memoirs are the most readable as works of literature, and often the most affecting emotionally; but rare indeed is the memoir that is not at least partly fictionalized.

American personal accounts of World War I have often been overshadowed by books written by European participants. They also attract little interest compared to American accounts of the Civil War or World War II. The importance of what Europeans call the Great War tends to be underestimated in this country, partly because of the brevity of American participation. The war did not have the same wrenching effect on the national psyche, perhaps, as the Civil War or Vietnam. Yet those American soldiers who experienced frontline combat were profoundly affected by what they saw. Their memoirs, diaries, and letters, which exist in greater quantity and quality than most people realize, and which were more likely to have been written by enlisted men than were European accounts, are well worth reading.

Many of them were published in the 1920s and 1930s, often by obscure local publishers, and are hard to find today. Reprints are rare as well. Other memoirs appeared in the 1960s during the 50-year anniversary of the war, as many aging veterans sought to record their memories before they passed away. In the last ten years, thanks particularly to the efforts of publishers like White Mane and Presidio, some very interesting memoirs have appeared.

Among the first wave of American war memoirs in the 1920s is one of the finest ever written in any country: Hervey Allen's *Toward the Flame: A War Diary*, first published in 1926, then in a revised edition in 1934. Since then it has been reprinted only once, in 1968 by the University of Pittsburgh Press. It desperately needs a new publisher. Allen, later a popular novelist and author of the bestselling *Anthony Adverse*, was a lieutenant in the 111th Infantry Regiment of the 28th Division, Pennsylvania National Guard. *Toward the Flame* covers a six-week period in July and August 1918 when his regiment fought in the Aisne-Marne battles near Château-Thierry. Allen was a conscientious young officer who cared deeply for his men and was exceptionally observant. His tone is realistic if slightly cynical throughout the book, which culminates in the final three chapters with the fighting for the doomed American bridgehead at Fismette. Without question this is one of the most powerful descriptions of combat ever written, and the final lines stayed with me for months after I first read them.

Other excellent American personal accounts published in the twenty years after the war include Norman Archibald's *Heaven High, Hell Deep*, an aviation memoir published in 1935; and Thomas Barber's *Along the Road*, a minor classic by a captain of pioneer troops of the 79th Division published in 1924. John Lewis Barkley, a Missourian in the 3rd Division who won the Congressional Medal of Honor, published his memoir *No Hard Feelings*! in 1930, another classic that has never been reprinted. Alden Brooks's *As I Saw It* (1930) is a fascinating book by an American serving with French heavy artillery; Albert Bartley's hard to find *Tales of the World War* (1935) and Chris Emmett's *Give 'Way to the Right* (1934) are two wonderful memoirs by Texans with the 90th Division; Harvey Cushing's *From a Surgeon's Journal* (1936) is an important medical memoir; and Kermit Roosevelt's *War in the Garden of Eden* (1919) is a fascinating book by the famous president's son who served in Rolls-Royce armored cars in Mesopotamia.

Among the more recently published books are some duds and some gems. Standing out among the gems is Elton Mackin's *Suddenly We*

Didn't Want to Die, published by Presidio Press in 1993. This is an extremely powerful and moving book by a private in the 5th Marines who served in the suicidal position of battalion runner but somehow survived.

In his recent book *Optimism at Armageddon: Voices of American Participants in the First World War*, historian Mark Meigs notes that most American soldiers never reached the state of war weariness that gripped many European soldiers. There are few American memoirs that depict real disillusionment, and many that reflect an enduringly strong patriotism. What would have happened to the American outlook if the war had lasted another one or two years is of course speculation. Perhaps the Americans would have developed much like the Australians, who in late 1918 were still the best troops in the British arsenal despite four years of war.

The Yanks and the Aussies took an immediate liking to each other at the front, fueled in part by their inveterate optimism, indiscipline, and contempt for the English. Many American soldiers remembered disliking and getting into fights with the Tommies, although this was mixed with a certain amount of respect. There is no question, however, that the Americans preferred to think of themselves as the saviors of France rather than the allies of the English. English soldiers, for their part, were happy to see Doughboys at the front but viewed the "can-do" optimism of the Yanks with a mixture of resentment and pity; a few months at the front, they believed, would convince the Americans that whipping the Hun would be no cup of tea.

Australian bitterness against the British army dated back to what they endured at Gallipoli, and persisted in France. Anzacs who witnessed the inertia of British troops at Suvla while Australians were massacred at Lone Pine nursed resentment for years to come. Sergeant Cyril Lawrence, an Australian who was there, decided after Suvla that the Tommies were little better than sheep, and it took two years in France before he would admit that they could be good soldiers in certain circumstances. For others the contempt was more easy-going. Some of the most amusing lines in these memoirs recount how Anzacs and Doughboys teamed up while on leave in Paris or other French cities to enrage British officers and the military police, while running riot with mademoiselles.

Aside from these similarities, Yanks and Aussies shared a reputation for taking no prisoners. If the diaries and memoirs of American and Australian soldiers are any indication, the reputation was justified. In most cases it was the killing of surrendering German snipers or machine-gunners in the heat of battle; an understandable reaction by soldiers who may have seen several of their comrades killed by these same Germans. Several Doughboys and Aussies whose memoirs I have read, however, remembered seeing individuals or small groups of German prisoners being shot on impulse by their captors behind the front. I do not want to over-generalize about this, and of course in any case it was the work of a small minority in both armies. Doughboys who recorded these incidents tended to treat these incidents as unavoidable, or perhaps even as beneficial in generating a reputation for American ruthlessness that would weaken German morale and thus hasten the end of the war. One American soldier wrote that the British and French had been wrong to fight by the rules given the magnitude of German atrocities, and that the best way to end the war was to give the Germans a dose of their own medicine. German memoirs speak with respect of the "gentlemanly" British code of warfare; but apparently they feared encounters with Australians or Americans in hand-to-hand combat.

A less than attractive strand running through many American accounts is racism. Again, memoirs, letters, and diaries testify to the pervasiveness of this in the American army. It is perhaps more evident in accounts by southern soldiers, such as Texan Chris Emmett's *Give 'Way to the Right*; but white men and women, northern and southern, all seem to have assumed that African Americans were inveterate cowards. I have yet to read a single account by a white American in favor of black soldiers. Memoirs by African American soldiers are rare, and those that exist have not been reprinted; but they too attest to the universality of a racism that dwelt on the failures of the 92nd Division but ignored the successes of the highly decorated 93rd Division, both African American formations.

There are few outstanding personal accounts by American women. It is here, strangely enough, that the brevity of American participation is most strongly reflected in the outlook of the authors. While the writings of British women who were nurses or ambulance drivers show thoughtfulness and understanding of the nature of the war, American women seem simply to have experienced too little of it to get beyond the naive jingoism that commonly characterizes their accounts. Every soldier is cheerful and plucky, every French civilian reflects the bleeding heart of France, every Hun is a barbaric baby killer. Even American nurses, heroic as they were for the time they served, rarely questioned the view of war that had been fed to them by popular propaganda; had they worked through the Somme or Verdun, perhaps they would have begun to think much like their English counterparts.

Many people have read Vera Brittain's pacifist classic *Testament of Youth*, one of the most moving books written about the war. Other accounts by British women that I would recommend are Elsie Corbett's *Red Cross in Serbia* (1964), Florence Farmborough's *Nurse at the Russian Front* (1974), Shirley Millard's *I Saw Them Die* (1936), and Olive King's *One Woman at War*, the letters of an Australian nurse and ambulance driver published in 1986.

Australians and New Zealanders wrote memoirs of extremely high quality, and out of all proportion to their numbers. On the whole, though my two favorite memoirs were written by an Irishman and an Englishman, I prefer the Anzacs to all others. They possess a combination of verve and thoughtfulness absent elsewhere, and depict warfare in an exotic range of locales, from the gullies of Gallipoli to the sands of Sinai to the mud of Flanders. I can also never help being charmed by the legendary Anzac humor and indiscipline.

Possibly the best Australian memoir is *The Desert Column*, published by the novelist and adventurer Ion Idriess in 1932. I cannot recommend this book enough. A fanatical diarist with incredible powers of observation, Idriess was a private in the Light Horse who spent several months at Gallipoli where he participated in hand-to-hand fighting. After the evacuation, to his disgust he then found himself fighting the Turks again, this time in the Sinai and Palestine, where he was severely wounded during the march on Jerusalem in December 1917. A useful sequel that takes the war in Palestine from December 1917 to the end of 1918 is Donald Black's *Red Dust: An Australian Trooper in Palestine*, published in 1931. Black, an introspective man who came to hate the war bitterly, was a cavalry trooper who also saw heavy combat.

C.E.W. Bean, the Australian war correspondent who wrote much of that country's official history of the war, was an interesting man whose sympathy with the common soldiers was legendary. *Gallipoli Correspondent: The Frontline Diary of C.E.W. Bean* is highly recommended. I also recommend two books by Sergeant Cyril Lawrence, *The Gallipoli Diary of Sergeant Lawrence* (1981), and *Sergeant Lawrence Goes to France* (1987), easier to find in this country than other Australian memoirs and well worth reading. Lawrence's contempt for the British and admiration for Americans is striking. A very good New Zealand memoir is Alexander Aitken's *Gallipoli to the Somme: Recollections of a New Zealand Infantryman* (1963), which contains priceless and realistic memories of combat on the Somme.

Among Canadian memoirs, the best is Will Bird's *Ghosts Have Warm Hands*, published in 1997. Bird was a private in the Canadian Black Watch and served in every major battle after 1916 except Vimy Ridge; an English friend tells me that "the manner of his story telling is incredible and left me dumb-founded." I also recommend *Letters of Agar Adamson, 1914 to 1919, Lieutenant Colonel, Princess Patricia's Canadian Light Infantry* (1997), Donald Fraser's *The Journal of Private Fraser, Canadian Expeditionary Force* (1998), and James Pedley's *Only This: A War Retrospect, 1917–1918*, published in 1927 and reprinted a few years ago.

My favorite British war memoir, is John Lucy's *There's a Devil in the Drum*. The original edition of 1938 is now quite rare, and the 1992 reprint by Naval and Military Press is almost as hard to find. Lucy was a poor Dublin boy who joined the regular army, the Royal Irish Rifles, along with his brother, a few months before the war began. The memoir vividly recounts his experiences at the front from the first days in August 1914 until the end of that year, a fascinating period that saw the eventual destruction of the old regular army. Lucy's writing is witty and understated, but often intensely moving, particularly in the description of his brother's death. It is a must read.

Another indispensable book that is equally rare in the original and reprint editions is F.C. Hitchcock's *Stand To! A Diary of the Trenches, 1915–18*, first published in 1937. Hitchcock was a subaltern with the 2nd Battalion of the Leinster Regiment, fighting in Flanders and in the later stages of the Battle of the Somme. This is one of the most complete and interesting war diaries ever published, with a wealth of detail and excellent contemporary maps and drawings. It is an essential source for study of the day-to-day routine and technical aspects of trench warfare.

Much easier to find, and among the top two or three of my favorites, is Edmund Blunden's *Undertones of War*, originally published in 1928. Blunden, a self-described "pastoralist at war," was a subaltern in the Royal Sussex Regiment who fought at the Somme and at Passchendaele. As a book that easily lends itself to academic literary analysis, *Undertones of War* has been misread and misused more than almost any other memoir. Perused without prejudice and preconception, it emerges as an extremely moving and thoughtful memoir that delves more deeply than almost any other book into the tragedy of modern warfare.

It is impossible not to recommend Siegfried Sassoon's trilogy *Memoirs of a Fox-Hunting Man* (1928), *Memoirs of an Infantry Officer* (1930), and *Sherston's Progress* (1936). Enough has been said about

Sassoon that I hardly need say any more. As one of the most important works in English literature of the twentieth century, it is unsurprising that Sassoon's slightly fictionalized memoir has been misused by literary critics who have seen it as a collective manifesto of English veterans of the war. It is better to see it for what it is: the memoir of a highly sensitive, intelligent, and brave individual who was shocked to the core of his soul by the suffering caused by the war. Sassoon's perceptiveness and deep moral sense makes for a highly profound and moving work; but again, read it on its own without reference to the literary critics. I have already mentioned Charles Carrington's *A Subaltern's War*, but it is worth pointing out again as an excellent memoir and useful counterbalance to Sassoon. Carrington saw as much of the war as did Sassoon, but left feeling very differently about what it all meant.

Very briefly, some of the other great British memoirs are *Old Soldiers Never Die* by Frank Richards (1933), *Salute of Guns* by Donald Boyd (1930), *The Ebb and Flow of Battle* by P.J. Campbell (1977), *Armageddon Road* by Billy Congreve (1982), *The Long Carry* by Frank Dunham (a stretcher bearer; 1970), *Gun Fodder* by A. Hamilton Gibbs (1919), *Into Battle* by John Glubb (1978), *Up to Mametz* by Wyn Griffith (1931), *A Subaltern's Odyssey* by R.B. Talbot Kelly (1980), *Of Those We Loved* by I.L. Read (1994), *Some Desperate Glory* by Edwin Campion Vaughan (1988), and *The Wet Flanders Plain* by Henry Williamson.

I have never seen a good Austro-Hungarian memoir; the few that exist in English are of generally poor quality and other apparently good ones have never been translated. The same is true with respect to Italian memoirs. Good French memoirs in English are also few and far between, though *A French Soldier's War Diary, 1914–1918* by Henri Desagneaux, published in English in 1975, is a good exception that I hope will presage more English translations of French memoirs. There are a few interesting Russian accounts, though most good books about that front in English were written by western observers. Accounts by Russians tend to be more about the Revolution and the Russian Civil War than the First World War.

The biggest standout among German memoirs, several of which have appeared in English, is Ernst Junger's *Storm of Steel*, published in 1929. It is a disturbing book. Junger believed the war to have been an enriching experience, and at times reveled in its violence and brutality. There is no doubt, however, that Junger experienced much more of the war than did Remarque or almost anyone else for that matter. His book is well worth reading. A lesser-known companion volume by Junger, *Copse 125*, enlarges on one incident in *Storm of Steel* and should be read in conjunction with it. *Forward March! Memoirs of a German Officer* by Ernst Rosenhainer, published two years ago by White Mane and still in print, is worth purchasing. Rosenhainer fought mainly on the Eastern Front.

Where can the historian or collector find war books? This is a serious question in the United States, where most of the best war books are very difficult to find. Major retail booksellers might have a few aviation memoirs squeezed in between the rows and rows of Civil War and World War II books. Used book stores may have a few First World War books, but aside from the common propaganda memoirs published in 1917 or 1918, good war memoirs are hard to find. The same is not true in Great Britain and Australia, where book dealers typically hold much larger stocks. Otherwise, the Internet—a boon to bibliophiles—is probably the best resource for finding them. New and used book dealers routinely advertise there, and almost every book in the following list is available on interlibrary loan.

Chapter 1

Australia and New Zealand

1. Adams, Alfred Sunderland. *Alf's Gallipoli: Letters from an Original Anzac and His Gallipoli Diary*. Hay, N.S.W.: Ollie Japp, 1984.

The author was a private in the 5th Battalion, A.I.F.

2. Adcock, Walter F. *Genuine War Letters: Written by an Australian to His People from the Battlefields of France*. Melbourne: National Press, 192–?. 288pp.

The author enlisted as a private in the 23rd Battalion, A.I.F., in January 1916.

3. Aitken, Alexander. *Gallipoli to the Somme: Recollections of a New Zealand Infantryman*. London: Oxford University Press, 1963. 177pp.

Memoir, August 1915–September 1916. Aitken rose from the rank of corporal to subaltern in the 1st Otago Battalion of the New Zealand Infantry Division. He was at Gallipoli for six weeks at the end of 1915, then fought near Armentières and on the Somme, where he was severely wounded on 27 September 1916. An exceptionally valuable and realistic memoir, particularly with respect to combat on the Somme in September 1916.

4. Auchterlonie, George. *The Best Fellows Anyone Could Wish to Meet: George Auchterlonie and the 8th Light Horse Regiment, A.I.F.* Leongotha, Vic.: A. Box, 1993. 34pp., illustrated.

The author enlisted as a private in July 1915.

5. Baensch, John. *War Diary 1915–1916*. Geelong, Vic.: Geelong Historical Society, 1993. 31pp., illustrated.

Private Baensch, 24th Battalion, A.I.F., was killed in August 1916.

6. Barrett, Keith Joy. *The Diary of an Australian Soldier*. Melbourne: Lothian Book Publishing Co., 1921. 111pp.

Diary, October 1914–February 1917. Barrett was a private in the Australian 2nd Field Ambulance from August 1914 to July 1915, when he was commissioned a lieutenant in the English 2nd Royal Fusiliers; he joined the 4th Royal Fusiliers in September and was promoted to captain three months later. He was mortally wounded in April 1917. Barrett was at Gallipoli for a month, and fought in France at Beaumont-Hamel and Arras; the diary is good for both periods.

7. Barton, Nathaniel Dunbar. *Nat D. Barton's Letters Home: 1914–1918 War*. Narromine, N.S.W.: Robyn Barclay, 1999. 250pp., illustrated.

Major Barton joined the 7th Light Horse Regiment in November 1914 and served to the end of the war. His unit fought at Gallipoli and in Egypt and Palestine.

8. Bean, C. E. W. *Gallipoli Correspondent: The Frontline Diary of C.E.W. Bean*. Sydney: George Allen & Unwin, 1983. 217pp., illustrated.

Diary, October 1914–December 1915. Fascinating account by Australia's official war correspondent who later became the official historian of the war. Bean, who experienced more of the front lines than perhaps any other journalist, was known for his sympathy for the soldiers and it shows in his diary. See also *Gallipoli Mission* (1948) by the same author.

9. Bishop, Bert. *The Hell, the Humour and the Heartbreak: A Private's View of World War 1*. Sydney: Brynwood House, 1990. 268pp., illustrated.

Memoir, August 1914–March 1919. Bishop was a private in the 55th Battalion of the 5th Division. He enlisted in 1915 and was posted for six months in Egypt before going to France, where he participated in the battles of Fromelles, Polygon Wood, Villers-Bretonneux, and Péronne. One of the best Australian memoirs, bringing out very well the attitudes and experiences of the enlisted men and the war-weariness of 1918. It deserves wider publication.

Black, Donald. *See* John Lyons Gray.

10. Bonnar, Malcolm Cornelius. *The Memoirs of M.C. Bonnar*. Adelaide: E.S. Wigg & Son, 1971.

The author, a lieutenant in the 2nd Divisional Signaling Company, enlisted in May 1915 and made it safely home.

11. Bostock, Henry P. *The Great Ride: The Diary of a Light Horse Brigade Scout, World War I*. Perth, W.A.: Artlook Books, 1982. 232pp., illustrated.

Memoir, August 1915–July 1919. Bostock was a private and corporal in the 10th Light Horse Regiment and the 3rd Light Horse Brigade Scout Troop. He served in Egypt, Sinai, Palestine, and Lebanon from 1915 until the end of the war, and then helped to put down the Egyptian rising in the spring of 1919. Either because of preference or a failing memory, Bostock is not forthcoming on the fighting he saw, preferring to summarize routine movements and episodes from his diary. Dull and not very readable, but good illustrations.

12. Boyce, George William. *A Prisoner of War, and How I Was Treated*. Sydney: W.J. Anderson, 1919. 36pp., illustrated.

The author enlisted as a private in the 5th Light Horse Regiment in December 1914.

13. Brereton, Cyprian Bridge. *Tales of Three Campaigns*. London: Selwyn & Blount, 1926. 290pp., illustrated.

Memoir, October 1914–1918. Major Brereton commanded New Zealand's 12th (Nelson) Company. Excellent memoir, well-illustrated, describing the Battle for the Suez Canal, Gallipoli, and the Somme.

14. Brown, Donald Forrester. *Your Loving Son, Don: Letters Home to North Otago from Sgt. Donald Brown VC*. Edited by Eunice P. Brown. Dunedin North, N.Z.: Otago Heritage Books, 1998. 48pp., illustrated.

Letters, January 1915–September 1916. Brown, a sergeant in the 2nd Otago Infantry Battalion of the New Zealand Division, won a posthumous Victoria Cross after being killed while sniping in High Wood in October 1916. Of local/family interest only.

15. Brown, James. *Turkish Days and Ways*. Sydney, London: Angus and Robertson, 1940. 288pp.

Memoir, April 1916–1918. Brown, a junior officer in an R.A.M.C.

Field Ambulance unit attached to a Yeomanry brigade, was captured in the Sinai in 1916. This intellectual memoir/history/travel book describes his subsequent experiences in Asia Minor and the Middle East.

16. Bull, Joseph Clarence. *One Airman's War: Aircraft Mechanic Joe Bull's Personal Diaries, 1916–1919.* Edited by Mark Lax. Maryborough, Qld.: Banner Books, 1997. 191pp., illustrated.

Diary, October 1916–April 1919. Bull was a First Class Aircraft Mechanic with No. 1 Squadron, A.F.C. He served in Egypt and Palestine, maintaining B.E.2 and other aircraft. Excellent, useful diary, very well annotated and illustrated.

17. Campbell, Harold, Wallace Campbell, William Scott Mair, and Arthur George Thynne. *Four Australians at War: Letters to Argyle, 1914–19.* Edited by Maurice Campbell and Graeme Hosken. Kenthurst, N.S.W.: Kangaroo Press, 1996. 216pp., illustrated.

Letters, September 1914–September 1919. The authors were all enlisted men and related. Harold Campbell of the 3rd Battalion, A.I.F., was killed on Anzac Ridge in October 1917. Wallace Campbell served in the 24th Company, Army Service Corps. William Scott Mair served in the 2nd, 33rd, and 54th Battalions, and was badly wounded at Fromelles in 1916. Arthur George Thynne served in the 20th Battalion and the 2nd Pioneer Battalion. Valuable letters, well-edited.

18. Carroll, Eric John Bernard. *A Letter from My Father: Through the Panama Canal to France, 1918.* Edited by Marcia E. Tanswell. Surrey Hills, Vic.: M.E. Tanswell, 1991. 48pp., illustrated.

Carroll enlisted in October 1917 as a driver in the 5th Mounted Transport Company.

19. Carthew, Noel. *Voices from the Trenches: Letters to Home.* London: New Holland Publishers, 2002. 244pp., illustrated.

Letters of three brothers, Charles (of the 8th Light Horse Regiment), Fred (10th Light Horse), and James Carthew (artillery), describing their experiences at Gallipoli, Palestine, and the Western Front.

20. Chandler, Les G. *Dear Homefolks: Letters Written by L.G. Chandler During the First World War.* Radcliffe, Vic.: M. Chandler, 1988. 193pp., illustrated.

Letters/Diary, July 1915–January 1919. Chandler, a noted naturalist and ornithologist, served as a corporal in the Army Medical Corps in Egypt and France. Lively, humorous letters supplemented by candid diary entries sometimes reminiscent of Blunden. Well illustrated with many original photos. Highly recommended.

21. Clay, Harold Richard. *Letters and Memoirs of the Late Sergeant Harold Richard Clay*. Blackburn, Vic.: T.J. Higham, 1928.

Clay, a sergeant in the 14th Field Artillery Brigade, enlisted in July 1915 and died of wounds in 1917.

22. Coates, Albert Ernest. *The Volunteer: The Diaries and Letters of Albert E. Coates, No. 23–7th Btn., 1st A.I.F. First World War 1914–18*. Melbourne: W. and W. Gherardin, 1995. 221pp., illustrated.

Letters/Diary, August 1914–December 1918. Fascinating, extensive materials, best on Egypt, Gallipoli, and the Somme, and deserving of wider publication.

23. Cobby, Arthur Henry. *High Adventure*. Melbourne: Robertson and Mullens, 1942. 232pp., illustrated.

Memoir, December 1916–November 1918. Cobby went to France in December 1917 as a lieutenant in A.F.C. No. 4 Squadron, fought through 1918, and eventually became a group captain. Witty, including exciting combat narratives.

24. Coghill, Eustace Halley. *Eustace Halley Coghill's Diaries*. v.1, *1916–1918, the First World War*. Melbourne: E. Carey, 1996. 104pp., illustrated.

Coghill was a gunner in the 11th Field Artillery Brigade.

25. Coker, Raymond H. *Incidents from a Soldier's Life*. Adelaide: Baring & Levy, 1921. 48pp.

Coker enlisted in February 1917 and became a lance corporal in the 2nd Light Railway Operating Company.

26. Conrick, Clive. *"The Flying Carpet Men."* Lucindale, S.A.: P. Conrick, 1993. 216pp., illustrated.

Diary, April 1918–February 1919. Conrick was a lieutenant in No. 1 Squadron of the Australian Flying Corps.

27. Cooper, Carolyn Ethel. *Behind the Lines: One Woman's War 1914–1918: The Letters of Caroline Ethel Cooper*. Edited by Decie Denholm. London: Jill Norman and Hobhouse, 1982. 311pp., illustrated.

Letters, July 1914–December 1918. Cooper lived in Leipzig, Germany, throughout the war, and reports honestly on civilian conditions there. Her letters were smuggled out of the country or concealed until the end of the war and thus avoided censorship.

28. Cozens, John David. *Round the World with the A.I.F. in Days of War and Peace, 1918–1919*. Brisbane: Robt. McGregor, 1920. 111pp., illustrated.

Private Cozens joined the 41st Battalion, A.I.F. in December 1917 and returned to Australia in August 1919.

29. Craven, Digger, and W.J. Blackledge. *Peninsula of Death: As Told to W.J. Blackledge by Digger Craven*. London: Sampson Low, Marston, 1936. 248pp., illustrated.

Memoir, 1915. An episodic, overly dramatized tale of the Gallipoli campaign.

30. Crossley, Lester. *Letters from Lester Crossley, 1915–1916*. Cobar, N.S.W.: N. Crossley, 2000. 60pp., illustrated.

Crossley, a private in the 4th Battalion of the 1st Australian Division, was killed at Pozières in July 1916.

31. Cull, William Ambrose. *At All Costs*. Melbourne: Australasian Authors' Agency, 1919. 203pp.

Captain Cull joined the 32nd Battalion, A.I.F. in May 1915. His unit participated in the Somme, Passchendaele, and other battles on the Western Front.

32. Cumberland, Oliver, and Joseph Cumberland. *The Anzac Letters of Oliver and Joseph Cumberland*. Scone, N.S.W.: Scone & Upper Hunter Historical Society, 1986. 45pp., illustrated.

Letters, October 1914–July 1915. Both men were privates in the 2nd Battalion, A.I.F. Oliver was killed in August 1915 at Lone Pine, and Joseph died in May 1915 of wounds received in the Gallipoli landing.

33. Davidson, John. *The Dinkum Oil of Light Horse and Camel Corps.*

Robina, Qld.: Bruce and Richard Davidson, 1996. 127pp., illustrated.
Memoir, August 1914–March 1919. A Boer War veteran, Davidson served as a Squadron Quartermaster Sergeant and second lieutenant with the Australian 1st Light Horse Regiment, and was wounded at Gallipoli. In July 1916 he joined the 12th Company of the Imperial Camel Corps, in which he became a first lieutenant. He fought in all of the Gaza battles to the capture of Jerusalem and Damascus. Fascinating memoir, albeit with more emphasis on personalities than on battles.

34. Demasson, Hubert P. *To All My Dear People: The Diary & Letters of Private Hubert P. Demasson 1916–1917.* Edited by Rachael Christensen. Fremantle, W.A.: Fremantle Arts Centre Press, 1988. 159pp., illustrated.
Letters/diary, July 1916–March 1917. Demasson was captured shortly after going to France with the 16th Battalion, A.I.F., in the spring of 1917, and died in prison that September. Unremarkable letters, good illustrations.

35. Denny, William Joseph. *The Diggers.* London: Hodder and Stoughton, 1919. 300pp., illustrated.
Memoir, March 1916–November 1918. Patriotic, vociferously anti-German musings of an Australian politician who was also a captain in the 9th Light Horse.

36. Dent, Arthur Ernest. *Fourteen Months a Prisoner of War.* Narrabri, N.S.W.: "The North Western Courier" Printing, 1919. 41pp.
Private Dent enlisted in the 6th Battalion, A.I.F. in July 1915.

37. Dinning, Hector. *Nile to Aleppo, with the Light Horse in the Middle East.* London: G. Allen & Unwin, 1920. 287pp., illustrated.
Memoir, roughly 1917–1918. Dinning was a captain in the Australian Light Horse. Beautifully illustrated, combination memoir and travelogue describing war in the Sinai and Palestine; includes extended references to T.E. Lawrence. Atmospheric, with little specific detail.

38. Doggett, John D. *The Story of an Anzac.* Lindisfarne, Tas.: N. Potter, 1999. 161pp., illustrated.
Doggett enlisted in January 1915 and served as a sergeant in the 42nd Battalion, A.I.F.

39. Donaldson, A. *The Amazing Cruise of the German Raider "Wolf." From the Log of Captain Donaldson, S.S. "Matunga."* Sydney: New Century Press, 1920. 138pp., illustrated.

Memoir, November 1916–December 1918. A confusing narrative, partly the translated memoirs of Captain Nerger of the *Wolf*, and partly Donaldson's memoirs after his ship's capture in August 1917.

40. Donnell, Anne. *Letters of an Australian Army Sister*. Sydney: Angus & Robertson, 1920.

Letters, June 1915–February 1919. Thoughtful, compassionate observations of a Red Cross nurse who served with the 3rd Australian General Hospital off Gallipoli, and in Egypt, Britain, and France.

41. Douglas, Keith Matheson. *Sapper 52: The Diary of Keith Matheson Douglas during the Gallipoli Campaign 1915*. Hyde Park, S.A.: D.R. Douglas, 1996. 37 leaves.

Matheson, who enlisted in August 1914, was a corporal in the Signaling Corps of the 1st Division. He survived Gallipoli.

42. Downing, Walter Hubert. *To the Last Ridge*. Melbourne: H.H. Champion, Australasian Authors' Agency, 1920. 192pp.

Memoir, July 1916–October 1918. Downing was a noncommissioned officer in the 57th Battalion, A.I.F. An episodic, semi-detached but often disturbing memoir describing some of the worst fighting on the Somme and in Flanders.

43. Duffell, William John. *Soldier Boy: The Letters of Gunner W.J. Duffell, 1915–18*. Edited by Gilbert Mant. Stevenage, Herts.: Spa Books, 1992. 163pp., illustrated.

Letters/memoir, December 1915–April 1919. Duffell served with the 2nd and 22nd Batteries of the 1st Australian Field Artillery Brigade. His letters are best on the Somme and Passchendaele.

44. Duguid, Charles [pseud. Scotty's Brother]. *The Desert Trail: With the Light Horse through Sinai to Palestine*. Adelaide: W.K. Thomas, 1919. 129pp., illustrated.

Memoir, includes author's diary, March 1917–April 1918. Duguid was a captain in the Light Horse. A disjointed, patriotic account, with some good illustrations and diary entries.

45. Dunbar, Arthur, and Emily Dunbar. *Arthur and Emily: Letters in Wartime*. Edited by Irene MacDonald and Susan Radvansky. Fitzroy, Vic.: McPhee Gribble, 1984. 94pp.

Letters, August 1915–January 1916. Of dubious authenticity, these purport to be letters between an infantryman based at Liverpool and his wife in Australia. Unexceptional.

46. Dunn, William. *Dear Mother*. Edited by Tom Austen. Perth, W.A.: St. George Books, 1990. 181pp., illustrated.

Letters, 1914–1915. Private William Dunn's experiences in Egypt and Gallipoli.

47. Edey, John F. *From Lone Pine to Murray Pine: The Story of a Mallee Soldier Settler*. Red Cliffs, Vic.: Sunnyland Press, 1981. 168pp., illustrated.

Autobiography, with about 50pp. dealing with World War I, when Edey was a sergeant in the 5th Battalion, 1st Division. From December 1914 to December 1917 he served in Egypt, Gallipoli, and the Ypres Salient, and was wounded twice. Good but disappointingly sparse on Edey's personal experiences.

48. Edmunds, George Bromfley. *Somme Memories: Memoir of an Australian Artillery Driver, 1916–1919*. Ilfracombe, Devon: Arthur H. Stockwell, 1955. 43pp.

Edmunds enlisted in the 8th Field Artillery Brigade in January 1916 and served to the end of the war.

49. Evans, Eric. *So Far from Home: The War Diary of Eric Evans*. Edited by Patrick Wilson. London: Leo Cooper, 2000. 256pp., illustrated.

Diary, February 1917–March 1919. Evans was a sergeant in the 13th Battalion, A.I.F. The only drawback to these excellent, readable, and carefully edited diaries is that they do not cover his early service at Gallipoli, where he was wounded, and at Passchendaele, which he fortunately missed by being hospitalized.

50. Evans, Gerald Vance. *Recollections of the 1914–1918 War*. Spring Hill, Qld.: G.V. Evans, 1982. 47pp., illustrated.

Memoir, October 1915–July 1919. Evans was a private in the 9th Battalion, 1st A.I.F. He left Australia in April 1916, stopping briefly in

Egypt and spending the rest of the war in France and Flanders. Short but very good memoir, apparently based on the author's diary.

51. Fenwick, Percival. *Gallipoli Diary: 24 April to 27 June, 1915.* Auckland: David Ling, 2000. 104pp., illustrated.

Lieutenant Colonel Fenwick was Deputy Assistant Director of Medical Services Headquarters in ANZAC. His sober diary describes the daily tedium and danger of the beaches at Gallipoli.

52. Forsyth, Reginald James Thomas. *Reginald James Thomas Forsyth, 1893–1918: Light Horseman, Budding Aviator, Much Loved Brother and Son.* Newport, N.S.W.: L.C. Forsyth, 1988. 128pp.

Diaries. Forsyth served in the 1st Light Horse Regiment and then became a second lieutenant in the 6th Squadron, A.F.C. He was killed in February 1918.

53. Fowler, John Ernest. *Looking Backward.* Canberra: Roebuck Society, 1979. 99pp., illustrated.

Autobiography, much of it dealing with trooper "Chook" Fowler's experiences as a member of the 12th Light Horse Regiment in Egypt, Gallipoli, Syria, and Palestine.

54. Fussell, J. C. *Brown Irishmen.* Auckland: Worthington, 1920. 23pp., illustrated.

A satirical memoir, in mock Maori English.

55. Gault, James A. *Padre Gault's Stunt Book.* London: Epworth Press, 1919. 188pp., illustrated.

Memoir of a Methodist chaplain who became well known to the Diggers in France.

56. Gaunt, Guy. *The Yield of the Years: A Story of Adventure Afloat and Ashore.* London: Hutchinson, 1940. 303pp., illustrated.

Autobiography, half on World War I. Gaunt, a native Australian, served throughout the war as Naval Attaché and Chief of the British Intelligence Service in the United States. Some insights on American counterespionage efforts.

57. Gray, John Lyons [pseud. Donald Black]. *Red Dust: An Australian*

Trooper in Palestine. London: Jonathan Cape, 1931. 303pp., illustrated.
Memoir, 1917–1918. Gray was a private in the 6th Light Horse. Introspective and antiwar, although the author also expresses contempt for stay-at-home 'shirkers.' He has some interesting comments on the British soldiery and military system. Black was involved in heavy combat and also experienced some of the most dreadful climates on earth. Not quite as good as Ion Idriess's *The Desert Column* but still worth reading.

58. Greville, Reginald Henry. *Memoirs of Reginald Henry Greville*. Edited by F.L. Carr. Auckland: Repro Graphics, 1997. 111pp., illustrated.
Autobiography, about half on World War I. Greville was a lieutenant in the New Zealand Cyclist Corps. His memoir is best on Passchendaele and the last battles of 1918.

59. Grose, Frank. *A Rough Y.M. Bloke*. Melbourne: Specialty Press, 1921. 180pp., illustrated.
Tale of a Y.M.C.A. representative.

60. Gum, Ray. *My Life Story with Experiences*. Prospect, S.A.: R. Gum, 1974. 423pp., illustrated.
The author enlisted as a private in the 9th Light Horse Regiment in August 1917.

61. Hadfield, Arthur. *What Did You do in the Great War, Dad!: The Diary of Sapper Arthur Hadfield, 25 October 1916 to 26 August 1919*. Orange, N.S.W.: I. McAndrew, 1996. 179pp., illustrated.
Hadfield was a private in the 1st Light Trench Mortar Battery.

62. Haig, Frederic William. *Frederic William Haig: An Autobiography: Exciting Experiences in Gallipoli, Australian Flying Corp, Turkish Prison, Qantas and Early Aviation*. Melbourne: Frederick's Publishing, 1996. 62pp., illustrated.
Haig was wounded at Gallipoli, and then joined A.F.C. No. 1 Squadron in Palestine, where he became a prisoner of war after crashing his Bristol fighter.

63. Hall, Joseph Rex. *The Desert Hath Pearls*. Melbourne: Hawthorne Press, 1975. 219pp., illustrated.
Autobiography, just over half on World War I. Hall served at

Gallipoli with the 1st Light Horse Field Ambulance, was commissioned a lieutenant in the 2nd Light Horse Regiment in July 1916, and then transferred to the Imperial Camel Corps. He remained with the Camel Corps until April 1918, when he became a staff captain in the 5th Light Horse Brigade in the Middle East. Includes long diary excerpts; excellent on Gallipoli and the Palestine campaign.

64. Hallenstein, Dalbert. *On Active Service with the A.I.F. Gallipoli and France*. Melbourne, 1919. 219pp., illustrated.

The author, a lieutenant in the 5th Machine Gun Battalion, was killed in action in September 1918.

65. Hallihan, Frank. *In the Hands of the Enemy: A Record of the Experiences of Frank Hallihan, 21st Battalion, in German Prison Camps*. Victoria: Robert W. Jones, 192–?. 32pp.

Private Hallihan enlisted in January 1915, was captured in 1916 near Cambrai, and made several escape attempts before returning to Australia March 1919.

66. Halpin, John. *Blood in the Mists*. Sydney: Macquarie Head Press, 1934. 277pp.

Grueling memoir of the sufferings of an Australian prisoner in Turkey.

67. Hamilton, Patrick M. *Riders of Destiny: The 4th Australian Light Horse Field Ambulance in the Palestine Campaign. An Autobiography*. Surrey Hills, Vic.: N. Sharp, 1985. 189pp., illustrated.

Memoir, February 1917–1918. Hamilton, a conscientious objector, served as a stretcher bearer in the 3rd Light Horse Field Ambulance in Egypt from 1915 to 1917, when he transferred to the 4th L.H.F.A. in Sinai and Palestine. Mostly transcribed diaries, not very readable but providing a good day-to-day account of the Palestine campaign. Good illustrations.

68. Handsley, George William. *Two and a Half Years a Prisoner in Turkey*. Brisbane: Jones & Hambly, 1920?. 64pp.

Handsley became a private in the 1st Light Horse Regiment in August 1915.

69. Harding, Edward Louis Stanley. *Stanley Harding World War One*

Letters: Father-Soldier-Farmer, 1893–1968. Nathalia, Vic.: Harding Family, 1995. 207pp., illustrated.

70. Harney, William Edward. *Bill Harney's War*. South Yarra, Vic.: Currey O'Neil, 1983. 59pp., illustrated.

Memoir, adapted from a radio documentary, roughly 1914–1918. Harney was a private in the 9th Battalion, serving in France. An old soldier's reminiscences, transcribed as spoken.

71. Haynes, Olive L. C. *We are Here, Too: The Diaries and Letters of Sister Olive L.C. Haynes, November 1914 to February 1918*. Edited by Margaret O. Young. Adelaide: Australian Down Syndrome Association, 1991. 277pp., illustrated.

Haynes joined the Australian Army Nursing Service in November 1914 and was discharged in December 1917.

72. Healy, Tim. *More Lives Than One: My Days of Hazard*. London: D. Appleton-Century Company, 1944. 426pp.

73. Henderson, Kenneth T. *Khaki and Cassock*. Melbourne: Melville & Mullen, 1919. 160pp., illustrated.

The author, a chaplain, returned to Australia in February 1918.

74. Hinckfuss, Harold. *Memories of a Signaller: The First World War, 1914–1919*. Melbourne: Dominion-Hedges & Bell, 1982. 182pp., illustrated.

Memoir, August 1914–April 1919. Hinckfuss was a corporal in the signaling section of the 26th Battalion, serving at Gallipoli and in France, where he was wounded. Readable, but with useful practical information on signaling work.

75. Hogue, Oliver. *The Cameliers*. London: Andrew Melrose, 1919. 280pp.

Memoir, 1917–1918. Novelized, episodic account by "Trooper Bluegum" of the Imperial Camel Corps in Palestine. Cheerful, patriotic, and not very useful as history.

76. Horner, H. *An Australian Prisoner of War in the Hands of the Hun*. Perth, W.A.: V.K. Jones and Company, 1919. 99pp., illustrated.

77. Host, John. *7016 Pte John Host, born 18 November, 1886, 16th Battalion, A.I.F.: Next of Kin, Wife, Mrs. J. Host, Seabarook, Northam, Western Australia.* Northam, W.A.: Host Publications, 1995. 50 leaves, illustrated.

Host enlisted in the 16th Battalion, A.I.F. in September 1916. Despite the title's implication, he survived and returned to Australia in February 1919.

78. Howell, Arthur G. *Signaller at the Front: The War Diary of Gunner Arthur G. Howell, MM First Australian Field Artillery Brigade and His Impressions of the Great War 1915–1918.* Carlisle, W.A.: Hesperian Press, 2001. 75pp.

Diary, November 1915–August 1918. Unannotated diary with some very good entries, especially relating to Pozières and the Somme battles.

79. Hurley, Frank. *Hurley at War: The Photography and Diaries of Frank Hurley in Two World Wars.* Broadway, N.S.W.: Fairfax Library in Association with Daniel O'Keefe, 1986. 160pp., illustrated.

Diaries/photos, mostly on World War I, 1917–1918. Hurley was appointed official photographer of the A.I.F. in 1917. This is a priceless visual record, sometimes in color, of Passchendaele and the latter stages of the Palestine Campaign.

80. Huxtable, Charles. *From the Somme to Singapore: A Medical Officer in Two World Wars.* Kenthurst, N.S.W.: Kangaroo Press, 1987. 168pp., illustrated.

Autobiography, with about 25pp. of Huxtable's recollections (transcribed from audio tapes) of his service in World War I. Huxtable, an Australian, was a captain in the R.A.M.C. and served at Loos, the Somme, and other battles before joining an A.I.F. hospital at Rouen in 1918.

81. Idriess, Ion Llewellyn. *The Desert Column: Leaves from the Diary of an Australian Trooper in Gallipoli, Sinai, and Palestine.* Sydney: Angus & Robertson, 1932. 388pp.

Memoir, 1914–1918. One of the best Australian accounts of the war. Idriess (who went on to become a noted adventurer and author of about 50 books) was a private in the 5th Light Horse Regiment. He spent several months at Gallipoli, where he was wounded and experienced hand-to-hand fighting. To his disgust he then found himself fighting the Turks in the harsh conditions of the Sinai peninsula, and remained in this theater of war until December 1917, when he was severely wounded fighting under Allenby in Palestine. One cannot help liking Idriess, who was a fanatical diarist with profound powers of observation. His accounts of mounted desert warfare and candid (but fair) commentaries on British soldiers and the high command make for an absorbing and highly recommended book. See also *Sniping: With an Episode from the Author's Experiences During the War of 1914–1918* (1942), by the same author.

82. Ingle, Judith. *From Duntroon to the Dardanelles: A Biography of Lieutenant William Dawkins: Including His Diaries and Selected Letters*. Canberra: J. Ingle, 1995. 319pp., illustrated.

Includes October 1914–April 1915 letters and diary of Dawkins, of the 2nd Field Company Engineers, who was killed at Gallipoli in May 1915. Some good entries on first days of Gallipoli landing.

83. Ison, Jack. *Dear Da*. Edited by Lynette Harrison and Graeme Hoskin. Dubbo, N.S.W.: L. Harrison, 1991. 147pp., illustrated.

Letters, December 1914–November 1917. Ison was a corporal in the 3rd Australian Infantry Battalion, serving in Egypt, Gallipoli, and France, and seeing heavy fighting before being killed in action at Passchendaele in November 1917. Moving, useful letters despite Ison's reticence on his combat experiences.

84. Jacob, John Gilbert. *Home Letters of a Soldier-Student*. Adelaide: G. Hassell & Son, 1919. 2 vols., 124 and 139pp., illustrated.

Letters, April 1916–July 1918. Jacob, a private in the 50th Battalion A.I.F., was killed near Hamel in July 1918. He described life at the front in as much detail as the censor would let him get away with.

85. Jones, T. M. *Watchdogs of the Deep: Life in a Submarine During the Great War*. Sydney: Angus & Robertson, 1935. 224pp., illustrated.

Memoir, 1916–1926. Able Seaman Jones was Leading Torpedoman on the submarine *J2*. This is a lively account of his experiences, which stretched across most of the western hemisphere.

86. Joseph, Erle James Hugh. *The Man Who Never Came Back*. Lindisfarne, Tas.: E. J. H. Joseph, 1983. 108pp.

Joseph served in the 12th Battalion, A.I.F., fought at Gallipoli, and lived to be Tasmania's last surviving Anzac.

87. Joynt, William D. *Saving the Channel Ports, 1918*. Melbourne: Wren, 1975. 233pp., illustrated. Sequel: *Breaking the Road for the Rest*. Melbourne: Hyland House, 1978. 206pp., illustrated.

Autobiography, most on World War I, when Joynt was a lieutenant in the 8th Battalion, A.I.F. He joined up in the summer of 1915, fought at Bullecourt and Passchendaele, and then won a V.C. at Herleville Wood in August 1918. Straightforward but compelling memoir.

88. Kaighin, Thomas Robert Livesay. *A Personal Account of World War 1*. Rowville, Vic.: R. Johnson, 2000. 82pp., illustrated.

Kaighin was a gunner in the 8th Field Artillery Brigade, 3rd Australian Division.

89. Kempe, Humphrey. *Participation*. Melbourne: Hawthorn Press, 1973. 200pp., illustrated.

Autobiography, most on World War I, when Kempe served in the 3rd Light Horse Regiment in Gallipoli, Sinai, and Palestine. Exceptionally interesting on his experiences at Gallipoli.

90. Kennedy, J. J. *The Whale Oil Guards*. Dublin: J. Duffy, 1919. 143pp.

A combination memoir/regimental history of the 53rd Battalion, A.I.F.

91. Keppie, Arthur Ernest. *Pte Arthur Ernest Keppie: His Diary, Letters and Postcards, 1914–1915*. Paterson, N.S.W.: Paterson Historical Society, 1999. 29pp., illustrated.

Keppie enlisted in the 4th Battalion, A.I.F. in August 1914 and was killed a day after the landing at Gallipoli. This book traces his training in Egypt and his family's attempts to learn about his death, which was not reported to them until August 1916.

92. Kerr, Peter William. *Behind the Lines: War Time Stories from 1914–1918 with the 5th Light Horse Regiment as Told by Peter William Kerr 1896–1984*. Brisbane: N. Wynn, 1997. 30pp., illustrated.

Private Kerr enlisted in the 2nd Light Horse Regiment in February 1916, and transferred to the 5th Light Horse as a machine gunner after his arrival in Egypt. He participated in the Sinai and Palestine campaigns through the end of the war. Humorous stories.

93. Kidd, Neville. *An Impression Which Will Never Fade: The True Story of an Original Anzac*. Pymble, N.S.W.: N. Kidd, 2000. 351pp., illustrated.

94. King, Olive. *One Woman at War: Letters of Olive King, 1915–1920*. Edited by Hazel King. Melbourne: Melbourne University Press, 1986. 220pp., illustrated.

Letters, May 1915–July 1922. King, who served as an ambulance driver in Belgium for the first few months of 1915, joined a Scottish Women's Hospital Unit in May of that year and followed it to Serbia. In the summer of 1916 she joined the Serbian Army Medical Service as a driver. Long, fascinating letters by a remarkable woman.

95. Kingsford, A. R. *Night Raiders of the Air: Being the Experiences of a Night Flying Pilot, Who Raided Hunland on Many Dark Nights During the War*. London: John Hamilton, 1935. 222pp., illustrated.

Memoir, 1915–November 1918. Kingsford, a New Zealander, transferred to the R.F.C. after infantry service that included surviving the sinking of his torpedoed troopship in 1915. In 1917–18 he flew F.E.2b aircraft with Squadron Nos. 33 and 100, service that included intercepting zeppelins and night bombing raids over Germany. Fast-paced.

96. Kirkcaldie, R. A. *In Gray and Scarlet*. Melbourne: Aleaxander McCubbin, 1922. 187pp., illustrated.

A nurse's medical narrative.

97. Knight, Bernard George, Herbert Augustine Knight, and William Douglas Knight. *My Dear Home: The Letters of Three Knight Brothers Who Gave Their Lives During WWI*. Edited by Nancy Croad. Auckland: N. Croad, 1995. 236pp.

Letters, May 1910–August 1918. Herbert, a private in the Otago Regiment, was killed at Gallipoli in May 1915. George served as an enlisted soldier and eventually became a second lieutenant in the 2nd Otago Battalion before being killed at Passchendaele in October 1917. William, an enlisted soldier in the Auckland Regiment, was killed near Bapaume in September 1918. Long, fascinating letters, carefully transcribed.

98. Koenig, Charles David, Thomas John Koening, and Tillie Koenig. *The Koenig Letters: The Correspondence of Charles, Thomas and Tillie Koenig During the First World War.* Edited by John Pearson Churchill. Churchill, Vic.: Centre for Gippsland Studies, 1990. 32pp., illustrated.

Charles and Thomas Koenig both joined the 31st Battalion, A.I.F. in July 1915. Thomas was killed in September 1917.

99. Laidlaw, James Maxwell. *For King and Country.* Bairnsdale, Vic.: J.G. Rogers, 1985. 222pp., illustrated.

Diary, January 1916–June 1919. Laidlaw served with the 9th Light Horse Regiment in Egypt and a variety of artillery and supply units in France before joining the 50th Battalion in August 1917. Excellent, well-illustrated diary, best on Passchendaele.

100. Laslett, George Sampson. *Reflections: Compiled from the Memoirs of George S. Laslett.* Mt. Gambier, S.A.: G.S. Laslett, 1981.

Sergeant Laslett joined the Machine Gun Squadron in January 1915.

101. Lawrence, Cyril. *The Gallipoli Diary of Sergeant Lawrence of the Australian Engineers, 1st A.I.F., 1915.* Carlton, Vic.: Melbourne University Press, 1981. 167pp., illustrated. Sequel, *Sergeant Lawrence Goes to France.* Melbourne: Melbourne University Press, 1987. 191pp., illustrated.

Lawrence was a sergeant and eventually a lieutenant in the 1st Division Engineers. The first book covers Lawrence's sojourn in Gallipoli through early 1916; the second describes the period from his arrival in France until the end of the war. Each volume is a priceless record of the Australian experience of the war and a testament to the indomitable spirit (and indiscipline!) of the Diggers. Harshly critical not only of the British war effort but also of the common English soldiers in 1915–16, though Lawrence later tones down his contempt. Lively and readable.

102. Lay, Percy. *The War Diaries of Captain Percy Lay, D.C.M., M.M., M.C., C. de G. (1914–1919).* Deer Park, Vic.: B & H, 1983. 195pp., illustrated.

Lay entered the army in August 1914 and served in the 8th Battalion, A.I.F.

103. Linton, John Stewart. *A Soldier's Tale: One Man's War, 16*

February 1916–12th June 1919: The Diary of Sergeant J.S. Linton, no. 29543, 3rd Divisional Ammunition Column, Australian Imperial Forces. Kalamunda, W.A.: J.S. Linton, 1997. 192pp., illustrated.

104. Lording, Rowland Edward [pseud. A. Tiveychoc]. *There and Back: The Story of an Australian Soldier, 1915–1935.* Sydney: Returned Sailors and Soldiers' Imperial League of Australia, 1935. 285pp.

Memoir, June 1915–1935. Extremely moving memoir, written in the third person, of a seventeen-year-old signaler of the 30th Battalion, A.I.F., in Egypt, on the Somme, and at home. Lording was gravely wounded, losing a lung as well as almost complete use of both arms, at Fromelles in July 1916. He describes his subsequent hospitalization, endless operations, morphine addiction, and the trials of life at home in graphic detail. Uncommon and therefore invaluable memoir from a casualty's point of view.

105. Lorimer, Patrick. *Patrick Lorimer: Letters from England and the Western Front 1916–1919.* Sydney: Pergola Press, 1997.

Lorimer became a private in the Army Veterinary Corps in August 1916.

106. Lowe, Charles H. *War Diary, 1916–1919: Spr. Charles H. Lowe, 4273 4th Pioneers.* Adelaide: E.M. Love, 1995.

107. Lushington, Reginald Francis. *A Prisoner with the Turks, 1915–1918.* London: Simpkin, Marshall, 1923. 101pp.

Lushington enlisted as a private in the 16th Battalion, A.I.F. in September 1914.

108. Lyall, Brian. *Letters from an ANZAC Gunner.* Edited by K.M. Lyall. East Kew, Vic.: Lyall's Yarns Pty Ltd, 1990. 214pp., illustrated.

Lyall enlisted in August 1914, served as a gunner in the 2nd Field Artillery Brigade, and died of wounds at Gallipoli in December 1915.

109. McBeath, William Frampton. *Diaries of Graves Detachment Digger William Frampton McBeath in the Years 1918–1919 of World War One: Pte. W. F. McBeath 61661 58th Battalion, 12th Reinforcements Australian Imperial Force.* Shepparton, Vic.: N.E. Harrison, 1994. 57pp., illustrated.

110. McCrea, Laurence. *Light Horse*. Brighton, S.A.: K.B. Printing Services, 1986. 108pp., illustrated.

Novelized, poorly written retelling by the author of his father's service with the 10th Light Horse Regiment in the Egypt and Palestine.

111. MacKenzie, Clutha. *The Tale of a Trooper*. London: John Lane, 1921. 200pp.

Memoir, August 1914–March 1919. Novelized memoir of a trooper in the Wellington Mounted Rifles, taking him from New Zealand to Egypt and Gallipoli, where he was blinded by a shell in August 1915. Better than most books in the "On Active Service Series," although MacKenzie's matter-of-fact reaction to his blinding is somewhat hard to swallow.

112. McKenzie, Stephen Nowell. *Stephen Nowell McKenzie: Recollections of a Centenarian*. Edited by Ian McKenzie. Canberra: I. McKenzie, 1995. 176pp., illustrated.

Autobiography, about 60pp. on World War I. McKenzie enlisted in July 1915 and was commissioned in March 1917; he served with the 16th Battalion in Egypt and the 48th Battalion in France and Belgium.

113. McLean, Archibald Lang. *War Vistas*. Sydney: Australasian Medical Publishing Co., 1928.

114. McLean, Duncan. *Still Alive and Kicking: Yelarbon, the Great War and Letters Home*. Tarragindi, Qld.: Duncan McLean, 2002. 248pp., illustrated.

Private McLean joined the 9th Battalion, A.I.F. in September 1916.

115. McLean, J. G. *War and Its Glories*. Melbourne: H.H. Champion, Australasian Authors' Agency, 1920. 86pp.

116. McMillan, David. *Stand to Arms: Lance Corporal David McMillan's War Diary, Australian 5th Field Co Engineers, 2nd Division, A.I.F. on the Western Front, 1916–1918*. Edited by Ronald Henderson. Berry, N.S.W.: R. Henderson, 1989. 125pp., illustrated.

Diary, February 1916–October 1917. McMillan's diary doesn't amount to much but it is well-presented here, with good illustrations.

117. McPhie, Victor Alexander Carpendale. *Victor Alexander Carpen-*

dale McPhie 1897–1983: Letters to his Family in 1917 and 1918. Australia: The Compiler, 1996. 78pp., illustrated.

McPhie joined the 2nd Field Artillery Brigade in August 1916.

118. Malcolm, William. *Boots, Belts, Rifle & Pack: A New Zealand Soldier at War, 1917–1919.* Edited by Dorothy McKenzie and Lindsay Malcolm. Dunedin, N.Z.: L.M. Malcolm, 1992. 167pp., illustrated.

Letters, July 1917–January 1919. Malcolm joined the Auckland Battalion of the New Zealand Division in France in March 1918, and left the front after being wounded in September. Interesting letters complemented by good illustrations and edited with restraint.

119. Malthus, Cecil. *Anzac: A Retrospect.* Christchurch: Whitcombe & Tombs, 1965. 159pp.

Memoir, August 1914–April 1916. Realistic, insightful memoir of an enlisted man in the New Zealand Canterbury Battalion, who participated in the defense of the Suez Canal against Turkish attack in December 1914 and landed at Gallipoli on April 26, 1915. One of the best memoirs of the Peninsula.

120. Maxwell, Joseph. *Hell's Bells and Mademoiselles.* Sydney: Angus & Robertson, 1932. 267pp.

Memoir, 1914–1919. The author enlisted in the 18th Battalion in February 1915 and served as an N.C.O. until being commissioned a second lieutenant in September 1917. Written from memory (Maxwell did not keep a diary) and at times rambling and overdramatized, but with valuable observations on Passchendaele and American efforts in 1918.

121. Miller, Eric. *Camps, Tramps & Trenches: The Diary of a New Zealand Sapper, 1917.* Dunedin and Wellington, N.Z.: A.H. and A.W. Reed, 1939. 207pp., illustrated.

Diary, January–December 1917. The author served in an engineer unit in France; this diary begins with his departure from New Zealand and contains many details of daily life in the trenches.

122. Miller, Len. *A Gallipoli Diary: Captain Len Miller of Ferny Creek.* Monbulk, Vic.: Monbulk Historical Society, 1995. 29pp., illustrated.

123. Mitchell, George Deane. *Backs to the Wall.* Sydney: Angus &

Robertson, 1937. 281pp.

Memoir, September 1916–December 1918. Mitchell, who was a private in the 10th and 48th Battalions, A.I.F., describes his post-Gallipoli experiences on the Somme and Flanders. His memoir seems slightly dramatized, but it provides an intimate view of the Digger's outlook on the war.

124. Moberly, Gertrude F. *Experiences of a "Dinki Di" R.R.C. Nurse.* Glebe, N.S.W.: Australian Medical Pub. Co., 1933. 121pp., illustrated.

Letters, July 1915–April 1919. Moberly spent most of the war in India, tending sick civilians and casualties from the East Africa campaign. Gushy letters "to her man, Peter."

125. Monash, John. *War Letters of General Monash.* Edited by F.M. Cutlack. Sydney: Angus & Robertson, 1934. 299pp., illustrated.

Letters, December 1914–December 1918. Monash began the war in command of the 4th A.I.F. Brigade and rose to command of the 3rd Australian Division before taking over the entire ANZAC force in 1918. Engaging and readable letters, which he wrote to his wife and daughter. See also *The Australian Victories in France in 1918* (1920), a memoir by the same author.

126. Morrow, Edgar. *Iron in the Fire.* Sydney: Angus & Robertson, 1934. 268pp.

Memoir, 1915–1918. Corporal Morrow served in the 28th Battalion, A.I.F., from May 1915 until the end of the war.

127. Nott, Lewis Windermere. *Somewhere in France: The Collected Letters of Lewis Windermere Nott, January–December 1916.* Sydney: HarperCollins, 1996. 334pp., illustrated.

Nott, a native Australian, was adjutant of the 15th Battalion, the Royal Scots. This book is composed of Nott's letters to his wife; those relating to the Battle of the Somme are especially interesting.

128. Old, Ernie. *By Bread Alone: The Autobiography of Veteran Cyclist Ernie Old.* Melbourne: Georgian House, 1950. 183pp., illustrated.

Autobiography, about 30pp. on World War I, when Old was a sergeant in the 13th Light Horse Regiment at Gallipoli and in Egypt and France. Best on Gallipoli.

129. Pacey, William L. *Anzac Diary*. Indooroopilly, Qld.: Roslyn Nicol, 1993. 64pp., illustrated.

Diary, September 1914–August 1915. Pacey served in the 3rd Australian Field Artillery Brigade and was killed at Gallipoli in August 1915. Good diaries, with a gap from February to the beginning of August, 1915.

130. Palmer, Alfred Brian. *Pedlar Palmer of Tobruk*. Canberra: Roebuck Society, 1981. 205pp., illustrated.

Autobiography, part on World War I, during which Palmer served in the Royal Navy and was wrecked on the Galapagos.

131. Palmer, Hartley Valentine. *The Trail I Followed*. Nelson, N.Z.: H.V. Palmer, 1970. 72pp., illustrated.

A New Zealand soldier's memoir.

132. Parton, Horace A. *The War Letters of Horace A. Parton (1891–1943), No. 3980 Co. 12 Rifles, H.Q. Signals, 5th Batt. 2nd. Brigade 1st Division A.I.F.* Whittington, Vic.: T. Parton, 1992. 95pp.

Letters, 1915–1919, describing the author's service in France.

133. Partridge, Eric. *Frank Honywood, Private: A Personal Record of the 1914–1918 War*. Carlton, Vic.: Melbourne University Press, 1987. 146pp.

Originally printed in R.H. Mottram, John Easton, and Eric Partridge, *Three Personal Records of the War*. London: The Scholartis Press, 1929. Memoir, April 1915–December 1918. The author, whose name was Eric Honywood Partridge, served in the 26th Battalion, A.I.F. at Gallipoli (briefly), the Somme, and Passchendaele. He was invalided sick in spring 1918. Very good, straightforward memoir.

134. Pilling, Ewen George. *An Anzac Memory: Extracts from a Rough Diary*. Dunedin, N.Z.: Stanton Brothers, 1933. 163pp., illustrated.

Lieutenant Pilling, a New Zealander of the 1st Otago Battalion, served in Egypt and Gallipoli and was killed near Messines in 1917.

135. Piper, Tom H. *Prisoner of War in Turkey in World War One: An Autobiography*. Lindsdale, Tas.: T.H. Piper, 1987. 91pp., illustrated.

136. Potter, R. C. *Not Theirs the Shame Who Fight: Edited Selections*

from the World War I Diaries, Poems and Letters of 6080 Private R.C. (Cleve) Potter, A Company 21st Battalion A.I.F. Charnwood, A.C.T.: Ginninderra Press, 1999. 210pp., illustrated.

Diary/letters, November 1916–January 1919. Thoughtful, introspective diary interspersed with amateur poems from the trenches, exceptionally revealing of the psychological impact of daily life at the front. Recommended.

137. Pretty, V. *Fragments from Gallipoli and France by a Returned Anzac*. Melbourne: Mitchell & Casey, 1926. 31pp.

Private Pretty served in the 24th Battalion, A.I.F., enlisting in March 1915 and returning to Australia in November 1917.

138. Prince, Thomas H. *Purple Patches. A Tale of the Sappers*. Sydney: Jackson and O'Sullivan, 1935. 304pp., illustrated.

Prince served in the 3rd Field Company of the Australian Engineers, and apparently later became a second lieutenant in the A.F.C.

139. Raws, Goldy, and John Alexander Raws. *Hail and Farewell: Letters from Two Brothers Killed in France in 1916*. Edited by Margaret Young and Bill Gammage. Kenthurst, N.S.W.: Kangaroo Press, 1995. 174pp., illustrated.

Letters, May 1915–August 1916. Alec and Goldy were brothers, both lieutenants in the 23rd Battalion, A.I.F., and both were killed near Pozières in the summer of 1916. Alec's letters were privately printed in 1931 in *Records of an Australian Lieutenant: A Story of Bravery, Devotion, and Self-Sacrifice, 1915–1916*.

Reid, Frank. *See* Vennard, Alexander.

140. Rentoul, Thomas Craike. *Prelude Fugue and Variations: Letters to a Loved One from Chaplain T.C. Rentoul in World War One*. Edited by Noni Faragher. Richmond, Vic.: Spectrum, 1989. 184pp., illustrated.

Letters, March 1916–November 1917. Mostly of family and religious interest, except for a few letters written from France in the spring of 1917.

141. Richardson, Thomas William Victor. *Sergeant Richardson's War: An Australian in World War 1*. Edited by A.D. Bell. Adelaide: Rigby, 1980. 98pp., illustrated.

Published in 1981 as *An ANZAC's War Diary*. Diary, November 1915–July 1919. Richardson served with the 106th Howitzer Battery on the Western Front. Skeletal diary, padded with a large helping of extraneous material.

142. Richer, Arthur. *Diary 1916–1918, Private A. Richer 59th Battalion*. Ballarat, Vic.: Genealogical Society of Victoria, Ballarat Group, for Lyn McKay, 1989. 18pp.

143. Roberts, James Henry. *Jim's Story, with the 37th Battalion A.I.F.* Melbourne: Spectrum Publications, 1982. 131pp., illustrated.

Corporal Roberts enlisted in March 1916 and returned to Australia in July 1917.

144. Robinson, Ira George Harold Augustus. *Dear Lizzie: A Kiwi Soldier Writes from the Battlefields of World War One*. Edited by Chrissie Ward. Auckland: HarperCollins, 2000. 142pp., illustrated.

Letters, January 1917–December 1918. Robinson was a corporal in the 2nd Battalion, New Zealand Rifle Brigade. Mostly commonplace letters with little on the front lines, although Robinson participated in Passchendaele and other major Western Front battles.

145. Rule, Edgar John. *Jacka's Mob*. Sydney: Angus & Robertson, 1933. 346pp.

Memoir, June 1915–December 1918. Rule was an enlisted soldier and lieutenant in the 14th Battalion, A.I.F., serving under Captain Albert Jacka, V.C., on the Western Front. One of the best Australian infantry memoirs, especially good on the Somme and with some revealing observations on Americans in 1918.

146. Sampson, Burford. *The Burford Sampson Great War Diary*. Glenorie, N.S.W.: Richard G. Sampson, 1997. 240pp., illustrated.

Sampson was a major in the 15th Battalion, A.I.F.

147. Savige, Stanley George. *Stalky's Forlorn Hope*. Melbourne: Alexander McCubbin, n.d. 176pp., illustrated.

Captain Savige served in the 24th Battalion, A.I.F., from March 1915 to January 1919.

148. Scrymgeour, James Tyndal Steuart. *Blue Eyes: A True Romance of the Desert Column*. Ilfracombe, Devon: Arthur H. Stockwell, 1961. 83pp.

Private Scrymgeour enlisted in October 1916 and served in the 2nd Light Horse Regiment until August 1918, when he returned to Australia.

149. Sharpe, C. P. M. *The Wanderings of a Rolling Stone*. Bloemfontein, S. Africa: A.C. White P. and P. Co., Ltd., 1923. 99pp., illustrated.

150. Sheldrake, William George. *Personal Diary: The Will of Sheldrake, Gallipoli 1915–1916*. Burswood, W.A.: D. Stone, 1999. 68pp., illustrated.

Private Shedrake enlisted in June 1915, serving in the 2nd Remount Unit until he returned to Australia in July 1916.

151. Sinclair, Ronald Augustine. *Dear Ad-Love Ron: The Complete Collection of the Handwritten Letters and Diary Entries of Ronald Augustine Sinclair, Australian Imperial Forces, Fifth Division Artillery, 14th Field Artillery Brigade, 114th Howitzer Battery on Active Service in Egypt, France and Belgium 1915–1919*. Singleton, N.S.W.: Sisters of Mercy, 1996. 180pp., illustrated.

152. Slater, William. *The War Diaries of William Slater*. Strathmore, Vic.: Astrovisuals, 2000. 268pp., illustrated.

Diaries, 1915–1917. Slater went to France in November 1916 as a stretcher bearer with the 10th Field Ambulance, and served eight months before being wounded and leaving for England. Antiwar; he later served as a prominent Australian Labor politician.

153. Sowden, William John. *The Roving Editors*. Adelaide: W.K. Thomas, 1919. 239pp., illustrated.

Memoir, 1918. Sowden, editor of "The Register," joined an official Delegation of Australian Editors on a tour of the French battlefields in the latter half of 1918.

154. Spencer, Percy E. *The Reminiscences of a Digger*. Perth: V.K. Jones, n.d. 116pp.

Spencer enlisted in December 1915 and served as a driver in the 8th Field Artillery Brigade through the end of the war.

155. Splivalo, Anthony. *The Home Fires*. Fremantle, W.A.: Fremantle

Arts Centre Press, 1982. 225pp., illustrated.

Memoir, 1914–1918. The author, a native Dalmatian from Austria-Hungary and therefore an "enemy alien," spent the war as an Australian internee, most notably at Holdsworthy concentration camp. Valuable perspective on wartime prejudice and jingoism in Australia.

156. Stewart, Alfred Robert Morison. *Diaries of an Unsung Hero*. Edited by Margaret Willmington. Blaxland, N.S.W.: M. Willmington, 1995. 276pp., illustrated.

Letters/diary, August 1915–September 1917. Stewart, a conscientious objector, served as a stretcher bearer with the 17th Battalion, A.I.F., and was killed in service in Polygon Wood in November 1917. Good, detailed entries.

157. Storer, Sam. *The War to End War and General Monash: As Seen by a Frontline Soldier*. Swan Hill, Vic.: Sunraysia Newspaper Services, 1977. 62pp., illustrated.

Memoir, March 1916–1918. Storer was a captain in the 14th Battalion, A.I.F. Vague, episodic reminiscences of the Western Front and the "great man," General Monash.

158. Strawbridge, Allan. *Suspect: The War Story of a Young Artist Accused of Espionage*. London: William Heinemann, 1936. 374pp.

Autobiography, mostly on World War I. Bitterly anti-German tale of a civilian interned in Germany for the war's duration, depicting his severe mistreatment at the hands of his captors.

159. Sutherland, L. W., and Norman Ellison. *Aces and Kings*. London: John Hamilton, 1936. 276pp., illustrated.

Sutherland was a flight lieutenant in No. 1 Squadron of the Australian Flying Corps, which operated in support of Allenby's offensive in Palestine. He flew a variety of aircraft, including the S.E.5a, R.E.8, D.H.6, and a Bristol fighter. Lighthearted memoir, emphasizing the camaraderie and adventure of the air service.

160. Suttor, Harold Bruce. *Journeys of a Light Horseman*. Edited by Andrew Shepherdson. Newtown, Tas.: A. Shepherdson, 2002. 202pp., illustrated.

Letters/diary. Suttor served with A Squadron of the N.S.W. Mounted

Rifles during the Boer War, and was commissioned major of the 7th Light Horse Regiment in 1914. Includes his wife's correspondence as a nurse at the Red Cross Hospital in Giza.

161. Taylor, Patrick Gordon, Sir. *Sopwith Scout 7309*. London: Cassell, 1968. 177pp., illustrated.

Memoir, May–September 1917. Taylor led A Flight of R.F.C. No. 66 Squadron, flying an obsolete Sopwith Scout over the Western Front against superior German aircraft. Excellent aviation memoir. See also *The Sky Beyond* (1963).

162. Taylor, Thomas E. *Peregrinations of an Australian Prisoner of War: The Experiences of an Australian Soldier in Germany and Bolshevic Russia*. Melbourne: E.W. Cole Book Arcade, 1920. 46pp.

Taylor, a soldier in the 14th Battalion, A.I.F., was captured near Bullecourt in April 1917, held a prisoner in Germany, and escaped via Bolshevik Russia. Severely critical observations on Communism and Russian society.

163. Telfer, Reginald. *Dad's War Diaries 1915–1919: Reg Telfer, Australian Medical Corps 27th Battalion*. Claire Taplin, 1996. 323pp., illustrated.

Diary, May 1915–May 1919. Very good diary of a medical orderly, best on the Somme but interesting throughout. Deserves wider publication.

164. Thorp, C. Hampton. *A Handful of Ausseys*. London: John Lane, 1919. 296pp., illustrated.

The author was a New Zealand native in an Australian unit. In this partially fictionalized memoir based on his own diary, he describes a typical Aussie recruit's life from the time he left home until he joined his battalion in France.

165. Tilton, May. *The Grey Battalion*. Sydney: Angus & Robertson, 1933. 310pp., illustrated.

Memoir, July 1915–November 1918. Tilton, an Australian Army nurse, landed in Egypt in September 1915 and served there until September 1916, when she transferred to a hospital in England. In May 1917 she went to France, and worked at hospital on the Western Front until leaving for South Africa in March 1918. Fascinating memoir of Tilton's varied experiences, based on her diaries.

166. Treadwell, Charles Archibald Lawrence. *Recollections of an Amateur Soldier*. New Plymouth, N.Z.: Thomas Avery & Sons, 1936. 252pp., illustrated.

Recollections of a New Zealand soldier at Gallipoli, and in Egypt and France.

167. Treloar, John Linton. *An Anzac Diary*. Armidale, N.S.W.: J.L. Treloar, 1993. 377pp., illustrated.

Diary, October 1914–March 1917. Treloar served as a sergeant on the staff of the 1st Australian Division from 1914 until January 1916, when he was commissioned a lieutenant in the No. 1 Squadron, Australian Flying Corps. In July 1916 he joined the headquarters of I Anzac Corps. Mostly mundane diaries, but with useful details on staff work and the Gallipoli landing.

168. Trotter, F. E. *Tales of Billzac: Being Extracts from a Digger's Diary*. Brisbane: R. McGregor, 1923. 46pp., illustrated.

Lieutenant Trotter served in the 5th Battalion, A.I.F.

169. Tubby, Alfred Herbert. *A Consulting Surgeon in the Near East*. London: Christopher, 1920. 279pp., illustrated.

Memoir, June 1915–March 1919. Tubby was Consulting Surgeon to the Mediterranean and Egyptian Expeditionary Forces, serving at Gallipoli and in Egypt and Palestine. A technical, administrative account.

170. Tuck, Stanley Thomas. *The War Diaries of Stanley Thomas Tuck, 1917 and 1918*. Edited by Gertrude Kirby. Geelong, Vic.: G. Kirby, 1989.

Private Tuck joined up in January 1917 and served in France with the 3rd Squadron, Australian Flying Corps.

171. Tucker, Gerard Kennedy. *As Private and Padre with the A.I.F.* London: The British-Australasian, Ltd., 1919. 162pp.

Chaplain Tucker served after August 1915.

172. Vennard, Alexander [pseud. Frank Reid]. *The Fighting Cameliers*. Sydney: Angus & Robertson, 1934. 226pp.

Memoir, 1916–1918, based on the author's own experiences in the 1st

Battalion of the Imperial Camel Corps in Palestine but written like a unit history.

173. Voss, W. J. *The Light of the Mind.* London: Chapman & Hall, 1935. 208pp.

Autobiography. The author (whose name may be a pseudonym) was an artillery officer. He begins with a wrenching description of his blinding at Ypres and recounts how he coped with it afterwards. Moving and well-written.

174. Watson, John Russell, and George Watson. *Dear Annie.* Edited by Elizabeth Elson. Mornington, Vic.: Elizabeth Elson, 1994. 111pp., illustrated.

Family history, with letters from cousins George and John Russell Watson, who served in Egypt and France. John served with the 5th Field Artillery Brigade and died of wounds in June 1918.

175. Watson, Stan H. *Gallipoli, the Tragic Truth: And Other Recollections of World War One.* Belair, S.A..: S.H. Watson, 1984. 34pp., illustrated.

Major Watson served with the 1st Division Engineers and returned to Australia in September 1918.

176. Webster, Bert. *Suvla to the Somme: The Wartime Letters of Bert Webster, R.A.N. Bridging Train & 23d Battalion, A.I.F.* Edited by Helen Mitchell. Wheelers Hill, Vic.: H. Mitchell, 2001. 193pp., illustrated.

177. Whitaker, Arthur George, and Charles Whitaker. *World War 1 Diaries of Two Brothers: Arthur George Whitaker & Charles Whitaker.* Edited by Helen Skinner. Frankston, Vic.: H. Skinner, 1998. 168pp., illustrated.

178. White, Thomas Alexander. *Diggers Abroad: Jottings By a Digger Officer.* Sydney: Angus & Robertson, 1920. 228pp., illustrated.

Memoir, 1917–1918. White, a captain in the 13th Battalion, A.I.F., provides a lighthearted description of his experiences on the Western Front, including Passchendaele, Cambrai, and the last battles of 1918.

179. White, Thomas Walter. *Guests of the Unspeakable: The Odyssey of*

an Australian Airman, Being a Record of Captivity and Escape in Turkey. Sydney: Angus & Robertson, 1932. 276pp., illustrated.

Memoir, 1914–1918. White, one of the first officers of the Australian Flying Corps, fought with the so-called "Half-Flight" Squadron in Mesopotamia in 1914–1915 before being shot down and captured near Baghdad in November 1915. He was held prisoner in the Middle East until 1918, when he escaped from Constantinople and trekked to freedom across the Balkans and Soviet Russia.

180. Whitelaw, Roy Melsyd. *Somewhere in France: Letters Home, the War Years of Sgt. Roy Whitelaw 1st A.I.F.* Fitzroy, Vic.: Five Mile Press, 1989. 169pp., illustrated.

Letters, 1915–1918. Whitelaw enlisted in August 1915, served in Egypt as an ambulance driver and then drove ammunition trucks in France with the 2nd Australian Motor Transport Company. His letters are records of daily life and leave in London and Paris.

181. Whiteside, Thomas Clair. *A Valley in France: World War I Letters to His Parents and Sister While on Active Service from Egypt, France and Great Britain, 1915–1918.* Beaconsfield, Vic.: E. Whiteside, 1999. 21pp., illustrated.

Whiteside enlisted in July 1915 and served as a corporal in the 59th Battalion, A.I.F. He was wounded in the head at Fromelles and returned home in December 1918.

182. Williams, Ernest Percival. *A New Zealander's Diary: Gallipoli and France, 1915–1917.* Christchurch, N.Z.: Cadsonbury, 1998. 272pp., illustrated.

Originally published in about a dozen copies at the end of the war. Diary, February 1915–November 1917. Williams, a lance-corporal in the 1st Canterbury Battalion, was killed while sniping in December 1917. Detailed, readable diary, with fascinating entries on Gallipoli and Passchendaele.

183. Williams, H. Richard. *The Gallant Company: An Australian Soldier's Story of 1915–18.* Sydney: Angus & Robertson, 1933. 275pp.

Memoir, July 1915–November 1918. Williams was sergeant and subaltern in the 56th Battalion, A.I.F. His memoir is realistically written but patriotic, best on the Somme and the battles of 1918. See also

Comrades of the Great Adventure (1935) by the same author.

184. Wilmer, Basil T. *The Path of Honour: Sgt. Basil T. Wilmer's Experiences in the Great War, 1914–1918*. Launceston, Tas.: A.W. Birchall, 1919. 160pp., illustrated.

Diaries/letters, 1914–1917. Wilmer enlisted in 1914, landed with the first wave at Gallipoli, and was killed in France in 1917 while serving with the 1st Field Artillery Brigade.

185. Wilson, Robert Adams. *A Two Years Interlude: France, 1916–1918*. Palmerston North, N.Z.: Keeling & Mundy, n.d. 115pp., illustrated.

Memoir, February 1916–November 1918. Wilson, a native New Zealander, served as captain and major in the British 116th Siege Battery, fighting at the Somme, Arras, and Passchendaele, and then joined the 5th and 6th Batteries of the 2nd New Zealand Army Brigade in 1918. A somewhat flat but detailed narrative.

186. Wilson, Walter Broughton. *Diary Written While on Active Service Abroad*. Crystal Brook, S.A.: A.K. Wilson, 1985. 33pp.

Sergeant Broughton served from 1915 to 1919 in the 27th Battalion, A.I.F., in Egypt, Gallipoli, and France.

187. Woodward, Oliver Holmes. *The War Story of Oliver Holmes Woodward, Captain, 1st Australian Tunnelling Co., Australian Imperial Force*. Adelaide: McDougalls, 1932. 171pp.

Woodward served on the Somme and other places on the Western Front.

188. Young, William Campbell. *Anderson Inlet Inverloch: World War 1 Diary of William Campbell Young*. Inverloch, Vic.: Published by Norman R. Deacon for the Inverloch Historical Society, 1999. 40pp., illustrated.

Corporal Young enlisted in July 1915 and served in the 2nd Machine Gun Company.

Chapter 2

Austria-Hungary

189. Ackermann, Wolfgang. *And We Are Civilized.* New York: Covici Friede, 1936. 276pp.

Memoir, June 1916–November 1918. Ackermann was a junior officer in an Austrian machine gun unit, fighting in Galicia in 1916–17 and ending the war on the Italian front. Paints a lurid picture of Austro-Hungarian demoralization, with soldiers shooting themselves and their officers in droves.

190. Gál, József. *In Death's Fortress.* Boulder, Colo.: East European Monographs, 1991. 195pp.

Fictionalized memoir, February to June 1916. Gál, a Hungarian, was a common soldier in the 82nd Székely Infantry Regiment. This book, written "on the basis of real episodes" but partly fictionalized, chronicles the experiences of a group of common soldiers in the Sixth Battle of the Isonzo in August 1916.

191. Horthy, Nicholas. *Memoirs.* New York: Robert Speller & Sons, 1957. 268pp., illustrated.

Although most of this memoir covers Horthy's postwar career as dictator of Hungary, a few chapters deal with his service in the Austro-Hungarian navy in World War I. Horthy was wounded at the Battle of Otranto in May 1917.

192. Imrey, Ferenc, and Lewis Stanton Palen. *Through Blood and Ice.* New York: E.P. Dutton, 1930. 353pp., illustrated.

Memoir, December 1913–1919. Imrey, a corporal in a Slovak regiment, describes the early battles of the war and his capture after being severely wounded later that year in the Carpathians. Most of this thoughtful book is about his imprisonment in Russia and subsequent escape after the revolution across Siberia to the Pacific Ocean.

193. Kelemen, Pál. *Hussar's Picture Book: From the Diary of a Hungarian Cavalry Officer in World War I.* Bloomington: Indiana University Press, 1972. 208pp.

Memoir/Diary, August 1914–November 1918. Kelemen fought with a Hussar regiment in the Carpathians and Serbia before being transferred to the 63rd Infantry Regiment in April 1917 and seeing action in the Tyrol. One of the few decent Austro-Hungarian memoirs.

194. Krist, Gustav. *Prisoner in the Forbidden Land.* Translated by E.O. Lorimer. London: Faber and Faber, 1938. 354pp.

Memoir, November 1914–December 1921. Angry account of privations that the author, an Austrian platoon leader, suffered after being captured in Galicia in November 1914. He was held in Central Asia for seven years, and witnessed firsthand the deaths of thousands of his fellow prisoners.

195. Reiter, Michael Maximilian. *Balkan Assault: The Diary of an Officer 1914–1918.* Translated by Shirley Granovetter. London: Historical Press, 1994. 32pp.

Diary, June 1914–October 1918, with gap from September 1915 to September 1917. Reiter, a Hungarian Jew, was a lieutenant in the 3/46th Infantry Battalion and fought in the Italian Alps. Sparse, with a few mildly interesting entries on Caporetto.

196. Spencer, Franz. *Battles of a Bystander.* New York: Liveright Publishing, 1941. 260pp.

Autobiography, about 60pp. on World War I, when Spencer served in a Czech regiment that never saw action because it kept dissolving as soon as it was assembled.

197. Stoffa, Paul. *Round the World to Freedom: Being the Escapes and Adventures of Major Paul Stoffa (of the Hungarian Army).* London: John Lane, 1933. 286pp., illustrated.

Adventures of an Austro-Hungarian officer who was interned for a time in England.

198. Triska, Jan. *The Great War's Forgotten Front: A Soldier's Diary and a Son's Reflections*. Boulder, Colo.: East European Monographs, 1998. 182pp.

Rewritten diary, November 1916–November 1919. Triska, a Czech, was drafted into the 1st Mountain Artillery Regiment in late 1916, and fought for the next two years on the Italian front. This disappointing book is not, alas, Triska's original diary, but son Jan F. Triska's retelling of the diary from the third person perspective, with tiresome additional commentary on subjects like globalization and the world economy.

Chapter 3

Canada

199. Adamson, Agar. *Letters of Agar Adamson, 1914 to 1919, Lieutenant Colonel, Princess Patricia's Canadian Light Infantry*. Edited by N.M. Christie. Nepean, Ont.: CEF Books, 1997. 368pp., illustrated.

Adamson, a Boer War veteran, began the war as a captain in Princess Patricia's Canadian Light Infantry despite being forty-eight years old and blind in one eye. He served at the Somme and commanded the regiment during Vimy Ridge and Passchendaele, where it was effectively destroyed.

200. Adamson, Richard H. *All for Nothing*. Kansas City, Mo.: Privately printed, 1987. 267pp.

Memoir of an infantryman who served for most of the war, most notably at Vimy Ridge and Ypres.

201. Antliff, William Shaw. *Letters Home, World War I, 1916–1919*. Kamloops, B.C.: Antliff Publishers, 1996. 2 vols., 441pp., illustrated.

Diaries, February 1916–March 1919. Antliff, a private in the 9th Field Ambulance, served throughout France and Belgium and was awarded the Military Medal.

202. Bagnall, Frederick William. *Not Mentioned in Despatches*. North Vancouver, B.C.: North Shore Press, 1933. 116pp.

By an "ex-Quaker" who became a sergeant in the infantry.

203. Barry, Arthur L. *Batman to Brigadier*. Newcastle, N.B.: Privately printed, 1965. 90pp.

Memoir, 1914–1919. Barry, a lieutenant and captain in the 26th Battalion, was also honorary colonel of the 2nd New Brunswick (North Shore) Regiment. A mixed account, providing some descriptions of battle on the Western Front and his personal relationships with other officers.

204. Becker, John Harold. *Memoir of John Harold Becker, 1894–1956: World War I Recollections*. Minneapolis, Minn.: C.J.B. Monroe, 1998. 227pp., illustrated.

Memoir, 1915–1919. Becker, a corporal in the 75th Canadian Infantry Battalion, joined his unit after Vimy Ridge. He was gassed at Passchendaele and served until being wounded at Le Quesnel in August 1918. Reissued in 2001 as *Silhouettes of the Great War: The Memoir of Corporal Harold Becker, 1915–1919.*

205. Beland, Henri. *My Three Years in a German Prison*. Toronto: William Briggs, 1919. 280pp., illustrated.

Memoir, July 1914–November 1918. The author was a Canadian doctor of Belgian extraction, and volunteered for the Belgian Army Medical Corps in August 1914. He was captured in October while serving at Antwerp and sent to prison in Germany. He was released to Holland in April 1918. Patriotic and anti-German.

206. Bird, Will R. *Ghosts Have Warm Hands: A Memoir of the Great War, 1916–1919*. Toronto: Clarke, Irwin, 1968. 255pp.

Memoir, July 1916–March 1919. Bird served in France and Belgium with the 42nd Royal Highlanders (Canadian Black Watch), participating in every major Canadian battle after Vimy Ridge, which he missed because of a case of the mumps. His actions include Passchendaele, Arras, and Cambrai. Brilliantly, absorbingly written—quite simply one of the best war memoirs from any country. See *And We Go On* (1930) by same author.

207. Black, Ernest Garside. *I Want One Volunteer*. Toronto: Ryerson Press, 1965. 183pp.

Memoir, 1916–1918. Black went to France in the summer of 1916 with an 18–pounder battery attached to the 3rd Canadian Division, and participated in the Somme, Arras, Vimy Ridge, and Passchendaele. An episodic, non-chronological narrative, full of fascinating details of life at the front but possibly exaggerated in some places.

208. Bongard, Ella Mae. *Nobody Ever Wins a War: The World War I Diaries of Ella Mae Bongard, R.N.* Edited by Eric C. Scott. Ottawa:

Janeric Enterprises, 1998. 70pp., illustrated.

Diary, August 1917–February 1919. Bongard was a native Canadian who trained in New York and joined the U.S. Army Nursing Corps with No. 2 Base Hospital at Etretat, France. Though often mundane, this is a wonderfully engaging diary, edited with a suitably light hand and with excellent illustrations.

209. Bramley-Moore, Alwyn. *The Path of Duty: The War Letters of Alwyn Bramley-Moore*. Calgary, Alta.: Historical Society of Alberta, Alberta Records Publication Board, 1998. 140pp., illustrated.

Letters, August 1914–March 1916. The author, a lance corporal and an original member of Princess Patricia's Canadian Light Infantry, fought in the first major battles of the war before being killed by a German sniper in Sanctuary Wood in March 1916.

210. Breckenridge, William. *From Vimy to Mons: An Historical Narrative*. Sherbrooke, Que.: 1919. 251pp.

Memoir, 1917–1918. Breckenridge served with the 42nd Royal Highlanders (Canadian Black Watch). A useful account of Vimy Ridge in particular.

211. Brophy, John Bernard, and Harold Price. *A Rattle of Pebbles: The First World War Diaries of Two Canadian Airmen*. Ottawa: Dept. of National Defence, 1987. 366pp., illustrated.

John Bernard "Don" Brophy was an R.F.C. pilot who was killed when his plane crashed in an accident in December 1916; Price flew in Mesopotamia.

212. Burns, Eedson Louis Millard. *General Mud: Memoirs of Two World Wars*. Toronto: Clarke, Irwin, 1970. 254pp., illustrated.

Autobiography, about one-third on World War I. Burns went to France in August 1916 as a signal officer in the 11th Canadian Infantry Brigade of the 4th Division, and saw fighting on the Somme, at Vimy Ridge, and Passchendaele. A fairly technical account, "especially of those episodes which seemed to show how troops should *not* be put into battle."

213. Chambers, Wallace. *"A Lovely Letter from Cecie": The 1907–1915 Vancouver Diary and World War I Letters of Wallace Chambers*. Vancouver: Peanut Butter Pub., 1998. 181pp., illustrated.

Chambers was killed at Ypres in 1915.

214. Clint, Mabel Brown. *Our Bit: Memories of War Service by a Canadian Nursing-Sister*. Montreal: Barwick, 1934. 177pp.

Memoir/diary, 1914–1919. Account of a nurse who served at Lemnos and in London and France.

215. Collis, Elsie Dorothy. *Excerpts from Nursing Sister Elsie Collis' First World War Diary: A 1911 Graduate from Victoria's Royal Jubilee Hospital Training School*. Edited by Anne Pearson. Victoria, B.C.: Anne Pearson, 1999. 51pp., illustrated.

216. Collishaw, Raymond, and R. V. Dodds. *Air Command: A Fighter Pilot's Story*. London: William Kimber, 1973. 256pp.

Autobiography, most on World War I. Collishaw trained for the R.N.A.S. in 1915 and became a flight sublieutenant of No. 3 (Naval) Wing in August 1916, flying a Sopwith escort fighter. After February 1917 he flew a Sopwith Pup with No. 3 (Naval) Squadron, and he became flight commander in No. 10 (Naval) Squadron in the summer of that year, flying a Sopwith triplane. In January 1918 he took command of No. 3 (Naval) Squadron, and finished the war with 61 victories, flying subsequently in Russia during the Allied intervention there. A somewhat dry, technical narrative of an epic career.

217. Cooke, Charles Lancelot. *Three Strikes and Not Out*. New York: Carleton Press, 1973. 31pp.

218. Craig, Grace Morris. *But This is Our War*. Toronto: University of Toronto Press, 1981. 148pp., illustrated.

Memoir, 1914–1920. Records the experiences of a young woman on the home front, with portions of her diary and letters from her family members at the front.

219. Dawson, Coningsby. *Living Bayonets: A Record of the Last Push*. Edited by Muriel Dawson. London: John Lane, 1919. 221pp.

Letters, 1918, of a lieutenant in the Canadian Field Artillery. Dawson, better known as the hyper-patriotic author of *Carry On* (1917) and *The Glory of the Trenches* (1918), became a favorite butt of disillusioned memoirists.

220. Dinesen, Thomas. *Merry Hell!: A Dane with the Canadians.* London: Jarrolds, 1930. 254pp., illustrated.

A native Dane, Dinesen was a private in the 42nd Royal Highlanders (Canadian Black Watch). He won the Victoria Cross near Amiens in August 1918.

221. Elvidge, Alfred Richard. *Memoirs of a Quiet Rebel.* Quyon, Quebec: Chesley House, 1997. 157pp., illustrated.

Autobiography, about 50pp. on World War I, when Elvidge served with the 4th Canadian Battalion in France. He was badly wounded at Ypres in May 1915 and never returned to the front; most of his memories concern his medical treatment.

222. England, Robert. *Recollections of a Nonagenarian of Service in the Royal Canadian Regiment, 1916–1919.* Victoria, B.C.: R. England, 1983. 36pp.

The author, a native Irishman, joined the army in 1916 and won the Military Cross in France.

223. Evans, James Lloyd. *My Darling Girl: Wartime Letters of James Lloyd Evans, 1914–1918.* Edited by Susan Evans Shaw. Hamilton, Ont.: Susan Evans Shaw, 1999. 120pp.

Captain Evans served in the 5th Battalion, 1st Division, and died in September 1918 near Arras.

224. Fallis, George O. *A Padre's Pilgrimage.* Toronto: Ryerson Press, 1953. 166pp.

Autobiography, 25pp. on World War I, when Fallis was chaplain of the 8th Brigade, 1914–1915. Mostly frivolous memories, and not very useful.

225. Ferguson, Frank Byron. *Gunner Ferguson's Diary: The Diary of Gunner Frank Byron Ferguson: 1st Canadian Siege Battery, Canadian Expeditionary Force, 1915–1918.* Hantsport, N.S.: Lancelot Press, 1985. 156pp., illustrated.

Diary, November 1915–June 1918. Ferguson's unit, equipped with 9.2–inch howitzers, participated in the initial bombardment of the Somme as well as Vimy Ridge and later engagements at Ypres. Feisty, quotable, and critical of Ferguson's officers and fellow soldiers.

226. Fraser, Donald. *The Journal of Private Fraser, Canadian Expeditionary Force*. Edited by Reginald H. Roy. Victoria, B.C.: Sono Nis Press, 1985. 334pp., illustrated.

Diary, September 1915–November 1917. Fraser enlisted in November 1914 and was assigned to the 31st (Alberta) Battalion. His first action at Kemmel came in September 1915, and he later fought at the Somme, Vimy, and Passchendaele, where he was badly wounded in November 1917. This diary contains long, interesting entries and provides one of the better Canadian accounts of the war.

227. Gass, Clare. *The War Diary of Clare Gass, 1915–1918*. Edited by Susan Mann. Montreal: McGill-Queen's University Press, 2000. 306pp., illustrated.

Diary, March 1915–December 1918. Gass was a lieutenant nursing sister with the Canadian Army Medical Corps, No. 3 Canadian General Hospital, serving at several locations during the war in France and England. Somewhat sparse diaries, but with excellent annotation and illustrations.

228. Gibbons, Arthur. *A Guest of the Kaiser: The Plain Story of a Lucky Soldier*. Toronto: J.M. Dent, 1919.

Memoir of a sergeant in the Toronto Regiment (3rd Battalion, 1st Division) who was captured by the Germans.

229. Goodwin, Vincent E. *Memories of the Forgotten War: The World War I Diary of Pte. V.E. Goodwin*. Port Elgin, N.B.: Baie Verte Editions, 1988. 290pp., illustrated.

Diary, 1917–1919. Goodwin served in the 2nd Canadian Motor Machine Gun Brigade and saw most of his action in the German March 1918 offensive and the Allied counteroffensive that ended the war.

230. Graves, Sandham. *Lost Diary: Being an Eye-Witness Account of the Service of the First Canadian Corps (1914–1917) and Pioneer Fighter Plane Service (1917–1918)*. Victoria, B.C.: Charles F. Banfield, 1941. 131pp.

Memoir, 1914–1918. Graves served in the Canadian Signal Corps before joining the R.F.C. in 1917 and flying over the Western Front, Italy, and the Near East.

231. Hallam, T. D. *The Spider Web: The Romance of a Flying-Boat Flight in the First World War*. Edinburgh: William Blackwood and Sons, 1919. 278pp., illustrated.

Memoir, August 1914–1919. The author commanded flying boat operations at Felixstowe Air Station from March 1917 until the end of the war, mostly in antisubmarine operations. Interesting if largely uneventful, with good illustrations.

232. Harris, Tom, and Christie Harris. *Mule Lib*. Toronto: McClelland and Stewart, 1972. 79pp., illustrated.

Gently humorous reminiscences of a man and his mule on the Western Front.

233. Hartney, Harold Evans. *Up and at 'Em*. Harrisburg, Pa.: Stackpole Sons, 1940. 333pp., illustrated.

Memoir, August 1914–November 1918. Hartney, a Canadian, flew a F.E. 2b pusher with the R.F.C. 20th Squadron until he was shot down and badly injured in in February 1917. After recovery, he was appointed a major in command of the U.S. 27th Aero Squadron, and in August 1918 he assumed command of the U.S. 1st Pursuit Group. One of the most notable aviation memoirs.

234. Hickson, Arthur Owen. *As it Was Then: Recollections, 1896–1930: A Memoir*. Wolfville, N.S.: Acadia University, 1988. 107pp.

Autobiography, partially dealing with Hickson's experiences as a private in the 26th Battalion from 1915 to 1918.

235. Howard, Gordon Scott. *The Memoirs of a Citizen Soldier, 1914–1945*. Regina, Sask.: Privately printed, 1970. 114pp., illustrated.

Autobiography, about 35pp. on World War I, when Howard was a sergeant in the 18th Battery, Canadian Field Artillery. A rough typescript, providing most detailed information on Vimy Ridge and Passchendaele.

236. Humphrey, James McGivern. *The Golden Bridge of Memoirs*. Don Mills, Ont.: Thomas Nelson & Sons, 1979. 182pp., illustrated.

Autobiography, about 50pp. on World War I, when Humphrey was a lieutenant in the 87th Battalion, Canadian Grenadier Guards. He went to

France in August 1916 and was wounded within a month. He returned to the front only in August 1918. Not much on his front line experiences.

237. Kentner, Robert George. *Some Recollections of the Battles of World War I.* Fredonia, N.Y.: I. Kentner Lawson, 1995. 164pp., illustrated.
Kentner served in the 46th Battalion.

238. Kerr, Wilifred Brenton. *"Shrieks and Crashes": Being Memories of Canada's Corps, 1917.* Toronto: Hunter Rose, 1929. 218pp. Sequel: *Arms and the Maple Leaf: Memories of Canada's Corps, 1918.* Seaforth, Ont.: The Huron Expositor Press, 1943. 90pp.
Memoir, June 1916–November 1918. Kerr went to France in January 1917 with the 67th Battery, Canadian Field Artillery, and transferred to the 11th Battery in April 1917, seeing action at Vimy Ridge and Passchendaele. Based on a diary, detailed but dense.

239. Lapointe, Arthur. *Soldier of Quebec (1916–1919).* Translated by R.C. Fetherstonhaugh. Montreal: Edouard Garand, 1931. 116pp. Published in French as *Souvenirs et Impressions de Ma Vie de Soldat (1916–1919).*
Diary, September 1916–February 1919. Lapointe served as a signaler and lieutenant (after October 1918) in the 22nd Battalion. Thoughtful, deeply religious but somewhat sparse diaries.

240. Lind, Francis T. *The Letters of Mayo Lind: Newfoundland's Unofficial War Correspondent, 1914–1916.* St. John's, Newfoundland: Robinson & Co., 1919. 175pp., illustrated.
Cheerful, unremarkable letters of a private in the Newfoundland Regiment who fought at Gallipoli and was killed at Beaumont Hamel in the summer of 1916.

241. McClare, Percy Winthrop. *The Letters of a Young Canadian Soldier During World War I: P. Winthrop McClare, of Mount Uniacke, N.S.* Kentville, N.S.: Brook House Press, 2000. 194pp., illustrated.
Letters, 1915–1917. McClare went to France with the 24th Canadian Infantry Battalion in February 1917 and was killed in action three months later near Fresnoy.

242. Macfie, Arthur, John Macfie, and Roy Macfie. *Letters Home.* Edited

by John Macfie. Parry Sound, Ont.: John Macfie, 1990. 219pp., illustrated.
Letters, 1914–1918. Mostly personal content in these letters of three enlisted soldiers in the 1st Battalion.

243. McKean, George Burdon. *Scouting Thrills*. New York: Macmillan, 1919. 235pp.
Memoir, 1916–1918. McKean was a lieutenant and captain in the 14th Battalion, and won a Victoria Cross near Vimy Ridge in April 1918. Patriotic, semi-Victorian stories of adventure written for boys.

244. MacKenzie, John Joseph. *Number 4 Canadian Hospital; The Letters of Professor J. J. Mackenzie from the Salonika Front*. Toronto: Macmillan, 1933. 247pp., illustrated.
Letters, May 1915–June 1916. MacKenzie served only briefly before returning home because of a heart infection. Mostly mundane, intellectual letters.

245. MacPherson, Donald Stuart. *A Soldier's Diary: The WWI Diaries of Donald MacPherson*. St. Catharines, Ont.: Vanwell, 2001.
McPherson went overseas with the Canadian Field Artillery in 1916 and fought at Vimy Ridge and Passchendaele before being commissioned in 1918.

246. Maxwell, George A. *Swan Song of a Rustic Moralist: Memoirs*. Hicksville, N.Y.: Exposition, 1975. 162pp., illustrated.
Maxwell was a private in the 49th Battalion.

247. Monaghan, Hugh Baird. *The Big Bombers of World War I*. Burlington, Ont.: Ray Gentle, 1976. 101pp., illustrated.
Memoir, August 1914–December 1918. Monaghan went to England with the 79th Canadian Battalion but illness kept him from going to France until 1918, when he became a second lieutenant in No. 215 Squadron, R.F.C. He flew a Handley Page in bombing raids over Germany until he was shot down and captured in September 1918. Dull until the last third of the book.

248. Murdoch, Benedict Joseph. *The Red Vineyard*. Cedar Rapids, Iowa: Torch Press, 1923. 313pp., illustrated.
Memoir, 1917–December 1918. Murdoch was Catholic chaplain of

the 3rd Canadian Infantry Brigade, and saw fighting at Amiens, Arras, and elsewhere in France. Honest view of religious life at the front.

249. Norman, Gisli P. *True Experiences in World War I*. Denare Beach, Sask.: G.P. Norman, 1988. 91pp.

250. O'Brien, Jack. *Into the Jaws of Death*. New York: Dodd, Mead and Company, 1919. 295pp., illustrated.

Memoir, 1914–1918. The author, a private and tunneler in the 28th Northwest Battalion, was captured at St. Eloi in 1916, held prisoner, and eventually escaped to Holland. Conversational, patriotic, and confusing narrative.

251. Ogilvie, William G. *Umty-iddy-umty: The Story of a Canadian Signaller in the First World War*. Erin, Ont.: Boston Mills Press, 1982. 59pp., illustrated.

Memoir, 1916–May 1919. Ogilvie went to France in the summer of 1917 as a signaler in the 21st Howitzer Battery, and saw action at Passchendaele and the major battles of 1918. Written from memory and therefore vague, but with good illustrations.

252. Pedley, James H. *Only this: A War Retrospect, 1917–1918*. Ottawa: Graphic Publishers, 1927. 371pp.

Memoir, 1917–1918. Pedley was a lieutenant in the 4th Battalion from late 1917 until the end of the war, serving at Lens, Hill 70, and other places before being wounded at Amiens in August 1918. An insightful account, revealing the friction that existed among officers and soldiers but also emphasizing their willingness to fight the enemy.

253. Pike, Stephen. *World War One Reminiscences of a New Brunswick Veteran*. Edited by Gene Dow. Hartland, N.B.: Gene Dow, 1990. 56pp., illustrated.

Memoir, 1915–1918, based on taped interviews conducted just before Pike's death. Pike served in France with the 26th Battalion. His obviously fading memory affects his narrative, which includes an account of an overzealous officer being shot by his men.

254. Pope, Maurice Arthur. *Letters from the Front, 1914–1919*. Edited by Joseph Pope. Toronto: Pope & Co., 1993. 154pp.

Letters, in English and French, August 1914–June 1919. Pope went to France in January 1916 as a lieutenant of the 4th Field Company Engineers, 2nd Division, and participated in the latter stages of the Somme. He became a staff officer in December 1916 and never returned to the front. Mildly interesting letters of a professional soldier.

255. Rabjohn, Russell Hughes. *A Diary: A Story of My Experience in France, and Belgium, During the World War, 1914–1918*. Burlington, Ont.: CDM Business Services, 1978. 139pp., illustrated.

256. Rawlinson, James H. *Through St. Dunstan's to Light*. Toronto: T. Allen, 1919. 86pp., illustrated.

Memoir of a blinded soldier from the 58th Battalion.

257. Rhude, S. Burton. *Gunner: A Few Reminiscences of Times with the Canadian Field Artillery, 1916–1919*. Sydney, N.S.: Privately printed, 1981. 130pp.

Rambling, sometimes incoherent account of Rhude's service with the 43rd Battery at Passchendaele and in the battles of 1918.

258. Richardson, Leonard Atwood. *Pilot's Log: The Flying Log, Diaries, Letters Home and Verse of Lt. Leonard Atwood Richardson, Royal Flying Corps, WWI, 1917–1918*. St. Catherines, Ont.: P. Heron, 1998. 257pp., illustrated.

Richardson flew S.E.5a aircraft in R.F.C. No. 74 Squadron.

259. Robinson, Jimmy. *The Life and Times of Jimmy Robinson*. Minneapolis: Associated Lithographers, 1973. 127pp., illustrated.

Autobiography. Robinson, later a well-known sportsman, served in the 44th Battalion and saw action at Vimy Ridge, which he describes in detail.

260. Scott, Frederick George. *The Great War as I Saw It*. Toronto: F.D. Goodchild, 1922. 327pp.

Memoir, 1914–1918. Scott served as Anglican chaplain with the 1st Canadian Division from the war's first battles until he was wounded near Cambrai in 1918. A classic religious memoir, most notable for Scott's devotion to his men and attempts to find his son's grave on the Somme.

261. Stacey, Anthony James, and Jean Edwards Stanley. *Memoirs of a Blue Puttee: The Newfoundland Regiment in World War One*. St. John's, Newfoundland: DRC Publishers, 2002. 190pp., illustrated.

Memoir/biography, October 1914–November 1918. Stacey, one of the first 500 volunteers in the Newfoundland Regiment, saw action at Gallipoli, the Somme, Arras, and Cambrai. Alas, his brief original memoir is buried within Stanley's potted history of World War I, which takes up most of the book. A prime example of over-editing.

262. Steele, Owen William. *Lieutenant Owen William Steele of the Newfoundland Regiment*. Edited by David R. Facey-Crowther. Montreal: McGill-Queen's University Press, 2003. 304pp.

Diary/letters, 1914–1916. Steele, one of the Newfoundland Regiment's "first 500," fought at Gallipoli and was killed at Beaumont Hamel in July 1916 along with most of his regiment. Good entries on Gallipoli in particular, along with general observations on war's psychological impact.

263. Stirrett, George. *A Soldier's Story, 1914–1918: A First Person Account of Captain George Stirrett, M.C., D.C.M., who Served with the First Hussars Through the Years of World War I*. 1974. 28pp.

264. Sutherland, Temple. *The Last Year of the Great War as Seen by Gunner Temple Sutherland*. Edited by George C. Bidlake. Fredericton, N.B.: South Devon Pub., 1996. 56pp., illustrated.

Diary, December 1917–January 1919. Sutherland was a gunner in No. 12 Siege Battery, which was equipped with 6-inch howitzers. He was gassed in October 1918 and spent the rest of the war in the hospital. Very sparse diary, augmented by photos and newspaper clippings.

265. Swanston, Victor N., and Ernest Swanston. *Who Said War is Hell!* Bulyea, Sask.: Yvonne and Ted Burgess, 1983. 62pp., illustrated.

Diaries, August 1914–April 1919. The Swanston brothers were both privates in the 5th Battalion; Victor worked in transport as a teamster. Roughly printed and edited, but with interesting details on front line life.

266. Teahan, John Patrick. *Diary Kid*. Edited by Grace Keenan Prince. Ottawa: Oberon Press, 1999. 197pp., illustrated.

Diary, November 1914–October 1916. Teahan began the war as a corporal in the Royal Canadian Dragoons and ended it as a second lieutenant in the 11th Battalion Sherwood Foresters when he was killed at Thiepval. He was an incredibly meticulous diarist, so much so that it remains fascinating even though the editor omitted about nine-tenths of it.

267. Tompkins, Stuart Ramsay. *A Canadian's Road to Russia: Letters from the Great War Decade*. Edited by Doris H. Pieroth. Edmonton: University of Alberta Press, 1989. 466pp., illustrated.

Letters, October 1912–May 1919. Tompkins was a lieutenant with the 31st Battalion of the 2nd Canadian Division, serving at the front from October 1916 until he was invalided out in April 1917 after Vimy Ridge. In 1919 he was with the 260th Rifle Battalion of the Canadian Expeditionary Corps in Siberia. A few gems exist in this otherwise lengthy, routine correspondence.

268. *Unknown Soldiers by One of Them*. New York: Vantage Press, 1959. 170pp.

Lurid tale of "incidents tragic, comic, horrifying, bawdy, shameful—being spattered with shreds of flesh, blood, and bone, when a shell blotted out a comrade; the horrors of being shelled in caving trenches," and "the sickness from living in cold, mud, and rain; and the sufferings of civilians as the author saw them in France."

269. Vanier, Georges P. *Georges Vanier, Soldier: The Wartime Letters and Diaries, 1915–1919*. Edited by Deborah Cowley. Toronto: Dundurn Press, 2000. 33pp., illustrated.

Letters/diary, May 1915–June 1919. Vanier rose from lieutenant to major of the 22nd (French-Canadian) Battalion before losing a leg near the end of the war. Carefully edited with many interesting entries, but frustratingly sparse at the most dramatic moments, like Vimy Ridge.

270. Walker, Thomas Earl. *A Soldier's Story: An Eyewitness Account from the Battlefield During WWI*. Edited by Bert Walker. Southampton, Ont.: B. Walker, 1997. 102pp., illustrated.

Biography/Letters, May 1915–November 1917. Thomas Walker served with the 26th and 17th Field Artillery Batteries, and was discharged after Passchendaele because of eardrum damage. Heavily edited and censored letters, primarily of personal interest.

271. Walker, Frank. *From a Stretcher Handle: The World War I Journal*

& Poems of Pte. Frank Walker. Edited by Mary Gaudet. Charlottetown, P.E.I.: Institute of Island Studies, University of Prince Edward Island, 2000. 143pp., illustrated.

Diary, 1914–1918. Walker served as a stretcher bearer in the Canadian Field Ambulance, serving at Vimy Ridge and Passchendaele.

272. Wheeler, Victor W. *The 50th Battalion in No Man's Land*. Calgary: Alberta Historical Resources Foundation, 1980. 327pp., illustrated.

Memoir, August 1916–June 1919. Wheeler was a signaler and saw action at the Somme, Lens, Vimy Ridge, Passchendaele, and in most of the major Canadian battles of 1918. He remained patriotic and religious despite some terrible experiences. A very good account, though not always well written.

273. Whiting, Francis James. *Getaway*. Victoria, B.C.: Trafford, 2000. 194pp.

Memoir, 1915–1918. Whiting joined Princess Patricia's Canadian Light Infantry in the spring of 1915 and fought at the Somme, Vimy Ridge, and Passchendaele. Already bitterly disillusioned, he was captured in August 1918 and subsequently escaped. An exciting, thoughtful and readable memoir.

274. Willson, Beckles. *From Quebec to Piccadilly and Other Places, Some Anglo-Canadian Memories*. London: Jonathan Cape, 1929. 366pp., illustrated.

Autobiography, about one-fourth on World War I, when Willson served as Assistant Record Officer for the C.E.F. He became a war correspondent in May 1916 and explored rear areas in France, Italy, and Palestine before the war ended.

275. Wilson-Simmie, Katherine M. *Lights Out: A Canadian Nursing Sister's Tale*. Belleville, Ont.: Mika Pub. Co., 1981. 168pp., illustrated.

Memoir, 1914–1918, of a nurse stationed in France during the war.

Chapter 4

France

276. Arnaud, René. *My Funny Little War*. South Brunswick, N.J.: Barnes, 1967. 154pp. Published in France in 1964 as *La Guerre 1914–1918: Tragédie Bouffe*.

Memoir, January 1915–June 1918. Arnaud was a second lieutenant in the 337th and 293rd Infantry Regiments, and fought in the Champagne in September 1915, Verdun, and the 1917 Nivelle Offensive. Unusual but interesting combination of comic and tragic elements.

277. Bloch, Marc. *Memoirs of War, 1914–15*. Translated by Carole Fink. Ithaca: Cornell University Press, 1980. 177pp., illustrated.

Memoir, August 1914–June 1915. Bloch, a noted historian, was a sergeant in the 272nd Reserve Infantry Regiment, fighting in the Battle of the Marne and then in the Argonne region. Fragmentary, brief memoir padded with much extraneous material; the introduction by Fink is longer than Bloch's memoir.

278. Bringolf, Hans. *I Have No Regrets: The Strange Life of a Diplomat-Vagrant, being the Memoirs of Lieutenant Bringolf*. Edited by Blaise Cendrars. Translated by Warre B. Wells. London: Jarrolds, 1931. 286pp., illustrated. German edition, *Der Lebensroman des Leutnant Bringolf*, published in 1927.

Autobiography, about one-third on World War I, when Bringolf served as a lieutenant in the 3rd Light Infantry, 1st Regiment, French Foreign Legion. He saw most of his fighting in the Balkans. Strange tale of a self-described adventurer.

279. Bunau-Varilla, Philippe. *From Panama to Verdun: My Fight for France*. Philadelphia: Dorrance, 1940. 277pp., illustrated. Published in

Paris, 1937, as *De Panama à Verdun; Mes Combats pour la France.*

Autobiography. The author was an engineer who became embroiled in the Panama Canal controversy and then developed a water-chlorination process used at Verdun.

280. Corday, Michel. *The Paris Front; An Unpublished Diary: 1914–1918.* London: Victor Gollancz, 1933. 395pp.

Diary, August 1914–November 1918. A lengthy account of wartime Parisian politics and society, highly critical of patriotic excesses and propaganda.

281. Desagneaux, Henri. *A French Soldier's War Diary, 1914–1918.* Edited by Jean Desagneaux. Translated by Godfrey Adams. Morley, Yorkshire: Elmfield Press, 1975. 112pp., illustrated. Published in France in 1971 as *Journal de Guerre 14–18.*

Diary, August 1914–February 1919. The author served as an assistant railway control officer until November 1915, when he became a company commander and eventually captain in the 129th Division. He saw action at Verdun, the Somme, the Vosges, Chemin des Dames, and Kemmel. Excellent and authentic, by far the best French account published in English.

282. Foch, Ferdinand. *The Memoirs of Marshal Foch.* Translated by T. Bentley Mott. Garden City, N.Y.: Doubleday, Doran, 1931. 517pp., illustrated.

Covers 1914–1918. Typical view from the top, with most detail on the first and last months of the war.

283. Fonck, René. *Ace of Aces.* Edited Stanley M. Ulanoff, translated by Martin H. Sabin and Stanley M. Ulanoff. Garden City, N.Y.: Doubleday, 1967. 156pp., illustrated. French edition, *Mes Combats*, originally published 1920.

Memoir, August 1914–November 1918. Lieutenant Fonck had 75 confirmed victories, more than any other Allied pilot. He flew Spad VII, XII, and XIII planes with C.47 and Spad 103 Squadrons. A fast-paced, enjoyable memoir.

284. Joffre, Joseph Jacques Césaire. *The Personal Memoirs of Joffre: Field Marshal of the French Army.* Translated by T. Bentley Mott. New

York: Harper & Brothers, 1932. 2 vols., 657pp., illustrated.

Covers 1910 to 1916. Useful especially for Joffre's discussion of Plan XVII and the first year of the war.

285. Lécluse, Henri de. *Comrades-in-Arms: The World War I Memoir of Captain Henri de Lécluse, Comte de Trévoëdal.* Edited by Roy E. Sandstrom. Kent, Ohio: Kent State University Press, 1998. 227pp., illustrated.

Memoir, January 1915–1918. Captain Lécluse commanded the 4th Squadron of the 9th Light Group, attached to the 9th Infantry Division until 1916, and fought in the Champagne and Lorraine. A disappointing, fragmentary memoir, padded with excessive annotation.

286. Pellissier, Robert. *A Good Idea of Hell: Letters from a Chasseur* à *Pied.* Edited by Joshua Brown. College Station, Tex.: Texas A&M University Press, 2003. 256pp., illustrated.

These letters were originally published in France in 1917, although the publisher does not make that fact clear.

287. Pétain, Henri Philippe. *Verdun.* Translated by Margaret MacVeagh. New York: Lincoln MacVeagh, The Dial Press, 1930. 235pp., illustrated.

Memoir, 1915–1916. An obviously biased but nonetheless crucial source for study of this pivotal battle.

288. Roy, René. *The Night's Candles.* New York: Macmillan, 1931. 158pp.

Roy was blinded on the Chemin des Dames; he describes his wounding, hospitalization, and eventual rehabilitation.

289. Rozier, Jean. *Souvenirs de Guerre: Some Reminiscences of My Experiences During the First World War.* Bloomington, Ill.: Scarlet Ibis Press, 1983. 23pp., illustrated. French text bound with English translation by Kathryn Wolfe.

290. Scapini, Georges. *A Challenge to Darkness: The Life Story of J. Georges Scapini.* Garden City, N.Y.: Doubleday, Doran, 1929. Translated by Helen Keller. 173pp.

Autobiography, most on World War I and aftermath. Scapini enlisted in the 39th Infantry Regiment and fought in the Ardennes in August 1914.

He was blinded near Artois in the autumn of 1915, and recounts his wounding, treatment, and recovery.

291. Teilhard de Chardin, Pierre. *The Making of a Mind: Letters from a Soldier-Priest, 1914–1919*. New York: Harper & Row, 1965. 315pp.

Mostly spiritual letters from this priest whose experiences of the First World War heavily influenced his thought. He in turn influenced the moral philosophy of Pope John Paul II.

292. Thenault, Georges. *The Story of the Lafayette Escadrille Told By Its Commander*. Translated by Walter Duranty. Boston: Small, Maynard, 1921. 172pp., illustrated.

Memoir, September 1914–January 1918. Captain Thenault emphasizes the personal relationships among the pilots rather than combat. Well illustrated.

293. Vendel, Henri Joseph. *Down the Red Lane*. Translated by Blair Taylor. Indianapolis: Bobbs-Merrill, 1930. 270pp.

Memoir, 1914–1918. Overwhelmingly sordid tale of an intellectual in the infantry who was disgusted to find himself "fallen among the mob" of the "common herd" of soldiers. He endured years of abject depression in the trenches before finally being evacuated because of illness near the end of the war. Romain Rolland provides an appropriately gloomy introduction.

294. Vibraye, Henri. *Old England: A French View*. Translated by Gerard Hopkins. London: Constable, 1941. 286pp.

General commentary on English popular and military culture, incorporating the author's experiences as an interpreter in the British Cavalry Corps from August 1914 until 1918.

Chapter 5

Germany

295. Bartels, Albert. *Fighting the French in Morocco*. London: A. Rivers, 1932. 255pp., illustrated.

Memoir, 1914–1918. Adventures of a German businessman who escaped French internment in 1914 to join Abdel Malek in guerrilla warfare until 1918. German edition titled *Auf Eigene Faust*.

296. Bensen, Walter. *Hindenburg's Soldier*. New York: Vantage Press, 1965. 177pp., illustrated.

Memoir, August 1914–November 1918. Bensen began the war as a noncommissioned officer in a field artillery regiment and was promoted to ensign in November 1914. He saw fighting in East Prussia, Galicia, and Serbia in 1914–15, and on the Western Front in 1918. The personal element in this memoir is disappointingly weak; it reads like more like a military history of the war.

297. Binding, Rudolf. *A Fatalist at War*. Translated by Ian F.D. Morrow. Boston: Houghton Mifflin, 1929. 246pp.

Memoir, October 1914–November 1918. Binding served as a cavalry officer in Flanders until August 1916, when he was "appointed A.D.C. on the Staff of one of the new divisions then being formed." Binding's contempt for common soldiers and frustration at the cavalry's inactivity makes it difficult to take his pessimism seriously. His book runs against the grain of most German memoirs published between the wars, but it does not justify the attention given to it by historians.

298. Bloem, Walter. *The Advance from Mons, 1914*. Translated by Graeme Chamley Wynne. London: Peter Davies, 1930. 211pp.

Memoir, August–September 1914. First published in Leipzig as

Vormarsch (1916). A brilliant account of the early months of the war by a reserve officer in the Brandenburg Grenadier Regiment, directly addressing the issue of German treatment of civilians as well as the fighting itself.

299. Bodenschatz, Karl. *Hunting with Richthofen*. London: Grub Street, 1996. Edited and translated by Jan Hayzlett. 224pp., illustrated. First published in Munich as *Jagd in Flanderns Himmel* (1935).

Diary, 1917–1918, of Richthofen's adjutant in Jasta 1, chronicling daily events and offering insight into the Red Baron's death. Foreword by Herman Göring.

300. Bucher, Georg. *In the Line: 1914–1918*. Translated by Norman Gullick. London: Jonathan Cape, 1932. 325pp.

German edition published in Leipzig (1930) as *Westfront 1914–1918, das Buch vom Frontkamaraden*, and made into a movie by Georg Pabst the same year. Memoir, 1914–1918, by a private soldier reliving his wartime experiences "in a kind of autonomous dream." Dark, dreary, and at least partially fictionalized.

301. Carossa, Hans. *A Roumanian Diary*. London: M. Secker, 1929. Translated by Agnes Neill Scott. 251pp.

Diary, October–December 1916. Atmospheric but uneventful story of a German doctor's service in the Carpathian mountains of Romania.

302. Degelow, Carl. *Germany's Last Knight of the Air: The Memoirs of Major Carl Degelow*. Translated by Peter Kilduff. London: W. Kimber, 1979. 218pp., illustrated.

Memoir, 1914–1918. Published in Germany as *Mit dem Weissen Hirsch Durch Dick und Dunn* (1920). Degelow served in the infantry until 1916, when he transferred to the air service. He served in Jastas 7, 36 and 40, ended the war as a squadron commander with 30 victories, and was awarded the coveted Blue Max. Good illustrations, and exciting accounts of air combat.

303. Doerflinger, Joseph. *Stepchild Pilot*. Tyler, Tex.: Robert R. Longo, 1959. 191pp.

Autobiography, including an account of his years with Jasta 10 in World War I.

304. Dwinger, Edwin Erich. *The Army Behind Barbed Wire: A Siberian Diary*. Translated by Ian F.D. Morrow. London: Allen & Unwin, 1930. 341pp. Published in Germany as *Die Armee Hinter Stacheldraht: das Sibirische Tagebuch* (1929).

Diary, 1915–1918, describing the hardships endured by German prisoners in Siberia.

305. Ebelshauser, G. A. *The Passage: A Tragedy of the First World War*. Edited by Richard Baumgartner. Huntington, W. Va.: Griffin Books, 1984. 176pp., illustrated.

Memoir, written in third person, August 1914–1920. The author was a Swiss who entered the German army in September 1915, and fought with the 17th Bavarian Infantry Regiment on the Somme and in Flanders before being captured by the British in April 1917. In his first year in the army Ebelshauser was sentenced to death for desertion, acquitted on a technicality, and later won the Iron Cross. A humane, balanced account.

306. Ehlers, Ludwig, and Edmund Gilligan. *One Lives to Tell the Tale*. London: Jonathan Cape, 1931. 356pp., illustrated.

Memoir by a seaman on the freighter *Java*, whose crew was captured by the British at Cape Town and interned in a South African prison camp. Only seventeen men survived the subsequent escape across Africa to German colonial territory.

307. Falkenhayn, Erich Georg Anton Sebastian von. *General Headquarters, 1914–1916, and its Critical Decisions*. London: Hutchinson, 1919. 299pp.

An important staff memoir, particularly for the Battle of Verdun.

308. Fürbringer, Werner. *Fips: Legendary U-Boat Commander, 1915–1918*. Translated by Geoffrey Brooks. London: Leo Cooper, 1999. 224pp., illustrated. Published in Germany as *Alarm! Tauchen! U-Boot in Kampf und Sturm* (1933).

Memoir, 1915–1918. The author was watch officer on the *U-20* but left for other service before that submarine sank the *Lusitania*. He commanded six U-boats before the end of the war. Anecdotal, often vague but exciting account of submarine warfare, accusing the English of at least one atrocity.

309. Heinz, Max. *Loretto, Sketches of a German Volunteer*. Translated by Charles Ashleigh. New York: H. Liveright, 1930. 316pp. Originally published in Berlin as *Loretto: Aufzeichnungen eines Kriegsfreiwilligen*.

Memoir, 1915–December 1918, mostly covering 1915 and 1917–1918. As a private and N.C.O., Heinz fought the French in the Champagne and the English at Loos and Hill 70. He returned to Flanders in April 1917 as a lieutenant, and participated in the March 1918 offensive before being badly gassed and partially blinded near the end of the war. Gripping, unjustly overlooked memoir, possibly the best German account in translation. Particularly interesting observations on the English troops and the 1918 offensive.

310. Hermanns, William. *The Holocaust: From a Survivor of Verdun*. New York: Harper & Row, 1972. 141pp., illustrated.

Memoir, August 1914–November 1916. Hermanns served with a machine gun company of the 67th Regiment. He spent over a year in the Argonne sector before being sent to fight in October 1916 near Verdun, where he was captured by the French. Deeply religious, he came to hate the war and even wrote a letter to the Kaiser in protest. Reveals the often cruel discipline and injustice that lay behind the efficiency of the German army.

311. Heydemarck, Georg Wilhelm. *Double-Decker C.666*. Translated by Claud W. Sykes. London: J. Hamilton, 1931. 207pp., illustrated. German edition, *Doppeldecker C.666*, published in 1916 and 1931.

Memoir, 1914–1918. The first volume covers Heydemarck's experiences as an observer; he later became a pilot over the Western Front and Macedonia. Heydemarck was an early Hitler supporter, and writes accordingly. See also the sequels, Sequels: *Flying Section 17* (*Flieger Abteilung 17*; 1934) and *War Flying in Macedonia* (1935).

312. Hindenburg, Paul von. *Out of My Life*. Translated by F. A. Holt. London: Cassell, 1920. 458pp. Published in Leipzig as *Aus Meinem Leben*. (1920).

Autobiography, with chapters discussing Hindenburg's role in World War I as Field Marshal and co-dictator with Ludendorff.

313. His, Wilhelm. *A German Doctor at the Front*. Washington, D.C.: The National Service Pub. Co., 1933. 230pp.

Memoir, August 1914–November 1918. Dry, technical account of the author's service as a doctor on the Eastern Front from 1914 to 1916 and in 1918, on the Western Front during 1916–1917, including at Cambrai, and on the frontiers of the Ottoman Empire in 1917.

314. Hoffman, Max. *The War of Lost Opportunities*. Translated by Alfred Edward Chamot. London: K. Paul, French, Trubner, 1924. 246pp.

Memoir, 1914–1918 of a German general who served as operations officer of the Eighth Army during the Battle of Tannenberg and spent most of the war on the Eastern Front.

315. Jünger, Ernst. *The Storm of Steel: From the Diary of a German Storm-Troop Officer on the Western Front*. Translated by Basil Creighton. London: Chatto & Windus, 1929. Published in Berlin (1925) as *In Stahlgewittern*. 319pp.

Memoir, January 1915–September 1918. Jünger was a lieutenant in the 73rd Hanoverian Fusilier Regiment and fought mainly against the English in Flanders. The most significant German memoir, and one of the more important of any nation. Frighteningly brutal, with a fervent nationalism of the sort that contributed to the myth that the German army had not been defeated but "stabbed in the back." Essential reading. See also *Copse 125* (1930) by the same author, a more detailed study of a particular episode in the latter part of the war.

316. Kohl, Hermann. *Airman's Escape: Being the Record of a German Airman's Escape from France in 1918*. Translated by Claud W. Sykes. London: John Lane, 1933. 236pp., illustrated.

Autobiography, describing Kohl's experiences as a bomber pilot over France and Italy before he was shot down over France in 1918. He escaped and lived to fly across the Atlantic Ocean in 1928.

317. Kröger, Theodor. *The Forgotten Village: Four Years in Siberia*. Translated by Crystal Herbert. London: Hutchinson, 1936. 320pp. Published in Berlin (1934) as *Das Vergessene Dorf: Vier Jahre Sibirien*.

Politicized tale of a German who tried to escape from Russia to Germany in 1914, was captured, and spent four harrowing years in Siberia.

318. Kühns, Edwin Valentine. *The Diary of a Young German Soldier, 1917–1918*. London: Avon Books, 1998. 52pp., illustrated.

Diary, June 1917–November 1918. Brief diary of a telephonist who served behind the lines at Douai and Bapaume before the armistice.

319. Lehmann, Ernest A. *Zeppelin: The Story of Lighter-Than-Air Craft*. London: Longmans, Green, 1937. 365pp.

Autobiography, half on World War I, when the author commanded zeppelin fleets and personally participated in raids on London and elsewhere. Arrogantly jingoistic, but intriguing, detailed, and readable.

320. Lettow-Vorbeck, Paul von. *My Reminiscences of East Africa*. London: Hurst and Blackett, 1920. Published in the United States as *East African Campaigns* (1957). 335pp., illustrated.

Memoir, January 1914–January 1919. Classic memoir by the commander of German forces in East Africa.

321. Ludendorff, Erich von. *Ludendorff's Own Story, August 1914–November 1918*. New York: Harper & Brothers, 1919. 2 volumes, 477, 473pp., illustrated. Published in Berlin (1919) as *Meine Kriegs-erinnerungen*.

Extremely biased but indispensable memoir of the most important German general of the war.

322. Martin, Alexander Gustav. *Mother Country, Fatherland: The Story of a British-Born German Soldier*. London: Macmillan, 1936. 391pp., illustrated.

Memoir, 1914–1918. The author, lieutenant colonel of the Prussian 6th Dragoons, concentrates on the first Marne campaign and his time as a prisoner in Siberia.

323. Mihaly, Jo. *There We'll Meet Again: A Young German Girl's Diary of the First World War*. Great Britain: W. Wright, 1998. 326pp., illustrated.

Diary, 1914–1918. The author was twelve years old when the war began, living in a village called Schneidemuhl in what is now Poland. Her diary chronicles her growing disgust with the war, culminating in lifelong pacifism.

324. Mücke, Hellmuth von. *The "Ayesha," a Great Adventure: The Escape of the Landing Squad of the "Emden."* Edited by J.C. Lockhard.

London: Philip Allan, 1930. 218pp., illustrated.

Memoir, 1914–1915, describing the adventures of the *Emden*'s landing party from Cocos-Keeling to Constantinople. Includes a description of the ship's career by the editor.

325. Nagel, Fritz. *Fritz: The World War I Memoirs of a German Lieutenant*. Edited by Richard A. Baumgartner. Huntington, W. Va.: Der Angriff, 1981. 116pp., illustrated.

Memoir, 1912–1921. Nagel joined Reserve Field Artillery Regiment No. 18 in August 1914 and participated in the Western Front's first battles before falling ill in October. In January 1915 he was reassigned to Flak Battery No. 54 and remained in that service until the end of the war, serving on the Eastern Front from 1915 until 1917 and in France in 1918, and shooting down two Allied airplanes. Modest, uneventful but very good memoir.

326. Niezychowski, Alfred von. *The Cruise of the Kronprinz Wilhelm*. Garden City, N.Y.: Doubleday, Doran, 1929. 304pp., illustrated.

Memoir, June 1914–April 1915. The author was a lieutenant on the raider *Kronprinz Wilhelm*, which made a celebrated 251–day cruise, capturing numerous ships, before escaping to the United States where ship and crew were interned. More realistic and therefore more interesting than the tales of Count Luckner by Lowell Thomas.

327. Noschke, Richard, and Rudulf Rocker. *Civilian Internment in Britain During the First World War*. Cookham, Berk., England: Anglo-German Family History Society, 1989. 60pp.

Noschke's diary and a short essay by Rocker describe their experiences as internees at places like Stratford and Alexandra Palace.

328. Plüschow, Gunther. *My Escape from Donington Hall, Preceded by an Account of the Siege of Kiao-Chow in 1915*. London: John Lane, 1922. 243pp., illustrated.

Memoir, 1914–1918. Exotic, fascinating account of a German airman who flew reconnaissance missions over the German colony of Tsingtao, China, until the enclave fell in 1915. He then escaped across China and by ship to the United States, and was captured by the British on his way back to Europe. He then escaped from England back to Germany.

329. Renn, Ludwig. *War*. Translated by Willa and Edwin Muir. London: Martin Secker, 1929. 364pp. Published in Frankfurt-am-Main (1929) as *Krieg*.

Fictionalized memoir, 1914–1918, of a career officer and aristocrat who spent much of the war at the front and later became a dedicated communist. One of the most important German war books, superior to *All Quiet on the Western Front*.

330. Rheinstein, Max. *Inside Germany, 1914–1918*. Chicago: Chicago Literary Club, 1942. 28pp.

Memoir, 1914–1918, of a young German soldier's road to disillusionment. Published for the obvious World War II propaganda value.

331. Richthofen, Kunigunde. *Mother of Eagles: The War Diary of Baroness von Richthofen*. Translated by Suzanne Hayes Fischer. Atlen, Pa.: Schiffer, 2001. 207pp., illustrated. Published in Berlin (1937) as *Mein Kriegstagebuch*.

Diary, 1914–1918. Originally published under the Nazi government and thus with a definite bias (in addition to the inevitable mother's bias!), this account provides some interesting information on the home front, and contains letters from and observations on the author's sons Manfred and Lothar.

332. Rieth, Albert Gustav. *War Memories: World War I Experience of Albert Rieth, Bugler, Regiment 169*. Translated by John Kurt Rieth. Williamsburg, Va.: Privately published, 2000. 118pp., illustrated.

333. Rintelen, Franz von. *The Dark Invader: Wartime Reminiscences of a German Naval Intelligence Officer*. London: Lovat Dickson, 1933. 288pp., illustrated.

Memoir, August 1914–February 1921. Rintelen recounts his work as a saboteur in the United States from April 1915 until August 1916, when he was captured in Britain, and his subsequent imprisonment and trial.

334. Rommel, Erwin. *Infantry Attacks*. Novato, Calif.: Presidio Press, 1990. 265pp., illustrated. German edition: *Infanterie Greift An* (1937).

Largely technical account of the lessons Rommel learned as an infantry officer in Italy in 1917. See also *Rommel: in His Own Words* (2003).

335. Rosenhainer, Ernst. *Forward March! Memoirs of a German Officer*. Translated by Ilse R. Hance. Shippensburg, Pa.: White Mane, 2000. 186pp., illustrated.

Memoir, 1914–1918. An excellent memoir, mostly describing Rosenhainer's experiences as an infantry officer on the Eastern Front.

336. Sanders, Liman von. *Five Years in Turkey*. Annapolis: United States Naval Institute, 1927. 325pp., illustrated.

Memoir, June 1913–August 1919. An indispensable source for study of the Gallipoli campaign and the war in the Middle East from the German and Turkish perspective.

337. Schröder, Hans. *An Airman Remembers*. Translated by Claud W. Sykes. London: John Hamilton, 1936. 320pp., illustrated. Published in Leipzig (1935) as *Deutsche Flieger in Krieg und Frieden*.

Memoir, January 1916–November 1918. The author served for most of 1916 on the Eastern Front in Jasta 58; at the beginning of 1917 that unit was renamed No. 248a and transferred to the Western Front, but Schröder was discharged that summer to become an air defense officer, ground observer, and air intelligence officer who interrogated captured enemy airmen. Well written and interesting.

338. Stark, Rudolf. *Wings of War: An Airman's Diary of the Last Year of the War*. London: Hamilton, 1933. 227pp.

Stark fought on the ground from 1914 to 1916 with Uhlan and machine gun units before transferring to flying in 1917. He initially flew in observation aircraft, but in January 1918 he joined Jasta 34b, scoring his first victory in March 1918, transferring to Jasta 77b in May and taking command of Jasta 35b in June. Besides scoring eleven victories, he became one of the war's most accomplished painters of aerial combat.

339. Steffens, Carl. *Krieg 1915–1916*. Orwell, Royston, England: Ellisons' Editions, 1988. 18pp., illustrated.

340. Stumpf, Richard. *War, Mutiny and Revolution in the German Navy: The World War I Diary of Seaman Richard Stumpf*. Edited by Daniel Horn. New Brunswick, N.J.: Rutgers University Press, 1967. 442pp., illustrated.

Diary, July 1914–November 1918. Seaman Stumpf served throughout the war on the battleship *Helgoland*. An extensive and well-annotated diary written in memoir form, with good accounts of Jutland and the German naval mutinies of November 1918.

341. Sulzbach, Herbert. *With the German Guns: Four Years on the Western Front 1914–1918*. Translated by Richard Thonger from *Zwei Lebende Mauern* (1935). London: Leo Cooper, 1973. 256pp., illustrated.

Diary, June 1914–December 1918. Sulzbach served as an enlisted soldier with the 63rd (Frankfurt) Field Artillery Regiment, mainly on the Western Front including the Somme in 1916. Unremittingly jingoistic and thus irritating, but representative of most German memoirs published in the same period. Ironically, Sulzbach was Jewish and fled Nazi Germany to serve with the British army in World War II.

342. Thomas, Lowell. *Count Luckner, the Sea Devil*. Garden City, N.Y.: Doubleday, Page, 1927. 308pp., illustrated. See also *The Sea Devil's Fo'c'sle* (1929) by the same author.

Tales of the captain of the raider *Seeadler*, as retold in a highly sensational style by the popular writer Thomas. The latter book includes an account of Luckner's experiences on the dreadnought *Kronprinz* during the battle of Jutland.

343. Tirpitz, Alfred von. *My Memoirs*. New York: Dodd, Mead, 1919. 2 vols., 377, 428pp., illustrated. Published in Leipzig (1919) as *Erinnerungen*.

Autobiography, a little over half on World War I, with special attention to the prewar Anglo-German naval rivalry and the submarine campaign.

344. Toller, Ernst. *I Was a German*. New York: William Morrow and Company, 1934. 294pp.

Memoir from the author's birth in 1893 to 1933. The young socialist student Toller escaped from France to Germany shortly after the declaration of war in 1914 to enlist as a private in the 1st Heavy Artillery Battalion, and late in 1915 he transferred to a machine gun unit as a corporal, serving near Verdun before being discharged due to illness. The chapters on World War I are powerful and reminiscent of Remarque.

345. Udet, Ernst. *Ace of the Black Cross*. Translated by Kenneth

Kirkness. London: Newnes, 1937. 251pp. Appears in later editions, translated by Stanley M. Ulanoff, as *Ace of the Iron Cross*. Published in Berlin (1935) as *Mein Fliegerleben*.

Autobiography of Germany's second-leading ace, who flew with Jastas 4, 11, 15, and 37 and scored 62 victories. Fast-paced and interesting, describing also his postwar adventures in Africa and North and South America.

346. Wild, Max. *Secret Service on the Russian Front*. New York: G.P. Putnam's Sons, 1932. 324pp.

Memoir, August 1914–November 1918. Wild participated in the Tannenberg campaign as Operations Orderly Officer of 8th Army Headquarters, and then as an espionage and counter-espionage officer on the Eastern Front for two years before his capture. After months in captivity he escaped across Siberia and eventually returned to Germany. Exciting, apparently honest, and very readable, with a good description of the first months of the war on the Eastern Front.

Chapter 6

Great Britain
(England, Ireland, Scotland, and Wales)

347. Abraham, James Johnston. *My Balkan Log*. London: Chapman & Hall, 1921. 311pp., illustrated.

Memoir, 1914–1915, when Abraham served with a Red Cross unit and as a major in the Serbian Army Medical Corps, fighting a typhus epidemic as Serbia battled Austria-Hungary.

348. Adam, Arthur Innes. *Arthur Innes Adam, 1894–1916. A Record Founded on His Letters*. Edited by Adela Marion Adam. Cambridge: Bowes & Bowes, 1920. 253pp., illustrated.

Adam, a captain in the 1st Battalion, Cambridgeshire Regiment, was killed in September 1916.

349. Adam, Helen Pearl. *Paris Sees it Through*. London: Hodder and Stoughton, 1919. 331pp., illustrated.

Memoir, 1914–1919. The author, who lived in Paris throughout the war, chronicles public moods, rationing, shelling, air raids, politics, soldiers marching to the front, and other events in the city during the war.

350. Adams, E. R. *My Travels in Foreign Lands, 1914–1918*. London: Adelphia Press, 1994. 41pp.

Memoir, 1914–1918. Adams became a stretcher bearer in the R.A.M.C. in August 1914, and served on the Western Front and Salonika. His memoirs, written at the age of 94, are confusing and inaccurate in some parts.

351. Adams, H. M. *A War Diary: 1916–1918*. Worcester: Baylis & Son, 1922.

Diary, May 1916–November 1918. Adams was a second lieutenant in the Worcesters. He transferred to the 183rd Light Trench Mortar Battery in July 1916, serving at Neuve Chapelle, the Somme, and Ypres. He then joined the Machine Gun Corps in Italy in February 1918, and remained on that front until the end of the war.

352. Adams, Ralph Edward Cadwallader. *The Modern Crusaders*. London: G. Routledge, 1920. 183pp., illustrated.

Diary, 1917–1918. The author was brigade major of the 231st Brigade Dismounted Yeomanry; he depicts Allenby's first offensive in Palestine. The diary ends when his division transferred to France after the March 1918 offensive. Humorous.

353. Airey, Fred. *The Time of the Soldier*. Fremantle, Western Australia: Fremantle Arts Centre Press, 1991. 211pp., illustrated.

Autobiography, including roughly thirty pages on 1914–1918 as well as Airey's experiences as a prisoner of the Japanese in World War II. During the First World War Airey, who bluffed his way into enlisting at age sixteen, was a decorated sergeant in the 55th (West Lancashire) Division, serving throughout the war in France before being hospitalized with trench feet in 1918.

354. Anderson, A. L. K. *The Unbreakable Coil*. Wolverhampton: Whitehead Bros., 1923. 86pp.

The author served in the 3rd Battalion of the South Staffordshire Regiment.

355. Andrews, Linton. *Haunting Years; The Commentaries of a War Territorial*. London: Hutchinson, 1930. 288pp.

Memoir, 1914–1918. Andrews, a Dundee journalist, joined the 1/4th Black Watch and went to France in February 1915. He served there until January 1918, when he returned home to join an officer's training course. Excellent accounts of Neuve Chapelle, Festubert, Loos, the Somme, and Passchendaele.

356. Andrews, Albert William. *Orders are Orders: A Manchester Pal on the Somme*. Edited by Sue Richardson. Manchester: Neil Richardson, 1987. 66pp., illustrated.

Memoir, September 1914–August 1917. Andrews was a private in the

19th Manchesters. He went into the trenches in December 1915, and was badly wounded and shell shocked during the Somme battles in August 1916. This account, which Andrews wrote during his convalescence in 1917, is short but worth reading.

357. Appleby, Eric. *Love Letters from the Front.* Dublin: Marino, 2000. 287pp., illustrated.

Letters, March 1915–October 1916. Love letters between Liverpudlian Appleby and Phyllis Kelly from the time he enlisted in the Royal Field Artillery until he was killed at the front in October 1916.

358. Aquila. *With the Cavalry in the West.* London: John Lane, 1922. 246pp., illustrated.

Memoir, August 1914–November 1918. The author, a lieutenant in an unnamed cavalry regiment, had his first taste of the front lines in December 1914 and participated in Arras and the British battles of 1918. More sober and realistic than most John Lane publications.

359. Armitage, Robert Linnell. *The Good Old Navy.* Vancouver, B.C.: Privately printed, n.d. post-World War II. 112pp., illustrated.

Memoir, 1914–1918. Rambling yarns of a battleship sailor in the Royal Navy.

360. Arnold, Charles. *From Mons to Messines and Beyond: The Great War Experiences of Sergeant Charles Arnold.* Studley, Warwickshire: K.A.F. Brewin, 1985. 63pp., illustrated.

Memoir, 1908–September 1918. Arnold enlisted in the 1st Battalion, East Surrey Regiment in 1909 and served mostly in Ireland until his regiment went to France in August 1914. He was wounded in the retreat from Mons, and returned to service in November 1915 with the 1st and 6th Battalions of the Border Regiment. After a brief posting in Egypt he saw fighting on the Somme and in Flanders, where mustard gas incapacitated him in July 1917. He wrote this sketchy memoir for his wife before the end of the war.

361. Ashley, R. S. *War Diary of Private R.S. (Jack) Ashley 2472: 7th London Regiment 1914–1918.* Buckhurst Hill: Philippa Stone, 1982. 103pp.

Diary, August 1914–December 1918. Ashley went with his regiment to France in March 1915 and participated in battles at Loos, Vimy Ridge, and the Somme, part of the time as brigade sniper, before he was captured in October 1916. Surprisingly good diary deserves a regular printing.

362. Ashmead-Bartlett, Ellis. *The Uncensored Dardanelles*. London: Hutchinson, 1928. 286pp., illustrated.

Memoir/diary, April 1915–January 1916. Ashmead-Bartlett, a war correspondent renowned for his opulent lifestyle, writes of the Gallipoli campaign from the top, and is highly critical of the British command. Best read in conjunction with the works of the Australian correspondent C.E.W. Bean.

363. Ashmead-Bartlett, Seabury H. *From the Somme to the Rhine*. London: John Lane, 1921. 205pp., illustrated.

Diary, August 1918–January 1919. The author was a staff officer in the 173rd Infantry Brigade, 58th Division. Not very exciting, but provides a reasonably good record of the 58th Division's movements in the last months of the war and the occupation of Germany.

364. Ashurst, George. *My Bit: A Lancashire Fusilier at War, 1914–1918*. Edited by Richard Holmes. Ramsbury, Wiltshire: The Crowood Press, 1987. 144pp., illustrated.

Memoir, August 1914–November 1918. Ashurst, a working-class soldier from Wigan, served as a noncommissioned officer in the 1st, 2nd, and 16th Lancashire Fusiliers. Excellent memoir, well-annotated, with striking accounts of the 1914 Christmas truce, the first day on the Somme at Beaumont Hamel, Passchendaele, and the creeping war-weariness in the British army of 1917.

365. Asquith, Herbert. *Moments of Memory: Recollections and Impressions*. London: Hutchinson, 1937. 382pp., illustrated.

Autobiography, about 150pp. on World War I. The author, Prime Minister Asquith's second son, was commissioned in a brigade of Royal Marine Artillery in late 1914 and served in Flanders in 1915. He sat out 1916 with an illness, and returned to the front as an officer in an R.F.A. in early 1917. He fought at Arras and Passchendaele as part of the 30th Division. Full of strategic and political observations as well as surprisingly candid personal reflections.

Assher, Ben. *See* Borradaile, Colin.

Ayscough, John. *See* Bickerstaffe-Drew, Francis Browning.

366. Bacon, Alban F. L. *The Wanderings of a Temporary Warrior: A Territorial Officer's Narrative of Service (and Sport) in Three Continents*. London: Witherby, 1922. 230pp., illustrated.

Bacon began the war as a second lieutenant in India. He went to Palestine in early 1917, took part in the Third Battle of Gaza, and went to France in time to help stem the final German offensive.

367. Bacon, Reginald. *From 1900 Onward*. London: Hutchinson, 1940. 398pp., illustrated.

Autobiography, part on World War I. Bacon resigned from the Royal Navy in 1909 as a rear-admiral, but returned to service in 1914. He commanded the Dover Patrol from 1915 to 1917, and subsequently became Controller of the Inventions Department. See also *The Dover Patrol 1915–1917* (1919) by the same author.

368. Bailey, Frederick Marshman. *Mission to Tashkent*. London: J. Cape, 1946. 312pp., illustrated.

Memoir, 1918–1919. Gripping tale of espionage by a man whom the Soviets accused of being the British master spy in Central Asia during the first stages of the Russian Civil War.

369. Baily, Francis Evans. *Twenty-Nine Years' Hard Labour*. London: Hutchinson, 1934. 287pp., illustrated.

Autobiography, about half on World War I. The author joined the army in 1916, serving in England as a private in military transport companies before being commissioned and sent to East Africa as a transport officer.

370. Bairnsfather, Bruce. *From Mud to Mufti: with Old Bill on All Fronts*. London: Grant Richards, 1919. 313pp., illustrated.

Amusing and revealing account by the soldiers' cartoonist of World War I, a lieutenant in the Royal Warwickshire Regiment, and a later inspiration to Bill Mauldin. Bairnsfather saw terrible fighting in 1914–1915, and was diagnosed at one point with shell shock. See also *Wide Canvas: An Autobiography* (1939) by the same author.

371. Baker-Carr, Christopher D'Arcy. *From Chauffeur to Brigadier*. London: Ernest Benn, 1930. 323pp., illustrated.

Memoir, August 1914–November 1918. The author, a retired officer of the Rifle Brigade, rejoined in August 1914 as a driver for G.H.Q., and witnessed the first battles in that capacity. In 1915 he was given responsibility for training British army machine-gunners, and ended up helping to establish the Machine Gun School and Corps. He finished the war in command of 1st Tank Brigade, and had the privilege of giving G.B. Shaw a ride in a tank. One of the best staff memoirs, entertaining and informative.

372. Balfour, Harold. *An Airman Marches*. London: Hutchinson, 1933. 282pp., illustrated.

Memoir, August 1914–1933. The author went to France in July 1915 as a subaltern in the King's Royal Rifle Corps, and transferred to R.F.C. Squadron No. 60 the following year. At the end of 1916 he was promoted to captain and made Flight Commander of No. 43 Squadron, where he remained until the end of the war. Several chapters relate his subsequent experiences in the Middle East and Canada.

373. Barber, Margaret H. *A British Nurse in Bolshevik Russia*. London: A.C. Fifield, 1920. 64pp.

Memoir/diary, April 1916–December 1919. Barber served as a Red Cross nurse in Moscow, Petrograd, and the Caucasus. In her memoir she is less concerned with documenting what she experienced than she is with proving that the Bolsheviks were a friendly crowd who committed no atrocities.

374. Baring, Maurice. *R.F.C. H.Q., 1914–1918*. London: G. Bell and Sons, 1920. 315pp.

Memoir, 1914–1918. Baring, a prominent English novelist and war correspondent, served as a staff officer in the Royal Flying Corps. See also *Dear Animated Bust: Letters to Lady Juliet Duff, France, 1915–1918* (1981), by the same author.

375. Barker, Albert W. *Memories of Macedonia*. London: A.H. Stockwell, 1921. 34pp.

376. Barker, George. *Agony's Anguish*. Manchester: Alf Eva, 1931. 96pp.

Rare memoir of a soldier in the 23rd Manchesters.

377. Barnett, George Henry. *With the 48th Division in Italy*. Edinburgh: William Blackwood and Sons, 1923. 162pp., illustrated.

Memoir, November 1917–March 1919. These reminiscences of the senior administrative officer of the 48th Division provide a useful narrative of the unit's activities in Italy.

378. Bartlett, Charles Philip Oldfield. *Bomber Pilot, 1916–1918*. London: Allan, 1974. 180pp., illustrated. Later editions titled *In the Teeth of the Wind*.

Memoir/diary, 1916–1918. Squadron Leader Bartlett served in R.N.A.S. No. 5 Squadron and in R.A.F. No. 205 Squadron, flying a D.H.4 and scoring eight victories over Belgium and France mostly in March 1918. Excellent illustrations.

379. Bayly, Hugh Wonsey. *Triple Challenge: or War, Whirligigs and Windmills. A Doctor's Memoir of the Years 1914–1929*. London: Hutchinson, 1935. 396pp., illustrated.

Bayly served in 1914 on HMS *Princess Royal* and then became Medical Officer of the 2nd Guards Brigade. He tended to Raymond Asquith, the Prime Minister's son, after his mortal wounding.

380. Bayly, Lewis. *Pull Together! The Memoirs of Admiral Sir Lewis Bayly*. London: G.G. Harrap, 1939. 299pp., illustrated.

Autobiography, part on World War I. Based at Queenstown (now Cobh, Ireland), Bayly commanded the Western Approaches from 1915 until the end of the war, collaborating closely with the American destroyers that began arriving there in 1917.

381. Baynes, Rory, and Joseph B. Maclean. *A Tale of Two Captains*. Edited by John Baynes and Hugh Maclean. Edinburgh: Pentland Press, 1990. 178pp., illustrated.

Memoir/letters,1914–1919. Baynes and Maclean were both captains in the Cameronians (Scottish Rifles) but otherwise unconnected. Baynes's account is in the form of a memoir dictated near the end of his life; Maclean's is a collection of letters, many of them more concerned with insurance than the war.

382. Beaman, Ardern Arthur Hume. *The Squadroon.* London: John Lane, 1920. 306pp.

Memoir, 1917–1918. Humorous but reticent memoir of a chaplain of a cavalry regiment, recording life behind the lines, Cambrai, the 1918 German offensive, and the Allied counteroffensive.

383. Beauman, Archibald Bentley. *Then a Soldier.* London: P.R. Macmillan, 1960. 186pp.

Autobiography, part on World War I, 1916–1918, when Beauman was a lieutenant colonel and commander of the South Staffordshire Regiment. He commanded the 69th Brigade in Italy in 1919.

384. Beaumont, Harry. *The Old Contemptible: A Personal Narrative.* London: Hutchinson, 1967. 224pp., illustrated.

Beaumont was an old regular and reservist in 1914, when he joined the Queen's Own Royal West Kent Regiment and went to Flanders. Wounded during the retreat from Mons, he was left for dead and taken up by Belgian civilians, who helped him escape to England nine months later. A unique and fascinating narrative.

385. Behrend, Arthur. *Make Me a Soldier: A Platoon Commander in Gallipoli.* London: Eyre & Spottiswoode, 1961. 156pp., illustrated. Sequel: *As from Kemmel Hill: An Adjutant in France and Flanders, 1917 & 1918.* London: Eyre & Spottiswoode, 1963. 176pp., illustrated.

Memoir, July 1914–November 1918. Behrend served in Egypt and at Gallipoli as a second lieutenant in the 1/4th Battalion, East Lancashire Regiment, until he was hospitalized with dysentery in June 1915. In 1917 he became an adjutant in the 90th Heavy Artillery Brigade, which was equipped with 6- and 9.2-inch guns and fought in France and Flanders. Behrend was an incorrigible optimist who (despite the many unpleasant aspects of war that he witnessed) looked back on his army years as a positive experience.

386. Bell, Henry Douglas. *A Soldier's Diary of the Great War.* London: Faber & Gwyer, 1929. 252pp.

Rewritten diary, August 1914–May 1917. Bell served with the London Regiment until the spring of 1915, when he joined a Scottish regiment as a junior officer, participating in Loos and the Somme. At the end of 1916 he became a pilot in the R.F.C. Plain, straightforward diary with an introduction by Henry Williamson.

387. Bell, John Keble. *An Author in Wonderland.* London: Chatto & Windus, 1919. 222pp.

Memoir, 1914–1918. Bell, a well-known author and playwright, served mainly on the home front, most notably as a propagandist although he was also a support officer in the R.F.C.

388. Bell, William. *A Scavenger in France: Being Extracts from the Diary of an Architect, 1917–19.* London: C.W. Daniel, 1920. 353pp.

Diary, May 1917–March 1919. The author served in France with the Friends Relief Committee, helping both refugees and battle casualties. He provides an account of that work as well as observations on architecture.

Benn, Wedgwood. *See* Stansgate, William Wedgwood Benn, Viscount.

389. Bennett, Septimus. *Septimus Bennett—Artist in Arms: A Sheffield Munitions Worker, 1915–18.* Edited by Martin Phillips and John Potter. Edinburgh: Pentland Press, 2001. 469pp., illustrated.

Biography, with journals dating May 1915–January 1919. Bennett was the younger brother of author Arnold Bennett. His journals provide an intriguing look at munitions work, but are unindexed.

390. Bentinck, Henry. *The Letters of Major Henry Bentinck: Coldstream Guards.* London: Robert Scott Roxburghe House, 1919. 138pp., illustrated.

Bentinck, of the 2nd Coldstream Guards, was killed on the Somme in October 1916.

391. Bentwich, Helen C. *If I Forget Thee: Some Chapters of Autobiography, 1912–1920.* London: Elek, 1973. 170pp., illustrated.

Bentwich was a Zionist and the wife of Norman Bentwich, who became the British Attorney General in Palestine. General observations on her service in the Women's Land Army and experiences in Palestine.

392. Bewsher, Paul. *"Green Balls": The Adventures of a Night-Bomber.* Edinburgh: William Blackwood and Sons, 1919. 309pp.

Memoir, roughly 1915–1918, describing Bewsher's experiences as an observer in R.N.A.S. Squadron No. 7, the first Handley-Page squadron, with a postscript relating his duties as a second-class air mechanic handling a kite balloon at the Dardanelles.

393. Bickerstaffe-Drew, Francis Browning [pseud. John Ayscough]. *John Ayscough's Letters to His Mother During 1914, 1915, and 1916*. Edited by Frank Bickerstaffe-Drew. London: Chatto & Windus, 1919. 323pp.

Letters, mainly on personal and religious topics by a Catholic chaplain in France, August 1914–February 1916.

394. Bidder, Harold Francis. *Three Chevrons*. London: John Lane, 1919. 240pp.

Letters, August 1914–November 1918. The author went to France in December 1914 as a captain in an infantry unit, stayed in or near the front lines in Flanders for most of 1915, fought on the Somme in 1916 as commander of a machine gun company, and took command of an infantry battalion in October 1916. One good letter on Bapaume in December 1916; otherwise lighthearted and not very useful.

395. Bingham, Edward Barry Stewart. *Falklands, Jutland and the Bight*. London: John Murray, 1919. 155pp., illustrated.

Memoir, August 1914–June 1916. Commander Bingham of HMS *Nestor* participated in the Battle of the Bight and the Falklands before being captured when his ship sank at Jutland. One of the most important British naval memoirs.

396. Bion, Wilfred R. *War Memoirs, 1917–1919*. Edited by Francesca Bion. London: Karnac Books, 1997. 312pp., illustrated.

Memoir, June 1917–January 1919. Bion, later a noted psychoanalyst, was a second lieutenant in Battalion "E" of the Royal Tank Corps, earning a D.S.O. at Cambrai on 20 November 1917. He wrote this memoir for his parents in 1919, and although it includes a great deal of useful technical information it excludes the more intimate details that he later recorded in *The Long Week-End 1897–1919: Part of a Life* (1982).

397. Bishop, H. C. W. *A Kut Prisoner*. London: John Lane, 1920. 243pp., illustrated.

Memoir, 1914–1917. The author was captured at Kut along with the remnants of the 6th Indian Division and subsequently escaped with a group of fellow prisoners, trekking on foot over the Anatolian Mountains to the Black Sea and the Crimea, where he finally arrived in October 1917.

398. Blackburne, Harry William. *This Also Happened on the Western Front: The Padre's Story*. London: Hodder and Stoughton, 1932. 191pp.

Diary/Letters, August 1914–1919. Blackburne witnessed the first battles of the war as chaplain of the 3rd Brigade, became Senior Chaplain of 1st Division in 1915, and Senior Chaplain of First Army in 1916. Best on 1914–15, when Blackburne worked more closely with the soldiers.

399. Blacker, Carlos Paton. *Have You Forgotten Yet? The First World War Memoirs of C.P. Blacker*. Edited by John Blacker. Barnsley: Leo Cooper, 2000. 321pp., illustrated.

Memoir, July 1914–November 1918. Blacker tried to join the army in 1914 despite his grave reservations about the righteousness of the Allied cause, but was rejected. He worked for a time as a courier for the Belgian Field Hospital, and in July 1915 was finally accepted in the Coldstream Guards, where he served as a lieutenant in the 4th and 2nd Battalions in France and Flanders. A dense (small print), intellectual, but rewarding memoir for those patient enough to read it.

400. Blackham, Robert James. *Scalpel, Sword and Stretcher: Forty Years of Work and Play*. London: Sampson Low, 1931. 240pp., illustrated.

Autobiography, part on World War I. Blackham, an Irishman, did medical work in India and Afghanistan before going to France and Italy as a colonel in the R.A.M.C.

401. Blackledge, William James. *The Legion of Marching Madmen*. London: Sampson Low, 1936. 244pp., illustrated.

Memoir, 1914–1919, of a soldier who was captured during the Mesopotamian Campaign and held prisoner by the Turks.

402. Blaser, Bernard. *Kilts Across the Jordan; Being Experiences and Impressions with the Second Battalion "London Scottish" in Palestine*. London: H. F. & G. Witherby, 1926. 252pp., illustrated. Preface by Field Marshal Allenby.

Essentially a unit history of the London Scottish told from the enlisted man's point of view.

403. Blunden, Edmund. *Undertones of War*. London: Richard Cobden-

Sanderson, 1928. 317pp.

Memoir, May 1916–March 1918. Blunden served as a second lieutenant with the 11th Battalion, Royal Sussex Regiment. He fought in the Battle of the Somme and Passchendaele. A moving, understated story of a "pastoralist at war," and arguably the best war memoir ever written. Although he is frequently regarded as an apostle of disillusionment, his attitude toward the war is ambiguous. For the observations of a soldier who met Blunden at the front, see entry #493.

404. Bombardier "X". *So This Was War!: The Truth about the Western and Eastern Fronts Revealed.* London: Hutchinson, 1930. 224pp., illustrated.

An explanation of the soldier's point of view for a civilian audience, debunking wartime propaganda and asserting the Tommies' respect for their enemies. First printed in the *Sunday Sun.*

405. Borradaile, Colin [pseud. Ben Assher]. *A Nomad Under Arms; The Chronicle of an Artillery-man from 1914 to the Armistice.* London: H.F. & G. Witherby, 1931. 368pp., illustrated.

Memoir, November 1914–1919. The author began the war as a second lieutenant and ended it as a battery commander of the 115th Heavy Battery, 2nd Corps. He served throughout France and Flanders, including at the Somme and Passchendaele. Oddly written but rewarding.

406. Borton, Arthur Close. *My Warrior Sons: The Borton Family Diary, 1914–1918.* Edited by Guy Slater. London: Peter Davies, 1973. 227pp., illustrated.

The author, a retired colonel, describes events on the home front and the exploits in Gallipoli and Palestine of his sons, Victoria Cross winner Arthur Borton of the 22nd London Regiment, and Amyas of the R.F.C. and Black Watch. Interesting and moving.

407. Bott, Alan. *Eastern Nights—and Flights: A Record of Oriental Adventure.* Garden City, N.Y.: Doubleday, Page, 1919. 298pp, illustrated.

Memoir, 1917–1918. Captain Bott describes being shot down over Palestine, his imprisonment in Constantinople, and his subsequent escape.

408. Boulnois, Helen Mary. *Some Soldiers and Little Mamma.* London: John Lane, 1919. 203pp.

Letters, June–September 1917. Almost intolerably cheery letters of a Y.M.C.A. worker, published as a souvenir for returning troops and dedicated to "my saviours and playfellows, the soldiers in France."

409. Bowen, Stephen. *Forsaken. Confessions of a Priest Who Returned.* London: Williams & Norgate, 1931. 300pp.

Bitter memoir of a priest who was so horrified by the war, and the loss of his brother at Gallipoli, that he lost his religious faith and left the priesthood.

410. Boyd, Donald. *Salute of Guns.* London: J. Cape, 1930. 389pp., illustrated.

Memoir, 1915–1918. Boyd served as an 18–pounder artillery subaltern. A testament of disillusionment, sometimes slow, and perhaps not up to the artistic standard of Sassoon or Blunden, but sincere and affecting nonetheless. Boyd writes that "the violence of the war in certain places was so great that it must have fastened to the earth those who died upon it. . . . Some part of us is still doing duty over there."

411. Bray, Norman Napier Evelyn. *Shifting Sands.* London: Unicorn Press, 1934. 312pp., illustrated.

Memoir, 1911–1918, with commentary on the postwar period. Bray, who was deeply involved in the Arab revolt, writes with equal parts admiration for the Arabs, particularly the House of Saud, and contempt for the "sensational" view of the war in the Middle East propagated by the British Press. He is also critical of T.E. Lawrence and other British officers involved with the Arabs.

412. Brenan, Gerald. *A Life of One's Own: Childhood and Youth.* London: Cambridge University Press, 1962. 244pp., illustrated.

Autobiography. Brenan, later a member of the Bloomsbury Group, served from August to December 1914 as a lieutenant in the 5th Gloucesters, then joined the 48th Divisional Cyclists Company (after 1916 the VIII Corps Cyclists Battalion). He witnessed the Somme, was wounded just before Passchendaele, and won the Military Cross during an admittedly dubious episode in the summer of 1918. Brenan apparently was a somewhat unpleasant man, but he had a fascinating life.

413. Bridges, Tom. *Alarms & Excursions: Reminiscences of a Soldier.*

London: Longmans, Green: 1938. 361pp.

Autobiography, over half on World War I. Bridges fought at Mons as lieutenant colonel of the 4th Hussars, after which he became Head of the Military Mission with the Belgian army. He commanded the 19th Division at the Somme, but has little to say about that episode before going on to describe his 1917–18 experiences in the United States and the Balkans.

414. Brittain, Vera. *Testament of Youth: An Autobiographical Study of the Years 1900–1925*. London: V. Gollancz, 1933. 661pp.

A classic memoir of bereavement, and one of the most important pieces of literature to emerge from the war. Brittain, a member of the "Bloomsbury Group" who would spend the rest of her life as a prominent peace activist, recounts her V.A.D. work, the pathos of the home front, and the loss of her loved ones. See also *Chronicle of Youth: War Diary 1913–1917* (1981) by the same author, and the next entry.

415. Brittain, Vera, et al. *Letters from a Lost Generation: The First World War Letters of Vera Brittain and Four Friends: Roland Leighton, Edward Brittain, Victor Richardson, Geoffrey Thurlow*. Edited by Alan Bishop and Mark Bostridge. Boston: Northeastern University Press, 1998. 427pp., illustrated.

Letters, September 1913–June 1918. Leighton was a second lieutenant in the 4th Norfolk and 7th Worcestershire regiments, killed 1915. Edward Brittain was a second lieutenant and captain in the 10th and 11th Sherwood Foresters, killed in Italy 1918. Richardson was a second lieutenant in the 4th Royal Sussex Regiment and 9th King's Royal Rifle Corps, mortally wounded at Arras 1917. Thurlow was a second lieutenant in the 10th Sherwood Foresters, killed 1917. A fascinating, well-illustrated, and informatively annotated volume.

416. Brocklebank, Henry Cyril Royds. *Tenth Cruiser Squadron, Northern Patrol: from the Diaries and Letters of Captain H. C. R. Brocklebank, C.B.E., Royal Navy, July 1914–August 1917*. Dorchester: Joan Brocklebank, 1974. 57pp., illustrated.

Fragmentary, uneventful diaries of the captain of the cruiser *Drake* and HMS *Changuinola*.

417. Brooke, Geoffrey Francis Heremon. *The Brotherhood of Arms*. London: William Clowes and Sons, 1941. 133pp., illustrated.

Memoir, August 1914–November 1918. In 1914 Brooke was appointed staff-captain to General Gough of the 3rd Cavalry Brigade, witnessing the B.E.F.'s first battles, and he served in a variety of staff positions for the rest of the war. Best on 1914–15.

418. Brown, Cedric Clifton. *Cedric's Letters During the Great War, 1914–1919*. London: William Clowes and Sons, 1926. 162pp., illustrated.

Letters, September 1915–February 1919. Brown served as a subaltern with the Sussex Yeomanry in Gallipoli and Egypt until February 1917, when he transferred to the Worcester Yeomanry in Palestine. He joined the Grenadier Guards in March 1918 and stayed with them until the end of the war, participating in the last British offensive with the Guards Division. Brown's letters are censored and restrained.

419. Brown, William Sorley. *My War Diary (1914–1919) Recollections of Gallipoli, Lemnos, Egypt, and Palestine*. Galashiels: J. McQueen & Sons, 1941. 134pp., illustrated.

The author was a lieutenant in the King's Own Scottish Borderers. Some very good entries, including Brown's experiences in the hospital and notes on war poets.

420. Brownrigg, Douglas. *Indiscretions of the Naval Censor*. London: Cassell, 1920. 279pp., illustrated.

Memoir, 1914–1918. Brownrigg, a retired rear-admiral, was the Admiralty's Chief Censor for the duration of the war. Mildly interesting comments on Jutland and various aspects of war propaganda and censorship, but not very revealing.

421. Bruce, Talbot Baines. *"Missing."* Edited by E.D. Cuming. Edinburgh: W. Blackwood & Sons, 1930. 246pp.

Story of an airman who was shot down over Belgium and eluded German attempts to find him for thirteen weeks.

422. Bruckshaw, Horace. *The Diaries of Private Horace Bruckshaw, 1915–1916*. London: Scolar Press, 1979. Edited by Martin Middlebrook. 229pp., illustrated.

Diary, January 1915–November 1916. Bruckshaw, a private in the Plymouth Battalion of the Royal Marine Light Infantry, served at Gallipoli, Salonika, and on the Western Front before being killed in 1917.

Surprisingly extensive and very well edited, with reproductions of some illustrated diary pages.

423. Bryson, Tom. *In Memoriam: Letters from Tom Bryson, 1917–1918.* London: Sunday School Union, 192–?. 96pp.

Letters from a soldier who died shortly after the end of the war.

424. Buchanan, Angus. *Three Years of War in East Africa.* London: John Murray, 1919. 247pp., illustrated.

Memoir, April 1915–November 1918. Captain Buchanan, a naturalist and explorer, was machine gun officer and map-maker with the 25th Royal Fusiliers in East Africa. An exciting tale of African adventure in the Victorian tradition.

425. Buckle, Elizabeth Braithwaite Turner. *"Triumphant Over Pain."* London: Longmans, Green, 1923. 128pp.

Memoir, 1914–1916, by a former South African War nurse who volunteered for hospital service at Netley in England. Consists mainly of essays on some of Buckle's individual patients.

426. Buckley, Francis. *Q6A and Other Places: Recollections of 1916, 1917 and 1918.* London: Spottiswoode, Ballantyne, 1920. 240pp., illustrated.

Memoir, 1916–1918. Captain Buckley went to France in January 1916 with the 3/7th Northumberland Fusiliers and later served as a bombing officer and brigade observer. He served at Hill 60, the Somme, Arras, and Passchendaele. Includes reproductions of some of his sketches of the front lines. Very interesting, understated memoir though with the "grim and ghastly" horrors suppressed.

427. Buckmaster, Owen Stanley. *Roundabout: The Autobiography of Viscount Buckmaster.* London: Witherby, 1969. 302pp., illustrated.

Autobiography, part on World War I, when Buckmaster served from 1915 to 1916 as a subaltern in the Duke of Cornwall's Light Infantry. He was wounded in early 1916 and posted to an officer cadet battalion.

428. Burgoyne, Gerald Achilles. *The Burgoyne Diaries.* London: Thomas Harmsworth, 1985. 249pp., illustrated.

Diaries, November 1914–May 1915. Burgoyne was a captain in the

2nd Battalion, Royal Irish Rifles. He served near Ypres and was wounded in May 1915 in an attack on Hill 60. Fascinating, detailed and candid diary entries with reproductions of the author's original drawings.

429. Burke, Mick. *Ancoats Lad: The Recollections of Mick Burke.* Swinton: Neil Richardson, 1985. 75pp., illustrated.

Autobiography, including memories gleaned from interviews of the author's wartime service with the 8th Battalion, Manchester Regiment, in Egypt, Gallipoli, and France.

430. Burr, Malcolm. *Slouch Hat.* London: George Allen & Unwin, 1935. 365pp., illustrated.

Autobiography of an Oxford scholar who found himself in command of No. 1 Civil Labor Battalion behind the Salonika front, which consisted of local hired laborers.

431. Bush, Eric Wheler. *Gallipoli.* London: Allen & Unwin, 1975. 335pp., illustrated.

History/memoir, February 1915–January 1916. Though mostly a general history of the Gallipoli campaign, the narrative is interspersed with Bush's memories as a young midshipman on the cruiser HMS *Bacchante.*

432. Butcher, Percy Edwin. *Skill and Devotion: A Personal History of the Famous No. 2 Squadron of the Royal Flying Corps.* Hampton Hill: Radio Modeller, 1971. 87pp., illustrated.

Memoir, August 1914–March 1918, of a mechanic in R.F.C. No. 2 Squadron, the first squadron to cross the channel and join the fighting in France.

433. Butler, Arthur Stanley George. *Plain Impressions.* London: The Aeroplane & General Publishing Company, 1919. 95pp.

Memoir. Butler was commissioned in the Royal Field Artillery in January 1915 and served at Ypres before being wounded in December of that year. He returned to the front in 1916 and was buried by a shell at Arras in April 1917, though he survived. Patriotic propaganda.

434. Butler, Patrick Richard. *A Galloper at Ypres and Some Subsequent Adventures.* London: T. F. Unwin, 1920. 276pp., illustrated.

Memoir, 1914–1915. Butler was lieutenant colonel of a cavalry unit in the 7th Division; this memoir takes him from landing in France to the 1st and 2nd Battles of Ypres.

435. Buxton, Anthony. *Sport in Peace and War*. London: Humphreys, 1920. 119pp.

Meditations and diversions of a cavalryman who found pleasure hunting and fishing behind the lines, with observations on the plants and animals living near the trenches.

436. Byrne, Charlie. *I Survived, Didn't I?: The Great War Reminiscences of Private "Ginger" Byrne.* Edited by Joy Cave. London: Leo Cooper, 1993.

Memoir, 1916–1918, of a member of the 2nd Hampshire Battalion from March 1916 until he transferred to the Machine Gun Battalion of the 29th Division that August. Some quite vivid scenes of life at the front.

437. Callwell, Charles Edward. *Experiences of a Dug-out, 1914–1918.* London: Constable, 1920. 339pp.

Memoir, August 1914–November 1918. Callwell was a retiree who served under Kitchener as Director of Military Operations in the War Office. Dry apologia for the War Office, and disquisition on strategic and political affairs.

438. Campbell, Gordon. *My Mystery Ships*. London: Hodder and Stoughton, 1928. 300pp., illustrated.

Memoir, September 1915–November 1918. Unusual story of Campbell's service on the "mystery ships," which allowed themselves to be torpedoed in order to lure U-boats within gun range. Other odd aspects of anti-submarine warfare are also discussed.

439. Campbell, Patrick James. *The Ebb and Flow of Battle*. London: Hamish Hamilton, 1977. 167pp.

Memoir, March–November 1918. Prequel: *In the Cannon's Mouth* (1979). Campbell was a subaltern in an 18-pounder battery of the Royal Field Artillery attached to the Fifth Army. Refreshingly self-deprecating account; *In the Cannon's Mouth* recounts Campbell's experiences at Passchendaele and *The Ebb and Flow of Battle* describes the German offensive of March 1918 and the British counteroffensive of September-November.

440. Cannan, May Wedderburn, and Bevil Quiller-Couch. *The Tears of War: The Love Story of a Young Poet and a War Hero*. Upavon, Wilts.: Cavalier Books, 2000. 176pp., illustrated.

Letters/Memoir, 1914–1919. Combined poetry, letters, and memoirs of Cannan, a distinguished poet, and Quiller-Couch, a major in the Royal Field Artillery who died of influenza during the occupation of Germany in 1919.

441. Carlisle, Montie. *My Own Darling: Letters from Montie to Kitty Carlisle*. Edited by Christopher Carlisle. London: Carlisle Books, 1989. 256pp., illustrated.

Letters, 1915–1918. Carlisle served as a lieutenant in the 8th (Service) Battalion of the Northumberland Fusiliers, seeing action at Gallipoli and on the Somme, where he was wounded in September 1916. After recovering he became a staff captain of the 101st Brigade. Little on the fighting, but some details of daily life.

442. Carpenter, Alfred Francis Blakeney. *The Blocking of Zeebrugge*. London: H. Jenkins, 1922. 295pp., illustrated.

Memoir, 1918. The author, captain of the cruiser HMS *Vindictive*, describes the blocking of Zeebrugge, a Belgian port and submarine base, in April 1918. Carpenter received one of eleven Victoria Crosses that were awarded after the battle. A good account, both authentic and exciting.

443. Carr, William. *A Time to Leave the Ploughshares: A Gunner Remembers, 1917–18*. London: R. Hale, 1985. 175pp., illustrated.

Memoir, 1917–1918. Carr, a subaltern in the 169th R.F.A. Brigade, participated in Cambrai before helping to stem the German March 1918 offensive. Written when Carr was 101 years old, and best on the battles of 1918.

444. Carrington, Charles [pseud. Charles Edmonds]. *A Subaltern's War: Being a Memoir of the Great War from the Point of View of a Romantic Young Man, with Candid Accounts of Two Particular Battles, Written Shortly After They Occurred, and an Essay on Militarism*. London: P. Davies, 1929. 224pp., illustrated.

Memoir, August 1914–November 1918, with most material relating to the Somme and Passchendaele. Carrington was a lieutenant in the 1/5th

Battalion of the Royal Warwickshire Regiment. An iconoclastic memoir written in opposition to the "disillusionment school," by a young officer who saw very heavy fighting and won the Military Cross. The "Essay on Militarism" is particularly important for providing an often-ignored veteran's perspective on the war. See also *Soldier from the Wars Returning* (1965) by the same author, with an epilogue commenting on the memoirs of Blunden, Graves, and Sassoon. Outspoken as always with respect to the "self-pitying school" of war memoirs, Carrington labels Remarque's *All Quiet on the Western Front* "a bad book inflated into a best-seller by the arts of publicity."

445. Carrothers, John Samuel. *Memoirs of a Young Lieutenant, 1898–1917*. Enniskillen: Print Factory, 1991. 88pp., illustrated.

Letters, June 1914–August 1917. Carrothers was commissioned a second lieutenant in the 3rd Battalion, Royal Inniskilling Fusiliers, in December 1916, and was killed at Passchendaele in August 1917. Some letters on the 1916 Dublin Easter Rising, but otherwise unremarkable.

446. Carton de Wiart, Adrian. *Happy Odyssey: The Memoirs of Lieutenant-General Sir Adrian Carton de Wiart*. London: Jonathan Cape, 1950. 287pp.

Autobiography, with a few chapters on World War I. At the start of the war the author was fighting Dervishes in Somalia, where he lost an eye. He went to France with the 4th Dragoon Guards in February 1915, and lost a hand at 2nd Ypres—"no worse than having a tooth out," he claimed—commanded the 8th Gloucesters at the Somme, and led the 8th North Staffordshires and the 12th Brigade, 4th Division in 1917–1918. Military biography in the Victorian style.

447. Casey, Edward. *The Misfit Soldier: Edward Casey's War Story, 1914–1932*. Edited by Joanna Bourke. Cork: Cork University Press, 1999. 77pp.

Tales of an Irish Cockney in the Royal Dublin Fusiliers, selected by the author of a book called *Dismembering the Male: Men's Bodies, Britain and the Great War* (1996). Bourke has a very definite postmodernist bone to pick and chooses her material accordingly. Readers interested in "military tourism" and Casey's supposed "personal and sexual insecurities" will find this book fascinating; others should look elsewhere.

448. Casson, Stanley. *Steady Drummer*. London: G. Bell & Sons, 1935. 281pp., illustrated.

Memoir, 1914–1918. Casson, an archaeologist, served in the 1st Battalion, East Lancashire Regiment in Flanders in 1915 and around Salonika from 1916 to 1918.

449. Cawston, Edward P. *Reminiscences of Incidents—and Problems Facing Young Officers in the Kaiser War 1914–1918*. St. Leonard's, Sussex: Kent & Sussex Author's Conclave, 1970. 219pp., illustrated.

450. Chandos, Oliver Lyttelton. *From Peace to War: A Study in Contrast 1857–1918*. London: Bodley Head, 1968. 208pp., illustrated.

Autobiography, with section on World War I based on the author's letters to his mother. Chandos served in 1914 with the 4th Battalion, the Bedfordshire Regiment, and joined the 2nd Battalion of the Grenadier Guards when he went to France in February 1915. By the end of the war he had become Brigade Major of the 4th Guards Brigade. Sketchy in places.

451. Channing-Renton, E. M. *A Subaltern in the Field*. London: Heath, Cranton, 1920. 63pp., illustrated.

This book seems also to have been published with the author's name as E.C. Matthews. The author was a lieutenant in the Duke of Cornwall's Light Infantry. See also *Letters from a Bohemian* (1940) by Channing-Renton.

452. Chapman, Guy. *A Passionate Prodigality: Fragments of Autobiography*. London: I. Nicholson and Watson, 1933. 346pp. 1966 first American edition has a new preface by Chapman.

Memoir, December 1914–January 1919. Chapman was an adjutant in the 13th Battalion Royal Fusiliers, City of London Regiment. He reached the Western Front in the summer of 1915 and participated in Arras, where he was badly gassed. An understated, valuable memoir; Chapman, who went on to become a distinguished historian, shows a depth of understanding rarely found elsewhere. See also *A Kind of Survivor: The Autobiography of Guy Chapman* (1975), which contains a chapter of the author's later reminiscences on the war.

453. Charteris, John. *At G.H.Q.* London: Cassell, 1931. 363pp.

Letters, 1914–1918. Charteris was G.H.Q. Chief of Intelligence from January 1916 until January 1918. Massive collection of Brigadier General Charteris's letters to his wife, including discussions of military intelligence, decision-making, and the personalities at Haig's headquarters, and references to less exalted matters such as the Angels of Mons.

454. Clapham, H. S. *Mud and Khaki: The Memories of an Incomplete Soldier*. London: Hutchinson, 1930. 224pp., illustrated.

Memoir, 1915, of a member of the 1st Honourable Artillery Company in Flanders in 1915. Excellent memoir, includes a harrowing account of a German gas attack in April of that year.

455. Clarke, Arthur Oldrid Temple. *Transport and Sport in the Great War Period*. London: Quality Press, 1938. 212pp., illustrated.

Memoir. Clarke served in the 66th Divisional Train, A.S.C., and in the Advanced Horse Transport Depot. Not particularly exciting but valuable memoir of the rear-area troops who kept the army working.

456. Clarkson, David. *Memoirs of a Company Runner: 1914–1918 War*. Edinburgh: Scottish National Institution for War Blinded, 1972. 43pp., illustrated.

Rare book, providing account of a common soldier in Flanders.

457. Clayton, Charles Pritchard. *The Hungry One*. Llandysul: Gomer Press, 1978. 244pp., illustrated.

The author served in the 1st Battalion of the Welsh Regiment and eventually became commanding officer of the 2nd Battalion. Includes valuable description of fighting on the Somme in Mametz Wood.

458. Clayton, Philip Thomas Byard. *Tales of Talbot House*. London: Chatto and Windus, 1919. 169pp., illustrated.

Padre "Tubby" Clayton founded the charity "Toc H" in Talbot House in Poperinghe, Belgium, as a rest center for soldiers. The first two books present various episodes of his experiences and the people he met; the last contains letters to his mother. See also *Plain Tales from Flanders* (1929); and *Letters from Flanders* (1932).

459. Cliff, Norman D. *To Hell and Back with the Guards*. Braunton: Merlin, 1988. 111pp.

Memoir, 1914–1918. This posthumously published memoir chronicles Cliff's experiences in the 1st Battalion of the Grenadier Guards at Loos, the Somme, Passchendaele, and elsewhere on the Western Front. The war left Cliff psychologically devastated, and he describes his feelings in a moving and harrowing manner.

460. Cliffe, Ida Elsie. *SRN at War: A Nurse's Memoirs of 1914–1918.* Birmingham: I.E. Cliffe, 1975. 26pp.

Brief memoir of a nurse's wartime service in Egypt, India, and Mesopotamia; comments on local sights and culture but little of interest.

461. Clouting, Benjamin. *Tickled to Death to Go: Memoirs of a Cavalryman in the First World War.* Edited by Richard Van Emden. Staplehurst: Spellmount, 1996. 178pp., illustrated.

Memoir, edited and transcribed from taped interviews, August 1914–June 1921. Clouting, who enlisted underage, was a trooper in the 4th Dragoon Guards, and his participation in the British army's first engagements around Mons makes up the best part of this book. Well-edited, and a fine tribute to one of the last veterans.

462. Cocker, Frank. *Comrades in Arms: The Letters of Frank Cocker, a Soldier in the Great War: Study in Evidence and Empathy.* Brighton: Tressell Publications, 1988. 45pp., illustrated.

Excerpted letters and diaries, September 1914–November 1918. Cocker served as a private and N.C.O. in the 1/4th Duke of Wellington's (West Riding) Regiment, and became a second lieutenant in the King's Own Yorkshire Light Infantry in September 1917, serving at Ypres and the Somme. Sparse material, heavily edited.

463. Coffey, James. *Active Service Diary Pte J. Coffey 31277 14th Hussars.* Edited by Michael Coffey and Margaret Coffey. Cambridge: Fieldfare Publications, 2001. 68pp., illustrated.

464. Coldicott, Rowlands. *London Men in Palestine and How They Marched to Jerusalem.* London: Edward Arnold, 1919. 232pp., illustrated.

Memoir, November–December 1917. Captain Coldicott, who apparently served in the 2/21st London Regiment of the 60th Division (although he fictionalizes names), realistically describes the capture of Jerusalem and the weeks leading up to it.

465. Colman, Jeremiah. *Reminiscences of the Great War, 1914–1918*. Norwich: Privately Printed, 1940. 104pp.

466. Colwill, Reginald. *Through Hell to Victory; from Passchendaele to Mons with the 2nd Devons in 1918*. Torquay, Devonshire, 1927. 272pp.

Memoir/Regimental History, 1918, describing the activities of the 2nd Devons in March 1918 and their defense of the Chemin des Dames in May.

467. Congreve, Billy. *Armageddon Road: A VC's Diary, 1914–16*. Edited by Terry Norman. London: William Kimber, 1982. 223pp., illustrated.

Diary, July 1914–January 1916, with gap September–November 1915. Congreve was a staff officer in the 3rd Battalion of the Rifle Brigade, and won the Victoria Cross posthumously after being killed on the Somme. Widely published, generally good diary with best passages on Neuve Chapelle, St. Eloi, and Hill 60.

468. Cook, Arthur Henry. *A Soldier's War: Being the Diary of the Late Arthur Henry Cook, Written during Four Years Service with the 1st Battalion. The Somerset Light Infantry, on the Western Front, France, during the Great War, 1914–18*. England: Goodman & Son, 1958. 90pp., illustrated.

Includes reminiscences of the Somme.

469. Cook, Charles St. G. *1914: Letters from a Volunteer*. Edited by Don Cook. Northwood: Don Cook, 1984. 40pp., illustrated.

Letters, October 1914–January 1915. Cook was a private in the 3rd and 10th Battalions, East Surrey Regiment. These letters only describe his training at Dover.

470. Cooke, E. D. M. H. [pseud. Arnewood]. *With the Guns West and East*. London: 1923. 95pp., illustrated.

Memoir, 1915–1918, reminiscing about Loos, the Somme, India, and Palestine. Cooke was one of the first to enter Jerusalem after the capture of the city.

471. Cooper, Matthew. *We Who Knew: The Journal of a Subaltern During the Great War*. Edited by A.M. Cooper. Sussex: The Books Guild, 1994. 102pp., illustrated.

Cooper enlisted in the 8th Royal Inniskilling Fusiliers in Dublin in September 1914, and was commissioned in April 1915. He went into the trenches at Loos in February 1916 and participated in the Battle of Messines that autumn. Sent home as medically unfit in July 1917, he returned to Flanders in April 1918.

472. Coppard, George. *With a Machine Gun to Cambrai: The Tale of a Young Tommy in Kitchener's Army 1914–1918*. London: H.M.S.O., 1969. 135pp., illustrated.

Memoir, based on diaries the author kept during service as a private and corporal in the 6th Battalion, Royal West Surrey Regiment and the Machine Gun Corps. He fought at Loos, the Somme, Arras, and Cambrai, where he was severely wounded. Coppard lied about his age to enlist at age sixteen. One of the best British war memoirs.

473. Corbett, Elsie. *Red Cross in Serbia, 1915–1919; A Personal Diary of Experiences*. Banbury, Oxon: Cheney & Sons, 1964. 186pp., illustrated.

Memoir/diary, May 1915–March 1919. The author was a Red Cross nurse in Serbia during 1915, and after being captured by the Austrians was repatriated and returned to drive an ambulance during the Salonika Campaign of 1916–18. Illustrates the squalid conditions on this front and the wretched state of the "hospitals" compared with the Western Front.

474. Cornelius, Frederick. *Path of Duty*. Portland: Southern Living, 2000. 156pp., illustrated.

Memoir of a soldier in the Royal Naval Division.

475. Courtney, Frank T. *The Eighth Sea*. Garden City, N.Y.: Doubleday, 1972. 297pp.

Autobiography, part on World War I. Courtney began as an air mechanic second class, joined R.F.C. No. 3 Squadron, and eventually became a flight commander. Among other things, he recounts coming out worst in a duel with the German ace Max Immelmann.

476. Cousland, Kenneth H. *The Great War, 1914–1918: A Former "Gunner" of the First World War Looks Back*. Privately printed, 1974.

Memoir, 1913–1919. Cousland recounts his service as a lieutenant and captain in the Royal Field Artillery, particulary around Vimy, Lens, and the Somme, May 1917–October 1918. Scarce.

477. Cowton, Albert E. *With the First in the Field.* Norwich: Privately printed, 1963. 496pp.

Autobiography, with four chapters on World War I. Cowton served with the No. 2 Kite Balloon Section in France and Belgium in 1915, and spent the next two years in Egypt and Mesopotamia with No. 14 Section. Dense, mainly of technical interest.

478. Cox, Sydney. *The Red Cross Launch Wessex on the River Tigris, 1916: Being the Diary of Sydney Cox.* Christchurch, N.Z.: Natula, 2002. 84pp., illustrated.

Diary, 1916. Intriguing diary of an officer on a hospital boat in the Mesopotamian campaign, with excellent photographs.

479. Coxon, Stanley William. *Dover During the Dark Days.* London: John Lane, 1919. 296pp., illustrated.

Memoir, 1914–1918. Commander Coxon describes, in vociferously patriotic language, the exploits and defeats of the Dover Patrol.

480. Creasy, Alfred B. *"It's War."* Seba Beach, Alta., Canada: Purple Wolf Pub., 1998. 296pp.

Reminiscences of a soldier in the Palestine campaign.

481. Creighton, Oswin. *Letters of Oswin Creighton, C.F., 1883–1918.* Edited by Louise von Glehn Creighton. London: Longmans, Green, 1920. 238pp., illustrated.

Creighton, a Church of England chaplain 4th class, served on the Western Front and died in France in April 1918.

482. Croft, William Denman. *Three Years with the 9th (Scottish) Division.* London: John Murray, 1919. 303pp., illustrated.

Memoir, 1915–December 1918. Croft was appointed to command the 11th Royal Scots in 1915, and led it through heavy fighting in Flanders and the Somme. He commanded the 27th (Lowland) Brigade from Passchendaele through the occupation of Germany. Very good memoir by an officer who apparently sympathized with his men.

483. Croney, Percy. *Soldier's Luck; Memoirs of a Soldier of the Great War.* Ilfracombe, Devon: Arthur H. Stockwell, 1965. 319pp., illustrated.

Memoir, 1916–1918. Croney served with the 2nd Cambridgeshire

Regiment at the Somme and subsequently transferred to the Essex Regiment.

484. Crozier, F. P. *A Brass Hat in No Man's Land.* London: Jonathan Cape, 1930. 270pp., illustrated.

Memoir, August 1914–November 1918. Crozier was colonel in command of the 9th Royal Irish Rifles until the autumn of 1916, when he was promoted to brigadier general and placed in command of the 119th Infantry Brigade of the 40th Division. Lauded by Robert Graves and others as one of the best war books, but sadly overrated. Crozier was an arrogant and cynical writer whose accusations (often obvious fabrications) amount to little more than indiscriminate mudslinging; and his wartime reputation as a martinet who cared little for the lives of his men was apparently well deserved.

485. Crundall, Eric D. *Fighter Pilot on the Western Front.* Edited by Chaz Bowyer. London: William Kimber, 1975. 192pp., illustrated.

Diary, 1916–1918. Captain Crundall joined R.N.A.S. No. 8 Squadron in early 1916 and flew Sopwith Triplanes with that unit until the summer of 1918, when he joined R.A.F. No 210 Squadron and flew Sopwith Camels. He eventually scored seven victories.

486. Crutchley, Charles. *Shilling a Day Soldier.* Bognor Regis: New Horizon, 1980. 128pp., illustrated.

Memoir of Gallipoli and the Palestine campaign.

487. Cuddeford, D. W. J. *And All for What?: Some War Time Experiences.* London: Heath Cranton, 1933. 226pp.

Cuddeford enrolled in the Nigerian Land Contingent in 1914, then sailed to England and joined the 3rd Battalion, Scots Guards, in early 1915. In January 1916 he was commissioned in the 12th Highland Light Infantry and saw service on the Somme and at Arras before being seconded to the King's African Rifles in July 1917 for service in East Africa.

488. Cumming, Hanway Robert. *A Brigadier in France, 1917–1918.* London: Jonathan Cape, 1922. 272pp.

Memoir, November 1916–May 1919. Cumming was appointed to command the 91st Infantry Brigade of the 7th Division in November 1916, and took over the 110th Brigade of the 21st Division in March 1918. In the latter capacity he was in the thick of the fight against the last German offensive of the war. Detached narrative, but useful for 1918.

489. Dalton, Hugh Dalton. *With British Guns in Italy, a Tribute to Italian Achievement*. London: Methuen, 1919. 267pp.

Memoir, 1917–1918. The author (who was Chancellor of the Exchequer under Clement Atlee's post-World War II Labour government), served as a subaltern with a siege battery in Italy from July 1917 to the end of the war.

490. Danby, Cyril. *Memories Preserved*. Ilfracombe, Devon: Arthur H. Stockwell, 1980. 61pp.

Memoir, August 1914–February 1919. Danby served as a private in the Machine Gun Corps at Salonika, attached to the 10th (Irish) Division. In 1917 his division was transferred to Palestine, and he participated in Allenby's Gaza battles. Some inaccuracies; apparently compiled from memory.

491. Dare, Jane, pseud. *Letters from the Forgotten Army*. London: Arthur H. Stockwell, 1920. 40pp.

Memories of a nurse at Salonika.

492. Darlington, Henry. *Letters from Helles*. London: Longmans, Green, 1936. 153pp.

Letters, May–September 1915. Lieutenant Colonel Darlington commanded the 1/5th Manchester Regiment in Egypt and Gallipoli. The letters describe his experiences at Gallipoli and the people he met there.

493. Davies, Emlyn. *Taffy Went to War*. Knutsford: Privately printed, 1976. 87pp.

Memoir, August 1914–February 1919. Davies enlisted in July 1915 in the 17th Royal Welch Fusiliers, went over the top at the Somme, and served as a wireless operator at Ypres and Passchendaele. He also met Edmund Blunden at the front. This humble, obscure memoir is remarkably interesting and detailed; it deserves a wider printing. Includes a description of a postwar visit to Ypres.

494. Davies, Richard Bell. *Sailor in the Air*. London: Peter Davies, 1967.

245pp., illustrated.

Autobiography, part on World War I, when Davies was Squadron Commander of No. 3 Squadron R.N.A.S., flying over France and Gallipoli. He won the Victoria Cross for his rescue of a downed pilot in Bulgaria in November 1915.

495. Davis, Arthur Henry. *Extracts from the Diaries of a Tommy (1916–19).* London: C. Palmer, 1932. 292pp., illustrated.

The author served in the Royal Engineers.

496. Davson, Harry Miller. *Memoirs of the Great War.* Aldershot: Gale & Polden, 1964. 172pp.

The author served on the Somme as commanding officer of the 159th Brigade, Royal Field Artillery, attached to the 35th Division. He also wrote the official history of that division, a Bantam unit.

497. Day, Henry Cyril. *A Cavalry Chaplain.* London: Heath, Cranton, 1922. 188pp., illustrated. Sequel: *Macedonian Memories* (1930).

Reminiscences of a Jesuit priest attached to the 2nd Mounted Division in Egypt and Gallipoli; after that unit was dissolved in 1916 he served on the Western Front and at Salonika.

498. Dearden, Harold. *Medicine and Duty: A War Diary.* London: Heinemann, 1928. 234pp.

Diary, approximately 1915–1918 (undated entries). The author, a doctor in the R.A.M.C., describes his service at various base hospitals behind the Western Front. Frequently graphic, with a surprisingly unsympathetic passage about a deserter.

499. DeHavilland, Geoffrey. *Sky Fever: The Autobiography of Sir Geoffrey DeHavilland.* London: Hamilton, 1961. 260pp.

Part of this book deals with DeHavilland's efforts as one of Britain's premier aircraft designers during the First World War.

500. De Lisle, Beauvoir. *Reminiscences of Sport and War.* London: Eyre & Spottiswoode, 1939. 276pp., illustrated.

Autobiography, with about 40pp. on World War I. He commanded the 2nd Cavalry Brigade at Mons, and went on to command the 1st Cavalry Division and the 15th Corps. Excessively self-effacing and therefore sketchy.

501. Denham, H. M. *Dardanelles: A Midshipman's Diary 1915–16*. London: John Murray, 1981. 200pp., illustrated.

Diary, August 1914–January 1916. Denham was a midshipman on the battleship *Agamemnon*. He was in the process of destroying his wartime diaries in his old age when a friend rescued the portion relating to the Gallipoli campaign. It was well worth saving, with excellent information on the naval bombardment of the Turkish forts and the landings. Very good illustrations.

502. Dennis, Gerald V. *A Kitchener Man's Bit: An Account of the Great War 1914–18*. Edited by Michael E. Hickes. Hemingborough, England: MERH Books, 1994. 280pp., illustrated.

Dennis served in the 21st Battalion of the King's Royal Rifle Corps in France and Italy.

503. Devas, Dominic. *From Cloister to Camp: Being Reminiscences of a Priest in France 1915 to 1918*. London: Sands, 1919. 199pp., illustrated.

The author witnessed some of the worst fighting on the Somme in the winter of 1916.

504. Dickson, William Edmund Ritchie. *East Persia: A Backwater of the Great War*. London: Edward Arnold, 1924. 279pp., illustrated.

Brigadier General Dickson went to Persia after the Russian Revolution as Director-General of Communications. Little on the war, mostly concerned with administrative matters and Near Eastern politics.

505. Dillon, Eric Fitzgerald Dillon. *Memories of Three Wars*. London: A. Wingate, 1951. 145pp., illustrated.

Autobiography, mostly on World War I, when Dillon served as a liaison officer to General Foch. Includes some interesting commentary on the high command.

506. Dixon, T. B. *The Enemy Fought Splendidly: Being the 1914–1915 Diary of the Battle of the Falklands & its Aftermath by Surgeon T.B. Dixon R.N.V.R. of HMS Kent*. Poole, Dorset: Blandford Press, 1983. 96pp., illustrated.

Diary, October 1914–May 1915. Absorbing diary of life aboard a

Monmouth-class British cruiser, including detailed descriptions of coaling, searching for German sea raiders, and explorations of the South American coast. Includes account of the Battle of the Falklands and the later destruction of the *Dresden.*

507. Dolden, A. Stuart. *Cannon Fodder: An Infantryman's Life on the Western Front, 1914–18.* Poole, Dorset: Blandford Press, 1980. 185pp., illustrated.

Memoir, November 1914–January 1919. Dolden was a private in the 1st Battalion London Scottish Regiment. Not a particularly bitter memoir, despite the title; good accounts of Loos, Hulloch, Somme, Arras, and other battles based on the author's wartime diaries.

508. Donohoe, Martin Henry. *With the Persian Expedition.* London: Edward Arnold, 1919. 276pp., illustrated.

Memoir, February–November 1918. Donohoe, a former war correspondent who became a major in the Army Intelligence Corps in 1918, describes his experiences as a Special Service Officer with the famed Dunsterforce in northwest Persia.

509. Doughty, Henry. *An Actor-Soldier, Henry Doughty ("Gunga Din"), Extracts from His Letters, 1914–1919.* London: Hutchinson, 1926. 86pp.

510. Douglas, William Sholto. *Years of Combat: The First Volume of the Autobiography of Sholto Douglas.* London: Collins, 1963. 384pp., illustrated.

Memoir, 1914–1918. Douglas began the war in the Royal Field Artillery but transferred to the R.F.C. in 1915, initially as an observer and eventually as commander of Squadron Nos. 43 and 84. Fascinating portrait of the early years of one of the most important figures in British military aviation.

511. Douie, Charles. *The Weary Road: Recollections of a Subaltern of Infantry.* London: John Murray, 1929. 226pp.

Memoir, 1915–1918. Douie was a subaltern in the 1st Dorsetshire Regiment. An insightful meditation on how soldiers experienced and remembered the war, and a critique of the disillusionment school of war writing. Douie does not provide a narrative of his day-to-day life at the front, which he considers too tedious to chronicle in detail, but illustrates his memoir with scenes from the Somme and Flanders, where he spent several weeks stationed on the Belgian coast. One of the best British memoirs.

512. Doyle, William Joseph Gabriel. *Father William Doyle, S.J.: A Spiritual Study*. London: Longmans, Green, 1925. 559pp., illustrated.

Diary/letters, 1914–1917. Doyle, a Jesuit priest attached to the 8th Royal Dublin Fusiliers of the 16th (Irish) Division, was killed at Langemarck in August 1917 while ministering to the dying. He had been ordered to the rear as a noncombatant, but refused. His posthumous nomination for the Victoria Cross was however declined.

513. Draper, Christopher. *The Mad Major: An Autobiography*. London: Air Review, 1962. 225pp., illustrated.

Autobiography, about 50pp. on World War I, when Draper was a Flight Commander of No. 8 Squadron, R.N.A.S. He later gained a reputation as a barnstormer; his wartime experiences will be of interest mainly to aviation enthusiasts.

514. Drobutt, Richard. *I Spy for the Empire*. London: Sampson Low, Marston & Co., 1939. 218pp.

Memoir, 1915–1918. Potboiler of an imperial spy in the Middle East and Asia.

515. Drury, William Edward. *Camp Follower: A Padre's Recollections of Nile, Somme and Tigris during the First World War*. Dublin: Exchequer Printers, 1968. 352pp., illustrated.

Memoir, 1914–1922. Drury was appointed a Church of England chaplain in July 1915 and went to Egypt with the London Rifle Brigade. He then joined the 56th Division in France and served behind the lines at the Somme before being wounded by a shell in May 1917. In November of that year he went to Mesopotamia, later serving in Persia. Dense, dull, and detailed.

516. Dugdale, Geoffrey. *"Langemarck" and "Cambrai": A War Narrative, 1914–1918*. Shrewsbury: Wilding & Son., 1932. 132pp., illustrated.

Memoir, July 1914–November 1918. Dugdale was commissioned a lieutenant in the 2/1 Shropshire Yeomanry in September 1914, but spent a year in England before his unit was shorn of horses and he joined the 6th King's Shropshire Light Infantry in France. After Langemarck, he commanded the Intelligence Department of 6th Division at Cambrai, where he admits to have suffered a nervous collapse. A restrained narrative, in writing which Dugdale "avoided as much as possible the gruesome and disgusting side of the war."

517. Duncan, George Simpson. *Douglas Haig as I Knew Him*. London: Allen & Unwin, 1966. 141pp., illustrated.

Memoir, 1915–1918. Duncan, a Church of Scotland army chaplain, was appointed to G.H.Q. in 1915 and developed a close personal relationship with Haig, who liked his sermons. Obviously biased but useful.

518. Duncan, Walter. *How I Escaped from Germany*. Liverpool: Privately printed, 1919. 108pp.

The author, a lieutenant in the King's Liverpool Regiment, was taken prisoner, escaped from Augustbad and Ingolstadt, and eventually made it to Holland. The hardships he endured hastened his death, which took place shortly after the war. Very anti-German.

519. Dundas, Henry Lancaster Nevill. *Henry Dundas, Scots Guards: A Memoir*. Edited by Robert Nevill Dundas. Edinburgh: William Blackwood and Sons, 1921. 253pp.

Letters, 1916–1918, with additional material by Henry's father and others. Henry, an Eton student at the beginning of the war, was commissioned in the Scots Guards and served on the Western Front from May 1916 until his death in 1918. Very interesting letters illustrating the ambivalence many soldiers felt about their service at the front.

520. Dunham, Frank. *The Long Carry: The Journal of Stretcher Bearer Frank Dunham, 1916–18*. Edited by R.H. Haigh and P.W. Turner. Oxford: Pergamon Press, 1970. 231pp., illustrated.

Diary, April 1916–December 1918. Dunham was a devout Baptist who volunteered for stretcher duty in the 7th Battalion, the London Regiment, serving at Messines and Cambrai, and during the German offensive of March 1918. Perhaps surprisingly, Dunham maintained a certain level of optimism through it all.

521. Dunsterville, Lionel Charles. *The Adventures of Dunsterforce*. London: Edward Arnold, 1920. 323pp., illustrated.

Memoir, January–September 1918. Intriguing memoir by the commander of the British Expeditionary Force that fought the Turks in the exotic surroundings of Persia, Mesopotamia, and the Caucasus in the last year of the war, culminating in the occupation of Baku.

522. Durnford, H. G. *The Tunnellers of Holzminden (With a Side-Issue)*. Cambridge: Cambridge University Press, 1920. 196pp., illustrated.

Memoir providing one of the war's best escape accounts. The author describes how he and others dug a tunnel under the wire at the Holzminden prison camp and eventually made it across Danish frontier.

523. Eades, Tom. *The War Diary and Letters of Corporal Tom Eades 1915–17*. Cambridge: Cambridge Aids to Learning, 1972. 47pp., illustrated.

Diary, October 1915–December 1917. Fragmentary; most detail relates to the author's service with the 27th Labour Company, Army Service Corps, at Gallipoli, where he unloaded supplies on the beaches. Some diary entries, and letters home, concern Egypt and Salonika in 1916–1917.

Easton, John. See entry #750.

524. Eberle, Victor Fuller. *My Sapper Venture*. London: Pitman, 1973. 208pp.

Memoir, autumn 1915–January 1917. Lieutenant Colonel Eberle describes his experiences with a field company of the Royal Engineers on the Somme and in Italy, including notes on the early development of the Bangalore Torpedo.

525. Eden, Anthony. *Another World, 1897–1917*. London: A. Lane, 1976. 156pp., illustrated.

Somewhat more than half of this memoir deals with Eden's service as a subaltern and adjutant with the 21st Battalion (Yeoman Rifles), King's Royal Rifle Corps during the war. He won a Military Cross at the Somme and eventually became a Brigade Major. An honest, moving account that shed's light on Eden's future career as Foreign Secretary and Prime Minister.

Edmonds, Charles. *See* Carrington, Charles.

526. Ellison, Norman F. *Remembrances of Hell: The First World War Diary of Naturalist, Writer and Broadcaster, Norman F. Ellison–"Nomad" of the BBC*. Edited by David R. Lewis. Shrewsbury: Airlife, 1997. 158pp., illustrated.

Memoir/diary, August 1914–January 1917. Ellison enlisted as a private in the 1/6th Battalion, The King's Liverpool Regiment, in August 1914 and saw action on the Somme and Flanders until trench foot ended his active service in January 1917. Heavily padded with extraneous material, but well illustrated and interesting.

527. Empson, C. C., ed. *Empson's War: A Collection of Letters*. Edinburgh: Pentland Press, 1995. 177pp., illustrated.

Letters, 1914–1918, from two brothers at the front, offering little of interest.

528. Evans, Alfred John. *The Escaping Club*. London: John Lane, 1921. 267pp., illustrated.

Considered one of the best entries in the long list of escape memoirs. Evans escaped from the infamous "Fort 9" at Ingolstadt, Germany, which had been established especially to holding most escape-prone prisoners. He made it to Switzerland, but after his return to service he was shot down over Palestine, falling into the hands of Arabs and Turks. His tale is said to have inspired many escapes in World War II.

529. Evans, Edward Radcliffe. *Keeping the Seas*. London: Sampson Low, Marston & Co., 1920. 326pp.

Memoir, August 1914–1919. Captain Evans commanded destroyers on the Dover Patrol, and was on HMS *Broke* during a battle with German raiders in March 1917.

530. Evans de Carbery, Francis Martin St. Helier. *Going Across; or, With the 9th Welch in the Butterfly Division; Being Extracts from the War Letters and Diary of M. St. Helier Evans*. Newport, Monmouth: R.H. Johns, 1952. 228pp., illustrated.

Combined letters and diaries, April 1916–May 1918. The author, a lieutenant, served at the Somme and Passchendaele before being captured in May 1918. Honest and realistic chronicle, with good descriptions of both major battles.

531. Ewart, Wilfrid Herbert Gore. *When Armageddon Came; Studies in Peace and War*. Edited by John Gawsworth. London: Rich and Cowan, 1933. 368pp.

Ewart served as a captain in the 2nd Scots Guards. This is a series of his essays on Ypres, Bourlon Wood, Neuve Chapelle, Arras, Aubers, and other episodes of the war. Ewart is better known for his novel about the war, *Way of Revelation* (1921); see also his book *Scots Guard* (1934).

532. *Experiences of a War Baby*. London: Gieves, 1920. 160pp., illustrated.

Memoir, 1914–1918. Memories of a young naval cadet who became a midshipman and acting sub-lieutenant, serving in the Grand Fleet at the Battle of Jutland.

533. Eyre, Giles Edward M. *Somme Harvest; Memories of a P.B.I. in the Summer of 1916*. London: Jarrolds, 1938. 255pp.

Memoir, May–July 1916. Eyre served in the 2nd King's Royal Rifle Corps. He describes here his terrible experiences at Loos and on the Somme, when his unit was shattered and he was taken prisoner. William Mariner, V.C., was blown apart in front of the author.

534. Farmborough, Florence. *Nurse at the Russian Front: A Diary, 1914–18*. London: Constable, 1974. 422pp., illustrated.

Diary, August 1914–April 1918. Farmborough had been living in Russia since 1908 when the war broke out, and she served as a Red Cross volunteer at the front until the Bolshevik Revolution forced her to leave the country. A harrowing and generally objective account of Russia's war effort despite the author's sometimes naive faith in the Czar. One of the best books about the Russian front, with excellent photographs. See also *Russian Album 1908–1918* by Farmborough, edited by John Joliffe (1979).

535. Fawcett, Margaret. *The First World War Papers of Margaret Fawcett: Letters and Diaries from Russia and Roumania 1916–1917*. Edited by Audrey Fawcett Cahill. Pietermaritzburg, South Africa: Wyllie Desktop Publishing, 1993. 144pp., illustrated.

536. Fedden, Marguerite. *Sisters' Quarters, Salonika*. London: Grant Richards, 1921. 221pp., illustrated.

Memoir, 1916. Tale of a V.A.D. who worked at Salonika during the summer and autumn of 1916.

537. Feilding, Rowland Charles. *War Letters to a Wife, France and Flanders, 1915–1919*. London: The Medici Society, 1929. 382pp., illustrated.

Letters, April 1915–May 1919. Feilding began the war as a company commander in the Coldstream Guards, became a battalion commander of 6th Connaught Rangers, and ended the war commanding the 1st/15th Battalion, Prince of Wales's Own Civil Service Rifles of the 47th Division. Very good letters, highly recommended.

538. Fergusson, Robert Menzies. *With the American Army in France (Diary of a Lecturing Tour)*. Paisley: Alexander Gardner, 1919. 62pp.

Patriotic musings of a Scottish author as he encouraged the troops.

539. Fisher, John Arbuthnot. *Memories and Records*. New York: George H. Doran, 1920. 2 volumes, 278 and 264pp., illustrated. Combined publication of *Memories* (1919) and *Records* (1919).

Autobiography of Admiral Lord Fisher, a fascinating man and an architect of the British Grand Fleet. Valuable though not very revealing.

540. Fisher, William. *Requiem for Will*. Wyesham, Monmouth, Gwent: E.H. Fisher, 1997. 115pp.

Diary, March 1915–June 1919. Fisher rose from sapper to sergeant in the Royal Engineers. Ill with tuberculosis—from which he died in 1922—and full of contempt for the "damned farce" of the war, Fisher nevertheless served bravely in active sectors at Ypres and the Somme. Candid front line diary entries.

541. Floyd, Thomas Hope. *At Ypres with Best-Dunkley*. London: John Lane, 1920. 234pp.

Memoir, 1914–1917. Lieutenant Colonel Bertram Best-Dunkley of the 2/5th Battalion, Lancashire Fusiliers, won a posthumous Victoria Cross for heroism on July 31, 1917, the first day of Passchendaele.

542. Foley, Henry Arthur. *Three Years on Active Service and Eight*

Months as Prisoner-of-War. Bridgewater: Walter Belcher, 1920. 185pp., illustrated.

Memoir, 1914–1918. Foley served in the 6th Somerset Light Infantry. He fought on the Somme and was wounded in September 1916.

543. Foot, Stephen. *Three Lives: An Autobiography*. London: William Heinemann, 1934. 355pp., illustrated.

Autobiography, about one-third on World War I. He was adjutant of the Royal Engineers, 21st Division, at the Somme; and was brigade major of the 2nd Brigade Tank Corps at Cambrai. In January 1918 he went to the War Office. He passes over the Somme and Cambrai too quickly to be very enlightening on either battle.

544. Forder, Archibald. *In Brigands' Hands and Turkish Prisons*. London: Marshall Brothers, 1920. 314pp.

Memoir, 1914–1918. Account of a missionary to the Bedouins of Jordan who was imprisoned in awful conditions by the Turks in Palestine and Syria.

545. Fox, Frank. *G.H.Q. (Montreuil-sur-Mer)*. London: Philip Allan, 1920. 306pp., illustrated.

The author was attached to the Quartermaster's Corps at G.H.Q. A purely administrative account.

546. Fraser, William. *In Good Company: The First World War Letters and Diaries of the Hon. William Fraser, Gordon Highlanders*. Edited by David Fraser. Salisbury: Michael Russell, 1990. 348pp., illustrated.

Letters/diaries, September 1914–March 1919. Fraser began the war as a subaltern in the 2nd Battalion, Gordon Highlanders, and ended it as Lieutenant Colonel of the 1st Battalion. Best on France in March–October 1918, but also contains some remarks on 1st and 3rd Ypres.

547. Fraser-Tytler, Neil. *With Lancashire Lads and Field Guns in France, 1915–1918*. Edited by Frederick Nolan Baker. Manchester: John Heywood, 1922. 287pp.

Letters, November 1915–August 1918. Lieutenant Colonel Fraser-Tytler was commanding officer of a battery in the 151st and 150th Howitzer Brigades. A thoroughly professional soldier, he even kept a "game-book," or scorecard, of his observed kills. He was badly gassed and died of the aftereffects in 1937.

548. French, Anthony. *Gone for a Soldier*. Kineton: Roundwood Press, 1972. 109pp., illustrated.

French served in the 1st/15th Prince of Wales's Own Civil Service Rifles, fighting on the Somme and elsewhere on the Western Front.

549. French, Fitzstephen John Featherston. *From Whitehall to the Caspian*. London: Odhams Press, 1920. 255pp., illustrated.

Memoir, July 1918–August 1919. Lieutenant Colonel French served with British forces in the Caucasus after the disbandment of the "Dunsterforce"; he describes the British occupation of Baku and the onset of the Russian Civil War.

550. French, John Denton Pinkstone. *1914*. London: Constable, 1919. 413pp.

Memoir, August–December 1914. French commanded the B.E.F. from August 1914 until December 1915. Profoundly biased, but one of the most important sources for the B.E.F. in the first months of the war.

551. Fry, William Maws. *Air of Battle*. London: William Kimber, 1974. 194pp., illustrated.

Memoir, 1914–1918. Fry had an exceptionally eventful military career. He served in France in 1914 as an infantry private and was commissioned in the Somerset Light Infantry, but transferred to the R.F.C. in December 1915. For the next two years he served with Squadron Nos. 12, 11, and 60—the latter under "Billy" Bishop—before returning to England in 1917. He returned to the front in 1918 with No. 87 Squadron, then took command of No. 23 Squadron, flying Spads. Before the end of the war he flew Sopwith Dolphins in No. 79 Squadron.

552. Fryer, E. R. M. *Reminiscences of a Grenadier, 1914–1919*. London: Digby, Long, 1921. 241pp.

Fryer began the war in the Honourable Artillery Company and was then commissioned in the Grenadier Guards.

553. Fuller, J. F. C. *Memoirs of an Unconventional Soldier*. London: Ivor Nicholson and Watson, 1936. 494pp., illustrated.

Autobiography, mostly on World War I, when Colonel Fuller most notably served as Chief of the General Staff of the Tank Corps. The definitive book on tanks in the war, with lasting influence on British military thinking.

554. *Fusilier Bluff; The Experiences of an Unprofessional Soldier in the Near East, 1918 to 1919*. London: Geoffrey Bles, 1934. 283pp.

The author served in Macedonia as well as Gallipoli and, at war's end, in Constantinople.

555. Fyfe, Henry Hamilton. *The Making of an Optimist*. London: Leonard Parsons, 1921. 279pp.

Memoir, 1914–1918. Fyfe, once a hardline Conservative and editor of the *Daily Mirror* newspaper, shifted allegiance to the Labour Party before the war. He covered Mons as a correspondent for the *Daily Mail* and immediately stirred up controversy by suggesting the battle had been a disaster. Later that year he made his way to the front by enlisting as a stretcher bearer for the French Red Cross and reported the war from that vantage point. He subsequently reported on the Eastern Front, and then again on the Western Front from 1917 until July 1918. This memoir suggests that the war's horrors converted him to pacifism, though as a Fabian he probably had been one already.

556. Gale, Richard. *Call to Arms: An Autobiography*. London: Hutchinson, 1968. 230pp., illustrated.

Autobiography, with about 50 pages relating to Gale's service in World War I. Gale served as a lieutenant and captain in the 164th and 126th companies of the Machine Gun Corps, and saw fighting at the Somme and Ypres as well as in the German 1918 offensive.

557. Gask, George Ernest. *A Surgeon in France: The Memoirs of Professor George E. Gask CMG, DSO, FRCS, 1914–1919*. Liskeard: Liskeard, 2002. 148pp., illustrated.

Unedited memoirs, originally written in 1920, of a doctor at St. Bartholomew's in London who went to serve at the front.

558. Gauld, H. Drummond. *The Truth from the Trenches*. London: Arthur H. Stockwell, 1922. 305pp.

Memoir, December 1916–November 1918. Bitter, meticulously realistic memoir of an enlisted soldier in the Berwickshires at Arras,

Passchendaele, and the 1918 battles in France and Flanders. Gauld is disdainful of the "multitude of bunglers" who led the British army. See also *Scotland Yet!* (1930) by the same author.

559. George, Gertrude A. *Eight Months with the Women's Royal Air Force (Immobile)*. London: Heath Cranton, 1920. Unpaginated, illustrated.

Memoir, 1918. Impressionistic memoir, nicely illustrated by the author with a foreword by Air Marshal Trenchard, describing daily life in a pioneering women's unit.

560. Gervis, Henry. *Arms & the Doctor: Being the Military Experiences of a Middle-Aged Medical Man*. London: C.W. Daniel, 1920. 85pp.

Gervis served in France as a captain in the R.A.M.C.

561. Gibbon, Monk. *Inglorious Soldier*. London: Hutchinson, 1968. 335pp., illustrated.

Memoir, January 1916–September 1918. Gibbon, a reluctant Irish soldier, was commissioned a subaltern in the Army Service Corps in January 1916. He participated in the suppression of the Dublin Easter Rising, and then served in France with the 31st Divisional Train. Although he became an ardent opponent of the war, Gibbon never saw much of the front, and he has more to say about politics and Irish affairs than the military.

562. Gibbons, John. *Roll On, Next War!: The Common Man's Guide to Army Life*. London: Frederick Muller, 1935. 186pp., illustrated.

Memoir, roughly 1914–1918. The author enlisted in December 1914 in a London Territorial Battalion. He provides vague, humorous observations on his experiences and the war in general. He either never ventured into the front lines or chose to say nothing about them.

563. Gibbs, A. Hamilton. *Gun Fodder: The Diary of Four Years of War*. Boston: Little, Brown, 1919. 313pp.

Memoir, June 1914–November 1918. Gibbs, younger brother of Philip Gibbs, enlisted in August 1914 as a trooper in the 9th Lancers, but at the end of the year he became a second lieutenant in the Royal Field Artillery, eventually rising to the rank of major and commanding his own battery of 18-pounders in 1918. His account of the Salonika campaign is suitably depressing, but his portrayal of the German 1918 offensive is frighteningly realistic and gripping. Gibbs emerged from the war extremely bitter and wholly disillusioned. Published in London, 1920 as *The Grey Wave*.

564. Gibbs, Gerald. *Survivor's Story*. London: Hutchinson, 1956. 182pp., illustrated.

Autobiography, part on World War I. Gibbs served in 1915 as a lieutenant in the 7th Battalion, Duke of Edinburgh's (Wiltshire Regiment). He transferred to the R.F.C. in 1916 and flew in No. 17 Squadron before becoming commanding officer of No. 29 Squadron in 1918.

565. Gibbs, Philip. *Realities of War*. London: W. Heinemann, 1920. 455pp.

Memoir, 1914–1918. Published in New York, 1920, as *Now it Can be Told*. Gibbs was one of the few war correspondents allowed to venture near the front lines. He was more conscientious than many of his colleagues, but his perspective on soldiers and the war was sometimes fatuous. Dense but rewarding. See also his books *The Hope of Europe* (London, 1921; published in New York, 1921, as *More that Must be Told*), and *The Pageant of the Years* (1946).

566. Gibbs, Stormont. *From the Somme to the Armistice: The Memoirs of Captain Stormont Gibbs, MC*. London: William Kimber, 1986. 206pp., illustrated.

Memoir, 1916–1918. Gibbs served in the 4th Suffolk Regiment at the Somme, Arras, Passchendaele, and in the German March 1918 offensive.

567. Gilbert, Vivian. *The Romance of the Last Crusade: With Allenby to Jerusalem*. New York: D. Appleton, 1923. 235pp.

Memoir, 1917–1918. The author enlisted in the 7th Battalion, Dorset Regiment, later part of the 180th Brigade, 60th Division, and fought with Allenby's 20th Corps in the Palestine Campaign. He witnessed the British entry into Jerusalem.

568. Gladden, Edgar Norman. *Ypres, 1917: A Personal Account*. London: Kimber, 1967. 192pp. Sequels: *Across the Piave; A Personal Account of the British Forces in Italy, 1917–1919* (1971); *The Somme, 1916: A Personal Account* (1974).

Memoir, May 1916–February 1919. Gladden served with the 7th

Battalion of the Northumberland Fusiliers on the Somme, and with the 11th Battalion of the same regiment at Ypres and in Italy. A remarkably engrossing memoir.

569. Glenn, Jane. *The Diary of Jane Glenn of Ruskington in the County of Lincoln for the Year 1917: from Monday 8th January 1917–Sunday 6 January 1918*. Edited by Derrick Wood. Boston, Lincs.: Richard Kay, 1996. 50pp., illustrated.

Diary of a farmer's daughter, describing rural life and the occasional wartime interruptions such as zeppelin raids.

570. Glockler, Henry W. *Interned in Turkey, 1914–1918*. Beirut: Sevan Press, 1969. 154pp.

Glockler, an Englishman born in Beirut, was interned for the war's duration at Ourfa in southeastern Turkey. From there he witnessed pogroms against the Armenians that eventually culminated in wholesale massacres.

571. Glubb, John. *Into Battle: A Soldier's Diary of the Great War*. London: Cassell, 1978. 223pp., illustrated.

Diary/Memoir, November 1915–December 1918. Glubb, later the renowned "Glubb Pasha" of the Arab Legion, was commissioned a second lieutenant in the Royal Engineers in April 1915. Glubb saw a great deal of fighting and was severely wounded in the jaw, but in his old age he looked back on the war as a tragic but necessary and even worthwhile endeavor. Very well written, with good maps.

572. Godley, Alexander John. *Life of an Irish Soldier: Reminiscences of General Sir Alexander Godley*. London: John Murray, 1939. 363pp., illustrated.

Autobiography, part on World War I. Godley served for the war's duration as commander of the New Zealand Expeditionary Force. Some useful comments on Gallipoli and the Western Front.

573. Goodland, Stanley. *Engaged in War: The Letters of Stanley Goodland, Somerset Light Infantry, 1914–1919*. Gomshall, Guildford: Twiga Books, 1999. 163pp., illustrated.

Letters, September 1914–December 1919. Goodland was a subaltern and captain in the 1/5th Somerset Light Infantry, stationed in India and

Mesopotamia during 1914–16, and in Egypt and Palestine from the spring of 1917. A lot of local color, but little of military interest.

574. Goodridge, Ernest. *The Same Stars Shine: The Great War Diary and Letters of Corporal Ernest Goodridge of Bentley, Yorkshire, with Contemporary Records and Illustrations*. Edited by Ernest N. Goodridge and John A. Goodridge. Loughborough: Teamprint, 2000. 190pp., illustrated.

Biography, with diary/letters dating December 1915–October 1916. Goodridge enlisted as a private in the 18th Battalion, King's Royal Rifle Corps, and was killed on the Somme in October 1916.

575. Goodyear, Frederick. *Frederick Goodyear: Letters and Remains, 1887–1917*. London: McBride, Nast & Co., 1920. 193pp.

Rare, transcribed letters of one of Britain's many blooming author/poets (an associate of Katherine Mansfield, D.H. Lawrence, and others) whose life was cut short by the war.

576. Gordon, Huntly. *The Unreturning Army: A Field-Gunner in Flanders, 1917–18*. London: J.M. Dent & Sons, 1967. 133pp., illustrated.

Memoir/Letters, June 1917–April 1918. Gordon, a second lieutenant in the 112th Brigade, Royal Field Artillery, was badly wounded in April 1918 and sat out the rest of the war. His book consists mostly of letters to his mother; the most interesting ones relate to Passchendaele.

577. Gosse, Philip. *Memoirs of a Camp-Follower*. London: Longmans, Green, 1934. 299pp.

Memoir, 1915–1918. Gosse, a naturalist and physician, served in the R.A.M.C. on the Western Front (part of the time with the unenviable status of Rat Officer for the 2nd Army) from 1915 until 1917, when he went to India. Interesting observations on flora, fauna, and sanitation in the trenches.

578. Gough, General Sir Hubert. *Soldiering On*. London: A. Barker, 1954. 260pp., illustrated.

Autobiography, about 70pp. on World War I. Gough began the war as commander of the 3rd Cavalry Brigade and in 1915 he commanded the 2nd Cavalry Division and the 7th Division. He led the First Army Corps during the Somme battles of 1916, and commanded the Fifth Army from

1916 until 1918, when he was sacked after his command shattered during the German March offensive. He concentrates here on vindicating himself from that disaster.

579. Gower, John William. *The Diary and Letters of Corporal (Acting Sergeant) John William Gower*. London: Family History Publications, 1994. 40pp.

Diary/letters, August 1914–May 1915. Gower enlisted in the Royal Field Artillery and arrived at the front in December 1914. This diary describes his experiences around Ypres in the first months of 1915. He entered the hospital in 1916 and remained there as a mental patient until 1950.

580. Gowland, John Stafford. *War is Like That*. London: John Hamilton, 1933. 239pp.

Memoir, October 1914–November 1918. In this novelized account Gowland recalls his experiences on the Western Front as an underage soldier in a territorial battalion, the Royal Engineers, and a signaling company. Best passages concern Neuve Chapelle. Broad view of the war, with vivid scenes of horror and destruction and fonder memories of comradeship and humor. "I have two sons and hope to God they will never be called upon to experience what we experienced during those dreadful years," Gowland writes, "but if those two boys are needed to defend Britain they will go . . . Yes, I shall go too."

581. Graham, Herbert W. *The Life of a Tunnelling Company, Being an Intimate Story of the Life of the 185th Tunnelling Company, Royal Engineers, in France, During the Great War, 1914–1918*. Hexham: J. Catherall, 1927. 180pp., illustrated.

Memoir/unit history, October 1915–November 1918. Graham's unit saw most of its action after April 1917, at Vimy Ridge, Hill 70, and the pursuit to Mons.

582. Graham, Stephen. *A Private in the Guards*. London: Macmillan, 1919. 356pp., illustrated.

Memoir, 1917–1919. One of the first widely read British war memoirs, reprinted in part from articles written during the war. Graham, a freelance journalist who served in the Scots Guards at the front beginning in April 1918, writes in the tradition of Ian Hay. "The life in

France was very arduous and full of dangers," he writes; "All was suffered cheerfully in the name of the great cause." Special attention given to American volunteers in the Guards. See also Graham's book of postwar musings, *The Challenge of the Dead a Vision of the War and the Life of the Common Soldier in France, Seen Two Years Afterwards between August and November, 1920* (1921).

583. Graves, Robert. *Good-bye to All That*. London: Jonathan Cape, 1929. 448pp., illustrated.

Autobiography, most on World War I, when Graves served in the 2nd Royal Welch Fusiliers. Perhaps the most widely read war memoir even though, by the author's own admission, his account is partly fictional. This fact blunts the effectiveness of the best passages, such as those describing the author's wounding at High Wood in July 1916 and the tribulations of his friend Siegfried Sassoon. An entertaining read, largely because of Graves's wit and writing skill, but of limited usefulness as a source of evidence for soldiers' experiences.

584. Gray, Frank. *The Confessions of a Private*. Oxford: B.H. Blackwell, 1920. 202pp.

The author was a member of the 8th Royal Berkshire Regiment.

585. Green, Arthur Frank Umfreville. *Evening Tattoo*. London: S. Paul, 1941. 288pp., illustrated.

Autobiography, most on World War I. Green served in 1914 as a captain in the 112th Heavy Battery of the Royal Garrison Artillery, fighting at 1st Ypres, and then went to 7th Division Headquarters as a Court Martial Officer. In 1915 he joined the staff of the 3rd Division, and in August 1915 transferred to the staff of XI Corps. He spent 1918 in Italy. Surprisingly interesting staff memoir.

586. Greenwell, Graham Hamilton. *An Infant in Arms: War Letters of a Company Officer, 1914–1918*. London: Dickson and Thompson, 1935. 304pp., illustrated.

Letters, September 1914–December 1918. Greenwell was a captain in the 4th Oxfordshire and Buckinghamshire Light Infantry, and saw fighting at the Somme and Passchendaele before his division was transferred to Italy. This book caused public outrage when first released because of the author's contention that he remembered "the years

1914–1918 as among the happiest I have ever spent."

587. Gregory, H. *Never Again; A Diary of the Great War*. London: A.H. Stockwell, 1934. 141pp.

588. Greig, Robert M. *Doing His Bit: A Shetland Soldier in the Great War*. Edited by Alex Cluness. Lerwick: Shetland Times, 1999. 87pp., illustrated.

A collection of articles originally printed in the *Shetland Times* in 1920–21, describing Greig's wartime experiences.

589. Griffith, Wyn. *Up to Mametz*. London: Faber and Faber, 1931. 238pp.

Memoir, November 1915–July 1916. Griffith was a lieutenant and captain in the 15th Royal Welch Fusiliers; during the Somme battles he was attached to the headquarters of the 115th Brigade. Most of this excellent memoir focuses on the capture of Mametz Wood in July 1916, in which the author's younger brother was killed. Griffith's experience working with staff officers convinced him that attacks on the "red tabs" by other authors usually were unjustified.

590. Grimshaw, Roly. *Indian Cavalry Officer, 1914–1915*. Edited by J. Wakefield and J.M. Weippert. Tunbridge Wells: Costello, 1986. 224pp., illustrated.

Diary, August 1914–June 1915. Captain Grimshaw saw action in 1st Ypres as a member of the 34th Poona Horse, then returned to England because of ill health. The second half of the book contains a fictionalized account of an Indian cavalry N.C.O. at the front in 1914.

591. Grinnell-Milne, Duncan William. *Wind in the Wires*. London: Hurst & Blackett, 1933. 288pp., illustrated. Numerous reprints.

Memoir, 1914–1918. The author transferred from the 7th Royal Fusiliers to the R.F.C. in 1915, flying a B.E.2 with No. 16 Squadron. He was shot down and captured later that year. He escaped in 1918 and took command of S.E.5a-equipped No. 56 Squadron. See also *An Escaper's Log* (1926), describing Grinnell-Milne's escape attempts from 1915 to 1917.

592. Groom, W. H. A. *Poor Bloody Infantry*. London: William Kimber,

1976. 185pp., illustrated.

Memoir, August 1914–November 1918. Groom was a private in the London Rifle Brigade, fighting at Arras, Passchendaele, Cambrai, and elsewhere. An extremely bitter, homiletic memoir overflowing with contempt for officers and all those responsible for the war.

593. Gurdon, John Everard. *Over and Above*. London: W. Collins Sons, 1919. 250pp.

Gurdon renames himself "Warton," a lieutenant and pilot in an unnamed squadron, in this novelized memoir written in the third person perspective.

594. Gurney, Ivor. *War Letters: A Selection*. Edited by R.K.R. Thornton. Ashington: Mid Northumberland Arts Group, 1983. 271pp., illustrated.

Letters, February 1915–November 1918. Gurney, a poet and composer, was a private in the 2/5th Gloucesters in 1916, and in the Machine Gun Corps in 1917. His letters are valuable for their literary and musical references, but contain relatively little on the war.

595. Gyte, Maria. *The Diaries of Maria Gyte of Sheldon, Derbyshire, 1913–1920*. Edited by Gerald Phizackerly. Cromford: Scarthin Books, 1999. 297pp., illustrated.

Moving diary of a simple country mother whose son, Tony Gyte, was killed in the war.

596. Hadlow, H. J. *The Experiences of a Volunteer in the First World War*. Eynsford: H. J. Hadlow, 1985. 134pp.

Memoir, September 1914–March 1919. Hadlow enlisted as a private in the 2/20th London Regiment in September 1914, at the age of sixteen. He went to France in June 1916 and served on the Somme before going to Salonika, where he remained for the first half of 1917. From June 1917 to June 1918 he saw fighting in Egypt and Palestine, and then returned to France.

597. Hague, Henry Joseph. *Memoirs of a L.A.C. in the R.F.C. and R.A.F.* Bath: H. Sharp and Sons, c.1960. 143pp.

Autobiography, mostly on World War I. Confusing memoir, in which Hague relates his experiences as an orderly in the R.A.M.C., and then as a Leading Aircraftsman Mechanic in the R.F.C. in Mesopotamia.

598. Haig, Douglas. *The Private Papers of Sir Douglas Haig*. Edited by Robert Blake. London: Eyre & Spottiswoode, 1952. 383pp.

Extracts from Haig's diaries, dating from July 1914, to April 1919. Perhaps significant as much for what Blake left out (only one-fifth of Haig's original diaries are transcribed) as for what he included, but invaluable nonetheless.

599. Hale, Alfred Matthew. *The Ordeal of Alfred M. Hale: The Memoirs of a Soldier Servant*. Edited by Paul Fussell. London: Cooper, 1975.

Memoir, 1916–1918. Hale, an Oxford-educated intellectual, was conscripted near the end of the war at the age of forty-one. He loathed the military life, which he was forced to endure as an officer's servant. An angry, bitter memoir, and thus inevitably singled out by Fussell.

600. Hamblin, Sidney Charles. *For Your Tomorrows: The First World War Letters of Private Sidney Hamblin*. Bungay, Suffolk: J. Garland, 1995. 102pp.

Letters, December 1917–March 1918. Hamblin, a private in the 7th Duke of Cornwall's Light Infantry, was killed in action on the Somme in late March 1918, shortly after his arrival at the front.

601. Hamilton, Ian. *Gallipoli Diary*. London: E. Arnold, 1920. 2 vols, 387 and 349pp., illustrated.

Diary, March–October 1915. A detailed, readable, and indispensable record of the Gallipoli campaign, by the commander in chief of the allied expedition.

602. Hamilton, Ralph G. A. *The War Diary of the Master of Belhaven, 1914–1918*. London: John Murray, 1924. 472pp.

Diary, January 1915–March 1918. Lieutenant Colonel Hamilton commanded the 106th Battery of the Royal Field Artillery, spending most of his time in the Ypres Salient before being killed at the end of March 1918. Dispassionate and quite detailed, an excellent record of daily life in the artillery.

603. Hankey, Maurice Pascal Alers Hankey. *The Supreme Command, 1914–1918*. London: Allen and Unwin, 1961. 2 volumes, 906pp., illustrated.

Dry but vitally important memoir of the Secretary to the Committee of Imperial Defence, providing one of the best available views of Britain's strategic and political conduct of the war.

604. Hannam-Clark, Theodore. *Some Experiences of a Court-Martial Officer*. Gloucester: Crypt House Press, 1932. 32pp.

Vague comments on the war, originally given as a dinner speech at the Gloucester Rotary Club in 1932.

605. Harbottle, George. *Civilian Soldier 1914–1919: A Period Relived.* Newcastle upon Tyne: Carlis Print, 1981. 132pp., illustrated.

Memoir, August 1914–November 1918. Harbottle enlisted in the 6th Battalion Northumberland Fusiliers in August 1914 and eventually rose to the rank of quartermaster sergeant; he gained a commission in the Machine Gun Corps in May 1917. Action in Flanders and on the Somme.

606. Harding, Geoffrey Parker. *Escape Fever*. London: J. Hamilton, 1932. 224pp., illustrated.

Memoir by an airman who was shot down by Richtofen's squadron and imprisoned at Karlsruhe, Strohen, and Holzminden before escaping to Holland.

607. Harding, Robert Henry. *From Archangel to New Zealand: The Diaries of Robert Henry Harding*. Edited by Gregor McShane. Hamilton, N.Z.: Rimu Publishing Company, 1985. 107pp., illustrated.

Diary, October 1914–May 1916, and April–November 1919. Harding was Chief ERA 2nd Class on HMS *Magnificent*, which served as a troopship during the Gallipoli campaign, and in 1919 he served on HMS *Cicala* at Archangel, Russia. Fragmentary diary with polemical material added by McShane.

608. Hardy, J. L. *I Escape*! London: John Lane, 1927. 260pp., illustrated. Introduction by Arthur Conan Doyle.

Memoir, December 1914–November 1918. Hardy, a captain in the Connaught Rangers, was captured in the war's first few months. Imprisoned in five different German prison camps, he escaped five times. Each attempt ended in recapture except the last in March 1918, when he made it from Schweidnitz in eastern Germany to Holland. Hardy returned to his regiment only to lose a leg and receive a bullet in the stomach in October 1918. One of the best POW stories ever published.

609. Harris, Lionel Herbert. *Signal Venture*. Aldershot: Gale & Polden, 1951. 278pp., illustrated.

Autobiography, about 40pp. on World War I, when Harris, a native Englishman, served in the Signal Section of the Australian 32nd Battalion in Gallipoli and France. Good technical information on signals work.

610. Harris, Temple. *Seventeen Letters to Tatham: A WWI Surgeon in East Africa*. Edited by Ann Crichton-Harris. Toronto: Keneggy West, 2001. 231pp., illustrated.

Letters, 1914–1918. The author was a surgeon with the Indian Medical Service, and witnessed the Battle of Tanga in November 1914. His seventeen letters to his brother in India are carefully annotated and researched, some on site at Tanga.

611. Harris, Tindall. *Motoring Memories in Peace & War*. London: St. Catherine Press, 1928. 91pp., illustrated.

612. Harrison, Michael Charles Cooper, and H. A. Cartwright. *Within Four Walls*. London: Edward Arnold, 1930. 306pp., illustrated.

Memoir, August 1914–November 1918. Harrison, an officer in the 2nd Royal Irish Regiment, was captured at Mons and held prisoner at Berg, Torgau, and Magdeburg before escaping from Strohen in 1917. He later became a major in the Royal Tank Corps. Cartwright, a captain in the Duke of Cambridge's Own (Middlesex Regiment), was captured at Mons and held at Burg, Halle, Magdeburg, and other prisons before escaping from Aachen near the end of the war. Straightforward narrative with wonderful cartoon illustrations.

613. Harvey, Frederick William. *Comrades in Captivity: A Record of Life in Seven German Prison Camps*. London: Sidgwick & Jackson, 1920. 319pp., illustrated.

Memoir, 1914–1918. Harvey enlisted in the 1st/5th Gloucestershire Regiment and went to France in 1915. He won the D.C.M. and a commission in August 1915 for his bravery during a patrol, and subsequently joined the 2nd Battalion before being captured in August 1916. He spent the rest of the war in seven prison camps throughout Germany.

614. Harvey, H. E. *Battle-line Narratives, 1915–1918*. London: Brentano's, 1928. 255pp.

Describes the author's experiences with the 17th and 22nd Battalions of the Royal Fusiliers at Festubert, the Somme, Cambrai, and elsewhere.

615. Harvey, W. J. [pseud. Night-Hawk]. *Rovers of the Night Sky*. London: Cassell, 1919. 204pp.

Memoir, 1916–1918. Partly reprinted from wartime newspaper articles. The author transferred from the Royal Engineers to the R.F.C. in late 1916, and scored a total of 26 victories flying a Bristol Fighter in No. 22 Squadron.

616. Haslam, A. D. *Cannon Fodder*. London: Hutchinson, 1930. 288pp.

Memoir, August 1914–December 1918. Haslam served in a Welsh regiment (the unit names are fictionalized) at the Somme and was captured in April 1918. Gently sarcastic and antiwar.

617. Hatton, Sydney Frank. *The Yarn of a Yeoman*. London: Hutchinson, 1930. 286pp., illustrated.

Memoir/unit history, 1914–1918. The author served in the Middlesex Yeomanry on British coastal duty at the beginning of the war and followed his regiment to Egypt, Gallipoli, Salonika, and Palestine. Vivid and interesting, particularly on Gallipoli.

618. Hawke, James. *From Private to Major*. London: Hutchinson, 1938. 254pp., illustrated.

Autobiography of a member of the Royal Signallers, Indian Army, before, during, and after World War I.

619. Hawkings, Frank. *From Ypres to Cambrai; The Diary of an Infantryman, 1914–1919*. Edited by Arthur Taylor. Morley: Elmfield Press, 1974. 144pp., illustrated.

The author enlisted in the 9th London Regiment (Queen Victoria Rifles) in 1914 at the age of sixteen. He fought at 2nd Ypres and was wounded at Gommecourt on July 1, 1916. After recovering he received a commission as a sub-lieutenant in the Royal Naval Division, and fought on the Hindenburg line in the summer of 1918 before being wounded again. Interesting diary but edited with a heavy hand and encased within a potted history of the Great War.

620. Haworth, Christopher. *March to Armistice, 1918*. London: William

Kimber, 1968. 172pp., illustrated.

Memoir, May 1917–November 1918. Haworth went to Flanders in April 1918 as a private in the 14th Argyll and Sutherland Highlanders, and remained at the front for the rest of the war. Good memoir, told in the present tense.

621. Hayward, Victor. *HMS Tiger at Bay: A Sailor's Memoir 1914–18*. London: William Kimber, 1977. 190pp., illustrated.

Memoir, Fall 1912–June 1919. Hayward joined the navy at age 15, serving on HMS *Impregnable* and HMS *Gibraltar* before joining the crew of the battle cruiser HMS *Tiger* in October 1914. He manned a 6-inch gun on the ship. Lively, readable memoir includes accounts of Dogger Bank and Jutland.

622. Head, Charles Octavius. *No Great Shakes: An Autobiography*. London: Robert Hale, 1943. 252pp., illustrated.

Part of this autobiography describes the author's experiences as an artillery officer during World War I; especially interesting memories of the capture of High Wood on July 14 during the Battle of the Somme.

623. Henson, Leslie Lincoln. *My Laugh Story: The Story of My Life, up to Date*. London: Hodder and Stoughton, 1926. 293pp.

Autobiography, part on World War I, when the author, a famous comic actor, helped to entertain the troops.

624. Herbert, Aubrey. *Mons, Anzac and Kut*. London: E. Arnold, 1919. 270pp.

Diary/memoir, August 1914–May 1916. Badly shortsighted, the author went to France at the beginning of the war as an interpreter, was wounded and captured during the retreat from Mons, exchanged, and then served as an intelligence officer in Egypt, Gallipoli, and Mesopotamia. Fascinating, straightforward, and very well written, best on Mons and Gallipoli.

625. Heron-Allen, Edward. *Edward Heron-Allen's Journal of the Great War: from Sussex Shore to Flanders Fields*. Edited by Brian W. Harvey and Carol Fitzgerald. Lewes: Sussex Record Society, 2002. 282pp., illustrated.

Diary, August 1914–July 1919. Good record of life on the home front in Sussex. The author also went to Flanders as a member of the Military Intelligence Department of the War Office.

626. Herringham, Wilmot. *A Physician in France*. London: E. Arnold, 1919. 293pp., illustrated.

Memoir, 1914–1918. Major General Herringham, a Vice Chancellor of the University of London and noted doctor, served as consulting physician at G.H.Q. and 3rd Army H.Q. He played an important role in the administrative development of the British R.A.M.C.

627. Hervey, H. E. *Cage-Birds*. Harmondsworth, Middlesex: Penguin Books, 1940. 155pp.

Potboiler of R.F.C. Lieutenant Hervey's experiences while attempting to escape from prison in Germany.

628. Hesketh-Prichard, Vernon Hesketh. *Sniping in France: with Notes on the Scientific Training of Scouts, Observers, and Snipers*. London: Hutchinson, 1920. 268pp.

Memoir, 1914–1918. The author, a former big game hunter, ran and developed the British army sniping program during the war; he describes in detail the techniques he taught.

629. Hickey, Daniel Edgar. *Rolling into Action: Memoirs of a Tank Corps Section Commander*. London: Hutchinson, 1936. 288pp., illustrated.

Memoir, August 1914–November 1918. Hickey was commissioned a lieutenant in the Suffolk Regiment in 1915, but a training accident kept him from active service. Instead, in December 1916 he joined the Machine-Gun Corps (Heavy Branch), later the Tank Corps, and became a captain in command of a section of H Battalion. Excellent first hand account of tank warfare at Passchendaele, Cambrai, and Amiens, with careful descriptions of practical issues.

630. Hill, Cedric Waters. *The Spook and the Commandant*. London: Kimber, 1975. 201pp.

Memoir, 1917–1918, by an R.F.C. officer who escaped from a Turkish prisoner of war camp by faking a spiritualist experience. His co-conspirator, E.H. Jones, gave his side of the story in *The Road to En-Dor* (1919; q.v.).

631. Hill, J. A. Sillitoe. *The Front Line and Beyond it; A Diary of 1917–18*. London: Houghton, 1930. 80pp.

632. Hilton, Richard. *Nine Lives: The Autobiography of an Old Soldier*. London: Hollis, 1955. 226pp.

Victorian-style autobiography of an adventurer who served during World War I as an observer in the R.F.C. over Flanders.

633. Hiscock, Eric C. *The Bells of Hell Go Ting-a-Ling-a-Ling: An Autobiographical Fragment Without Maps*. London: Arlington Books, 1976.

Memoir, 1914–1919. Hiscock joined the Royal Fusiliers in 1914 by lying about his age—he was only fifteen. He went to Flanders in 1917 and experienced the horrors of Passchendaele, the last battles of 1918, and the occupation of Germany. Darkly humorous and intriguing.

634. Hitchcock, F. C. *Stand To! A Diary of the Trenches, 1915–18*. London: Hurst & Blackett, 1937. 358pp., illustrated.

Diary, May 1915–December 1918. Hitchcock was a subaltern with the 2nd Battalion of the Leinster Regiment, fighting near Ypres and in the later stages of the Battle of the Somme. He was in England from February 1917 to August 1918. One of the most complete and interesting war diaries ever published, with a wealth of detail and excellent contemporary maps and drawings. An essential source for study of the day-to-day routine and technical aspects of trench warfare.

635. Hodges, Goderic. *Memoirs of an Old Balloonatic*. London: Kimber, 1972. 175pp., illustrated.

Autobiography, part on World War I, when Hodges served in the R.F.C. and transferred to balloon service. Written for enthusiasts.

636. Hodgson, Clarence F. *From Hell to the Himalayas*. Westville, South Africa: King & Wilks, 1983. 206pp., illustrated.

Autobiography, part on World War I, when the author served in the Royal Field Artillery.

637. Hody, E. H. *With "the Mad 17th" to Italy*. London: George Allen & Unwin, 1920. 159pp., illustrated.

Memoir/unit history, 1917–1918. The author served as a major in the

17th Divisional Supply Column.

638. Holtom, Ernest Charles. *Two Years' Captivity in German East Africa: Being the Personal Experiences of Surgeon E.C.H., Royal Navy.* London: Hutchinson, 1919. 239pp.

Memoir, July 1914–December 1916. Holtom describes German brutality toward prisoners and natives in East Africa.

639. Home, Archibald. *The Diary of a World War I Cavalry Officer.* Edited by Diana Briscoe. Tunbridge Wells: Costello, 1985. 222pp., illustrated.

Memoir, August 1914–November 1918. Home joined the 11th Hussars in France in August 1914 and became a brigadier general of the Cavalry Corps in September 1916. Excellent view of the high command combines tactical insights into battles like Messines and Cambrai with more personal observations on himself and his men.

640. Hope, Thomas Suthren. *The Winding Road Unfolds.* London: Putnam, 1937. 340pp.

Memoir based on a diary, July–December 1917. Describes the author's service at Ypres, his wounding, and subsequent recovery in the hospital.

641. Horn, Trevor. *Lancer Dig In: 1914 Diary—the Marne.* Orwell, Cambs.: Ellison's Editions, 1983. 47pp., illustrated.

Diary, August–October 1914. Intriguing diary of a lieutenant of the 16th Queen's Lancers at Kemmel, Mons, the Marne, and Messines.

642. Hornsey, Frank Haydn. *Hell on Earth.* London: Chapman & Hall, 1930. 243pp.

643. Horrocks, Brian. *Escape to Action.* New York: St. Martin's Press, 1961. 320pp.

Autobiography, about 40pp. on World War I, when Horrocks fought at Mons as a lieutenant in the Middlesex Regiment, was captured, and made several attempts to escape.

644. Horton, A. E. *When I Became a Man: Private Memoir of Two Years' Overseas Service.* London: Houghton, 1931. 248pp.

Memoir, June 1916–December 1918. Horton went to France with a machine gun company in December 1916 and fought at Hill 60 but luckily missed Passchendaele while on leave. His unit went to Italy in November 1917 and helped to stem the Austrian June 1918 offensive. Elegantly written; Horton claims the war helped him to grow up and become a man.

645. Hunter, John Templeton. *Hell at Ypres*. San Antonio, Texas: The Naylor Company, 1934. 209pp.

Memoir, 1914–1918. The author, a Belfast native, joined the Royal Engineers as a sapper in June 1915 and fought in the Ypres Salient and in France. Lively, readable, and realistic chronicle from an enlisted soldier's point of view.

646. Hutchison, Graham Seton. *Footslogger: An Autobiography*. London: Hutchinson, 1931. 399pp., illustrated.

Autobiography, about 100pp. on World War I. Hutchison came from Africa in 1914 to serve in France as a lieutenant in the 2nd Argyll and Sutherland Highlanders, and had some trouble getting used to war on the Western Front. He fought at the Somme as a captain in the Machine Gun Corps, 100th Brigade, and subsequently became lieutenant colonel and Machine Gun Officer of the 33rd Division, before being "blown up" near the end of the war. A pleasure to read; somehow, Hutchison's boastfulness never becomes annoying. See also *Warrior* (1932) and *Pilgrimage* (1935), by the same author; and *Biography of a Batman* (1929) written under the name Graham Seton.

647. Hutton, Isabel Galloway Emslie. *With a Woman's Unit in Serbia, Salonika and Sebastopol*. London: Williams and Norgate, 1928. 302pp., illustrated.

Memoir by a member of the Scottish Women's War Hospitals organization.

648. Hyndson, James Gerard Wyndham. *From Mons to the First Battle of Ypres*. London: Wyman & Sons, 1932. 128pp.

Diary, August 1914–February 1915. Hyndson was a captain of the 1st Loyal North Lancashire Regiment; because of declining health, he was invalided back to England in February 1915. Valuable record of the B.E.F.'s first battles of the war.

649. *In Spite of All Rejoicing: A Soldier's Diary of the Great War*. New York: Duffield and Company, 1929. 260pp.

Diary, August 1914–May 1917. Straightforward diary of trench life on the Western Front, and later of flying in the R.F.C.

650. Inchbald, Geoffrey. *Camels and Others*. London: Johnson, 1968. 184pp.

Memoir, 1916–1918. Inchbald's Berkshire Yeomanry Regiment was incorporated into the Imperial Camel Corps in 1916, and he served in that unit from Egypt through almost the entire Palestine campaign. Includes quotations from and numerous references to T.E. Lawrence.

651. Ingrey, Corporal. *Shoesmith to the Gunners: A Private Unofficial Diary of a Cambridgeshire Shoesmith, 1916–1917, on the Somme and at Ypres*. Orwell, Camb.: Ellison's Editions, 1988. 20pp.

652. Insall, Algernon J. *Observer: Memoirs of the R.F.C., 1915–1918*. London: Kimber, 1970. 208pp.

Insall served as an observer in R.F.C. Squadron No. 11, flying Vickers FB5s, until May 1916, when he became adjutant of the Third Corps Wing. He later served as R.F.C. liaison to French aircraft manufacturers. Best on Insall's service with No. 11 Squadron.

653. Iron, John. *Keeper of the Gate: The Reminiscences of Captain John Iron, Harbour Master of Dover*. London: Sampson Low, Marston, c.1936. 246pp., illustrated.

Memories of the Dover Patrol.

654. Ironside, Edmund. *Archangel 1918–1919*. London: Constable, 1953. 220pp., illustrated.

Memoir, September 1918–November 1919. Ironside was a temporary brigadier general commanding the 99th Brigade of the 2nd Division in September 1918, when was sent to Archangel and placed in command of the Allied forces in North Russia. He returned to Britain a major general in September 1919. A readable and important account of the Allied intervention in Russia.

655. Irwin, Noel Mackintosh Stuart. *Infantry Officer, 1914–1918: The Record of Service as a Young Officer in the First World War*. Torquay:

Goss Albion, 1943. 24pp., illustrated.

The author graduated from Sandhurst two months before the war began and fought the war's first battles in France and Flanders.

656. Jabotinsky, Vladimir. *The Story of the Jewish Legion*. Translated by Samuel Katz. New York: Bernard Ackerman, 1945. 191pp.

Memoir, December 1914–August 1919. Jabotinsky was a Russian Zionist and founder of the Jewish Legion. He traces the development of the Legion in this memoir, including its participation in the Palestine campaign.

657. Jack, James Lochhead. *General Jack's Diary, 1914–1918; The Trench Diary of Brigadier-General J. L. Jack, D. S. O.* Edited by John Terraine. London: Eyre & Spottiswoode, 1964. 319pp., illustrated.

Jack served as a captain of the 1st Cameronians, Scottish Rifles, and the West Yorkshire Regiment before becoming commander of the 28th Brigade. Remarkably complete diary, providing excellent descriptions of the war's first and last battles and almost everything in between. Characteristically iconoclastic editing by Terraine.

658. James, Frank. *Faraway Campaign*. London: Grayson & Grayson, 1934. 281pp.

Account of the war in Central Asia.

659. Jerrold, Douglas. *Georgian Adventure*. London: Collins, 1937. 398pp., illustrated.

Autobiography, with section on World War I covering August 1914–November 1916. Jerrold was a lieutenant in the Hawke Battalion of the Royal Naval Division, serving at Gallipoli and on the Somme, where he was severely wounded in November 1916. A Catholic activist who later became one of the most prominent British supporters of General Francisco Franco, Jerrold also led a lonely campaign against the "disillusionment" school of war writing. See his pamphlet *The Lie About the War* (1930).

660. Johnston, Maurice Andrew Brackenreed, and Kenneth Darlaston Yearsley. *Four-Fifty Miles to Freedom*. Edinburgh: W. Blackwood, 1919. 295pp., illustrated.

Memoir, 1914–1918. The authors, both captains, were captured at Kut and imprisoned in Turkey. After an elaborately prepared escape they made it with eight other officers to Cyprus.

661. Jones, E. H. *The Road to En-Dor: Being an Account of How Two Prisoners of War at Yozgad in Turkey Won Their Way to Freedom.* London: John Lane, 1919. 351pp., illustrated.

Memoir, February 1917–October 1918. Strange story of how Lieutenant Jones and his fellow captive, Lieutenant C.W. Hill of the R.F.C., escaped a Turkish prisoner of war camp by faking spiritualism. See also Hill's memoir, *The Spook and the Commandant* (1975).

662. Jones, James Ira. *Air Fighter's Scrap-Book.* London: Nicholson and Watson, 1938. 332pp.

Memoir, 1914–1918. A hodgepodge of chapters on various aviation subjects intermingles with "Taffy" Jones's account of his own service from May to August 1918 with R.F.C. No. 74 Squadron, during which period he scored 37 victories.

663. Joubert de la Ferté, Philip Bennet. *The Fated Sky: An Autobiography.* London: Hutchinson, 1952. 280pp., illustrated.

Autobiography, about 40pp. on World War I. Joubert joined the R.F.C. in 1913, and flew with No. 1 Squadron from August 1914 until he took command of No. 1 Squadron the following year. He took over 5th Wing on the Suez Canal in 1916 and returned to England in 1917. Joubert should have devoted a separate book to his experiences in 1914; he only skims them here.

664. Keable, Robert. *Standing By: War Time Reflections in France and Flanders.* London: Nisbet, 1919. 260pp.

Memoir, 1914–1918. Keable served before the war as an Anglican missionary in Africa, and went to France as chaplain to a group of South African laborers. He created a scandal by having an affair, converting to Catholicism, running away to Tahiti, and becoming an advocate of open marriages.

665. Keeling, Edward Herbert. *Adventures in Turkey and Russia.* London: J. Murray, 1924. 240pp., illustrated.

Memoir, in which the author describes his capture at Kut, imprisonment in Turkey, and subsequent escape to the Crimea.

666. Kelly, David. *39 Months with the "Tigers," 1915–1918*. London: Ernest Benn, 1930. 160pp., illustrated.

Memoir, July 1915–November 1918. Kelly was a captain on the staff of the 110th Infantry Brigade, consisting of four battalions of the Leicester Regiment. He begins with an angry assault on disillusionment war books, constituting what he calls a "flood of pornography," but provides little more than a staff officer's view of unit movements from the Somme to the Armistice.

667. Kelly, R. B. Talbot. *A Subaltern's Odyssey: Memoirs of the Great War, 1915–1917*. London: Kimber, 1980. 192pp., illustrated.

The editor of this account writes in the introduction that "those who believe that it is dangerous, perhaps wicked, to publish anything that declares there was another side to the war will disapprove of Talbot Kelly's memoirs." Kelly—a gunner officer in the 9th (Scottish) Division—believed that the results of the war, spiritually and otherwise, were not all bad. As the memoirs show, no one could accuse Kelly, who fought at Loos, the Somme, Arras, and Passchendaele, of not having experienced the worst the war had to offer! Nicely illustrated.

668. Kennet, Edward Hilton Young, 1st Baron. *By Sea and Land: Some Naval Doings*. London: T.C. & E.C. Jack, 1920. 362pp.

Memoir, 1914–1918. The author served during the war as a naval cipher officer, and lost his right arm during the attack on Zeebrugge in 1918.

669. Kerr, Charles Lester. *All in the Day's Work*. London: Rich & Cowan, 1939. 314pp., illustrated.

The author served as an officer in the Royal Navy, commanding shore batteries in Flanders and Salonika and then managing convoys to and from Egypt.

670. Kerr, Mark E. *Land, Sea, and Air: The Reminiscences of Mark Kerr*. London: Longmans, Green, 1927. 406pp., illustrated.

Autobiography, about 40pp. on World War I, when Kerr commanded the British Adriatic Squadron. Disappointingly brief.

671. Keyes, Roger. *The Naval Memoirs of Admiral of the Fleet Sir Roger Keyes*. Volume 1, *The Narrow Seas to the Dardanelles, 1910–1915*.

London: Thornton Butterworth, 1934. 538pp., illustrated. Volume 2, *Scapa Flow to the Dover Straits, 1916–1918*. London: Thornton Butterworth, 1935. 416pp., illustrated.

Detailed and useful memoirs of one of the most important figures in the British navy, who was involved in planning for Gallipoli and the Zeebrugge raid of April 1918, among other actions.

672. Keynes, Geoffrey. *Gates of Memory*. Oxford: Clarendon Press, 1981. 428pp., illustrated.

Autobiography, with one chapter about the author's experiences in World War I and two more chapters on Rupert Brooke and Siegfried Sasson, whom he knew. Keynes, the brother of John Maynard Keynes, became a lieutenant in the R.A.M.C. in August 1914, and was appointed a captain and medical officer to the 23rd Brigade of the Royal Field Artillery in August 1915. He saw service at Ypres and the Somme before taking over a Casualty Clearing Station near Albert in 1916, where he remained for the rest of the war.

673. Kiernan, Reginald Hugh. *Little Brother Goes Soldiering*. London: Constable, 1930. 136pp.

Diary, December 1917–September 1918. Very good diary, describing combat during the German March 1918 offensive, and day-to-day life in the trenches.

674. Kirkbride, Alec. *An Awakening: The Arab Campaign 1917–18*. Tavistock: University Press of Arabia, 1971. 134pp., illustrated.

Memoir, January 1916–1920. Kirkbride, who had lived in Egypt from childhood, served in 1916–17 in the Royal Engineers and the Egyptian Labour Corps. In 1918 he was attached to the army of Faisal Hussein, and participated in the Arab uprising. Densely written but useful for research.

675. Knight, Gerald Featherstone. *"Brother Bosch": An Airman's Escape from Germany*. London: William Heinemann, 1919. 176pp.

Memoir, November 1916–1917. Knight, a captain in the R.F.C., describes being shot down near Cambrai, his capture, and subsequent attempts to escape until he finally made it to Holland. Humorous and exciting.

676. Knox, Alfred William Fortescue. *With the Russian Army,*

1914–1917: Being Chiefly Extracts from the Diary of a Military Attaché. 2 vols. London: Hutchinson, 1921. 752pp., illustrated.

Memoir/Diary, August 1914–January 1918. Before the war Knox was military attaché to the British embassy in St. Petersburg, and from 1914 to 1917 he accompanied the headquarters of various Russian armies on several fronts. Invaluable perspective on the Russian high command, rich in detail, but without much on what the war was like for common soldiers.

677. Laird, Frank M. *Personal Experiences of the Great War: (An Unfinished Manuscript).* Dublin: Eason & Son, c.1925. 200pp.

Memoir, July 1914–December 1918. Laird enlisted in the 7th Royal Dublin Fusiliers at the end of 1914, and was wounded at Suvla Bay, Gallipoli, in August 1915. He became a second lieutenant that autumn, served with the 10th Royal Dublin Fusiliers during the 1916 Easter Rising, and then went to France with the 8th Battalion of the same regiment in early 1917. He was wounded during the Messines Offensive in June 1917, and the Germans captured him in their March 1918 offensive. Engrossing, multifaceted memoir.

678. Lambert, Arthur. *Over-the-Top: A "P.B.I." in the H.A.C.* London: John Long, 1930. 224pp.

3rd person memoir, 1917–December 1918. Lambert was drafted in 1917 and served as a private in the 2nd Battalion, Honourable Artillery Company, in Flanders and Italy. Lambert claims to "tone down scenes inconceivably ghastly" and record "every possible instance of bravery and cheerfulness," but his narrative remains powerful and, apparently, realistic.

679. Landau, Henry. *All's Fair: The Story of the British Secret Service Behind German Lines.* New York: G.P. Putnam's Sons, 1934. 329pp., illustrated.

Memoir, 1914–1918. Landau commanded the British secret service's Military Division in Holland after 1916, and directed espionage activities in France and Belgium. His tales are of questionable authenticity.

680. Lascelles, Alan. *End of an Era: Letters and Journals of Sir Alan Lascelles 1887–1920.* Edited by Duff Hart-Davis. London: Hamish Hamilton, 1986. 348pp., illustrated.

The author's wartime letters concern his service—almost all behind the lines—in the Bedfordshire Yeomanry. Mainly of personal and literary interest.

681. Latham, Bryan. *A Territorial Soldier's War*. Aldershot: Gale & Polden, 1967. 133pp., illustrated.

Memoir, 1914–1918. Latham enlisted in the London Rifle Brigade in 1913 and went to France with the 4th Division in November 1914, participating in that year's Christmas Truce. He served as a stretcher bearer in the Second Battle of Ypres in April 1915, and was wounded. He returned to the front that autumn as a lieutenant in the 3/17th London Regiment and took command of a Stokes mortar battery, serving at Vimy Ridge before joining the Indian army in 1917. In 1918 he participated in the Palestine campaign in the 2/19th Punjabis of the 60th Division. Good memoir, well illustrated.

682. Latymer, Hugh Burdett Money-Coutts. *Chances and Changes*. Edinburgh: W. Blackwood, 1931. 328pp.

The author served from 1915 to 1917 as a captain in the Royal North Devon Hussars in Gallipoli and Egypt.

683. Law, Francis. *A Man at Arms: Memoirs of Two World Wars*. London: Collins, 1983. 238pp.

Autobiography with about 60 pages covering 1914–1918. Law was a lieutenant and captain in the 1st Battalion, Irish Guards, and participated in battles at Loos, the Somme, and Passchendaele. Surprisingly candid memories of a professional soldier.

684. Lawrence, Brian. *Letters from the Front: The Great War Correspondence of Lieutenant Brian Lawrence, 1916–17*. Edited by Ian Fletcher. Tunbridge Wells: Parapress, 1993. 128pp., illustrated.

Lawrence served with the 1st Grenadier Guards on the Somme and elsewhere on the Western Front.

685. Lawrence, T. E. *The Seven Pillars of Wisdom: A Triumph*. Privately printed, 1926; numerous reprints. 659pp., illustrated. Abridged as *Revolt in the Desert* in 1927.

The classic story of Lawrence's involvement in the Arab revolt against the Turks. See also *The Letters of T. E. Lawrence* (1938) and *The Home Letters of T. E. Lawrence and His Brothers* (1954).

686. Lawson, Henry Brailsford. *Vignettes of the Western Front: Reflections of an Infantry Subaltern in France and Belgium, 1917–1918*. Edited by Andrew Lawson. Oxford: Positif Press, 1979. 96pp., illustrated.

Episodic, non-chronological memories of Passchendaele, the March 1918 offensive, and various aspects of daily life on the Western Front.

687. Lawson, James Burnett. *A Cameronian Officer: Being a Memoir of Lieutenant James Burnett Lawson, Second Cameronians (Scottish Rifles)*. Glasgow: John Smith & Son, 1921. 255pp.

Biography with letters and poems, August 1914–November 1919. This is a kind of double memoir of Lieutenant Lawson, who was killed in the March 1918 offensive, and his father, who describes in an extremely moving manner the anguish he felt at his son's death and the subsequent, ultimately futile attempts to retrieve his body.

688. Lawson, John Cuthbert. *Tales of Ægean Intrigue*. London: Chatto and Windus, 1920. 271pp., illustrated.

Memoir, August 1914–March 1917. A Cambridge don, Lawson was appointed a naval intelligence officer at the beginning of the war and hunted spies and influenced governments in the Aegean region. Read in conjunction with Compton MacKenzie's *Aegean Memories* (1940).

689. Lee, Arthur Stanley Gould. *No Parachute: A Fighter Pilot in World War I; Letters Written in 1917*. London: Jarrolds, 1968. 234pp.

Letters, May 1917–January 1918. Lee, a former lieutenant in the Sherwood Foresters, joined R.F.C. No 46 Squadron and flew over Messines, Vimy Ridge, Passchendaele, and Cambrai. Detailed, well-written letters make this collection read like a memoir. See also *Open Cockpit: A Pilot of the Royal Flying Corps* (1969).

690. Lewis, Cecil. *Sagittarius Rising*. London: Peter Davies, 1936. 331pp.

Memoir, 1915–1921. Captain Lewis served in R.F.C. Squadron Nos. 3, 44, 56, 61, and 152, but scored all eight of his victories flying an S.E.5a for No. 56 Squadron in May–June 1917. Many consider this book to be the best aviation memoir ever written, and it has been reprinted numerous times. See also *All My Yesterdays: An Autobiography* (1993).

691. Lewis, Gwilym Hugh. *Wings Over the Somme, 1916–1918*. London:

Kimber, 1976. 205pp., illustrated.

Diary, 1916–1918. The author joined the R.F.C. in 1915 and was posted to No. 32 Squadron, equipped with D.H.2 aircraft, the following year. In 1917 he became Flight Commander of No. 40 Squadron, and rounded out his total of twelve victories flying an S.E.5.

692. Lewis, Saunders. *Letters to Margaret Gilcriest.* Edited by Mair Saunders Jones, Ned Thomas, and Harri Pritchard Jones. Cardiff: University of Wales Press, 1993. 636pp.

Letters, November 1914–August 1937. These letters from Saunders (a prominent Welsh nationalist and writer) to his future wife chronicle his wartime service as a lieutenant in the 12th South Wales Borderers, and his eventual disillusionment.

693. Lewis, Wyndham. *Blasting & Bombadiering.* London: Eyre & Spottiswoode, 1937. 312pp., illustrated.

Memoir, 1914–1926. Lewis served as a second lieutenant and bombardier in several batteries of the Royal Field Artillery on the Western Front. He describes his experiences at Ypres, and breaks them down into their component elements, analyzing each in his own idiosyncratic manner. Very important memoir by a Vorticist artist and intellectual who associated with some of Britain's most important literary figures and later became a fascist sympathizer.

694. Liddell Hart, Basil Henry. *The Memoirs of Captain Liddell Hart.* London: Cassell, 1965. 2 volumes, 434 and 334pp., illustrated.

Autobiography, with unfortunately only a short chapter on Liddell Hart's wartime service in the 2nd, 3rd, 6th, and 9th King's Own Yorkshire Light Infantry, the R.F.C., and the Gloucestershire Regiment. The vast majority of the work concerns his later development as a military theorist.

695. Linzell, Harold Harding. *Fallen on the Somme: The War Diary of 2nd Lieutenant Harold Harding Linzell M.C. 7th Border Regiment.* Edited by M. A. Argyle. North Devon: Aycliffe Press, 1981. 54pp., illustrated.

Diary, January–June 1916. Fairly routine diary, stopping just short of the Somme, in which Linzell was killed.

696. Livermore, Bernard. *Long 'un: A Damn Bad Soldier.* Batley: Harry Hayes, 1974. 179pp., illustrated.

Memoir, 1914–1918. The author was a private in the 2/20th Battalion of the London Regiment, and served as part of the 60th Division on the Western Front, Salonika, and Palestine. A humorous account.

697. Livingston, Guy. *Hot Air in Cold Blood*. London: Selwyn & Blount, 1933. 288pp., illustrated.

Autobiography, mostly on World War I, when Livingston was Director of Air Organization in the War Office, and inspected the budding American air service in 1918. Remarkably opinionated administrative memoir, closing with a diatribe against "puerile politicians."

698. Livock, G. E. *To the Ends of the Air*. London: H.M. Stationery Office, 1973.

Memoir, 1914–1931. Livock joined the Royal Naval Air Service in 1914 and flew a Felixstowe F2a over the North Sea from the air station at Great Yarmouth.

699. Lloyd, Percival St. Lawrence. *The Wood of Death and Beyond: The First World War Recollections of Major P. St. L. Lloyd O.B.E.* Edited by R.J. Lloyd. Ockham: Ockham Books, 1997. 111pp.

Memoir, August 1914–1919. Lloyd was commissioned a subaltern in August 1917 and joined the 22nd Royal Fusiliers outside Bethune. His memoir is best on the Battle of Cambrai, in which he was wounded.

700. Lloyd, Robert Alleyn. *A Trooper in the "Tins": Autobiography of a Lifeguardsman*. London: Hurst & Blackett, 1938. 320pp.

Memoir, 1911–1918. Lloyd enlisted as a trooper in the 1st Battalion of The Life Guards in 1911 and served at Antwerp, Ypres, the Somme, Arras, and Cambrai before he was wounded in May 1918.

701. Lloyd, Thomas. *The Blazing Trail of Flanders*. London: Heath Cranton, 1933. 255pp., illustrated.

Memoir, October 1914–November 1918. Lloyd, a lieutenant in the Cheshires, describes his experiences in Aden, India, and Passchendaele in between chapters on the closing battles of the war. Worthwhile despite the odd arrangement.

702. Lockhart, John Gilbert. *Palestine Days and Nights: Sketches of the Campaign in the Holy Land*. London: R. Scott, 1920. 140pp.

Memoir, 1917–1918. The author served as a junior officer in Palestine during the final campaigns of 1917–1918.

703. Long, Bernard Wilfrid. *First World War Letters of 2nd Lt. Bernard Wilfrid Long, 1896–1917*. London: David Hawgood, 1995. 59pp.

Letters, 1916–1917. Long went to France in July 1916 as a second lieutenant in the 16th Battalion ("Bradford Pals") of the West Yorkshire Regiment, serving as an intelligence officer until a German sniper wounded him near Givenchy in September. He went back to France in June 1917 as a member of the 2nd West Yorkshire Regiment, and was killed at Langemarck in August 1917. Sincere, honest, and moving letters.

704. Long, Selden Herbert. *In the Blue*. London: John Lane, 1920. 204pp.

Memoir, December 1914–1918. "Tubby" Long served in R.F.C. Squadron Nos. 24, 29, 46, and 111, flying a B.E.2c at Loos and other planes in France, Flanders, and Palestine. He ended the war with 9 victories and the rank of major.

705. Longmore, Arthur. *From Sea to Sky, 1910–1945*. London: Geoffrey Bles, 1946. 304pp., illustrated.

Autobiography, about 45pp. on World War I. Longmore formed and commanded R.N.A.S. Squadron No. 1 in 1914–15, and was appointed lieutenant commander of HMS *Tiger* in January 1916. In April 1918 he was appointed a lieutenant colonel in the R.A.F. and served the last months of the war in the Mediterranean.

706. Luard, K. E. *Unknown Warriors: Extracts from the Letters of K. E. Luard, R.R.C., Nursing Sister in France, 1914–1918*. London: Chatto and Windus, 1930. 306pp., illustrated.

Letters, October 1915–August 1918. Luard was in charge of nursing at various casualty clearing stations, tending wounded from Arras, Passchendaele, and the March 1918 offensive, as well as the daily toll from the trenches. A good documentary record, exuding continual optimism despite the length of Luard's service.

707. Lucy, John. *There's a Devil in the Drum*. London: Faber and Faber, 1938. 393pp.

Memoir, August–December 1914. Lucy was a private in the 2nd Royal Irish Rifles. Possibly the best war memoir ever written, but difficult to find even in reprint editions. Lucy was a poor Dublin boy who along with his brother joined the Regular Army before the war began. This book vividly recounts his experiences in the B.E.F. from August 1914 until the end of the year. Lucy's writing is witty and understated, but often intensely moving, particularly in the description of his brother's death. Highly recommended, and deserving a larger reprint edition.

708. Lushington, Franklin [pseud. Mark Severn]. *The Gambardier: Giving Some Account of the Heavy and Siege Artillery in France, 1914–1918*. London: Benn, 1930. 224pp., illustrated.

Lushington served as a major in the Royal Garrison Artillery.

709. Lytton, Neville. *The Press and the General Staff*. London: W. Collins Sons, 1920. 231pp., illustrated.

Memoir, 1914–1918. Lytton served as an officer in the 11th Royal Sussex Regiment, on the staff of the 39th Division, at G.H.Q., and then coordinated war correspondents for the staff. He describes his and the correspondents' struggles in obeying the dictates of the General Staff while trying to remain true to the facts of life at the front. He was a friend of Edmund Blunden.

710. McCudden, James Thomas Byford. *Five Years in the Royal Flying Corps*. Edited by C.G. Grey. London: Aeroplane, 1919. 348pp.

Memoir, 1914–1918. McCudden joined the Royal Engineers as a fifteen-year-old bugler in 1910, and had become a mechanic in the R.F.C. by the outbreak of the war. He rose to the rank of major, serving in Squadron Nos. 3, 20, 29, 56, and 66, and scored fifty-seven victories. He won the Victoria Cross in April 1918, but was killed in a flying accident in July. Reprinted in numerous editions; some have the title *Flying Fury: Five Years in the Royal Flying Corps*.

711. McDermott, Frank. *Confessions of an Old Soldier*. Worthing, West Sussex: Churchman, 1984. 146pp., illustrated.

Autobiography, mostly on World War I, when McDermott went to France in September 1916 as a second lieutenant in the 1/4th Royal Berkshire Regiment and served on the Somme. He later transferred to the 2nd Battalion of the same regiment as a signaling officer, and after coming down with trench feet in the spring of 1917 he left for India. Especially good on fighting in March 1917.

712. MacKenzie, Compton. *Gallipoli Memories*. London: Cassell, 1929. 405pp.

Memoir, August 1914–August 1915. MacKenzie, at the beginning of the war already a well-known author, served as an intelligence officer during the Gallipoli campaign and, though he visited the peninsula, saw little actual fighting. This memoir is full of odd characters and tricky situations, and reads like a novel. Useful also for its glimpses of Sir Ian Hamilton and the rest of the British staff's handling of the campaign. Mackenzie's subsequent service through 1916 in Greece and the Aegean is covered in *First Athenian Memories* (1931), *Greek Memories* (1939), and *Aegean Memories* (1940).

713. McLanachan, W. [pseud. McScotch]. *Fighter Pilot*. London: G. Routledge & Son, 1936. 248pp., illustrated.

Memoir, 1917–1918. The author became a lieutenant in R.F.C. No. 40 Squadron in 1917 and eventually scored seven victories.

714. Macmillan, Harold. *Winds of Change, 1914–1939*. London: Macmillan, 1966. 664pp., illustrated.

Autobiography, with only one chapter on World War I, but that is a very good chapter, describing the future Prime Minister's experiences as a second lieutenant in the 19th King's Royal Rifle Corps and the 4th and 2nd Battalions of the Grenadier Guards. He fought at Loos and was badly wounded in the pelvis on the Somme.

715. MacMillan, Norman. *Into the Blue*. London: Duckworth, 1929. 213pp.

Memoir, 1916–1919. The author was a captain in R.F.C. No. 45 Squadron, and scored nine victories flying Sopwith Camels and Snipes over the Western Front and Italy. Exciting and well-written.

716. MacNaughtan, Sarah. *My War Experiences in Two Continents*. London: J. Murray, 1919. 286pp., illustrated.

Memoir, 1914–1916. The author, a novelist, did hospital and canteen work in Belgium, Russia, and Persia until she died in 1916. Opinionated and critical of the war.

717. Malins, Geoffrey H. *How I Filmed the War: A Record of the Extraordinary Experiences of the Man Who Filmed the Great Somme*

Battles, etc. New York: Frederick A. Stokes, 1919. 307pp., illustrated.

Memoir, August 1914–March 1917. Malins, a film maker and "showman," filmed independently on the Western Front until October 1915, when G.H.Q. appointed him the B.E.F.'s official cameraman. Among his many works was the famous *Battle of the Somme*. A fascinating but not entirely honest memoir, since many of Malins's shots were staged. Written in 1917 but published after the war.

718. Mann, Hugh Wallace, and Jessie Reid. *Under the Shadow: Letters of Love and War, 1911–1917: The Poignant Testimony and Story of Captain Hugh Wallace Mann, 7th & 5th Battalions, the Queen's Own Cameron Highlanders and Jessie Reid.* Dunfermline: Cialann Press, 1999. 192pp., illustrated.

Letters, 1911–1917. Mann fought at Loos and died in November 1917 from wounds received at Passchendaele. These are love letters between Mann and Reid, more interesting for their moving personal relationship than for any details provided of the front lines.

719. Mann, James Saumarez. *An Administrator in the Making, James Saumerez Mann, 1893–1920.* London: Longmans, Green, 1921. 330pp., illustrated.

Letters chronicling the author's administrative service in Mesopotamia.

720. Mannock, Edward. *The Personal Diary of Major Edward "Mick" Mannock.* Edited by Frederick Oughton. London: Spearman, 1966. 221pp.

Diary, 1917–1918. Mannock was one of Britain's best and most intriguing fighter pilots. He joined R.F.C. No. 40 Squadron in April 1917, flying a Nieuport Scout, and flew an S.E.5a as flight commander of No. 74 Squadron from February to July 1918. He took over No. 85 Squadron from William Bishop in July 1918 and was killed later that month after having scored a total of 61 victories.

721. Mappin, Kenneth George. *My Father's War: Kenneth George Mappin in the Great War, 1914–1918: A Selection from His Diaries.* Edited by John Mappin. Montreal: John Mappin, 1997. 59pp.

Mappin was commissioned a second lieutenant in the 1st Battalion, North Staffordshire Regiment in August 1914 and served until 1917, when he was promoted to captain and transferred to R.F.C. No. 27 Squadron.

722. Marks, Thomas Penrose. *The Laughter Goes from Life: in the Trenches of the First World War*. London: Kimber, 1977. 190pp.

Memoir, 1917–1918. The author served in the Gloucestershire Regiment attached to the 55th Division, serving at the La Bassée Canal and at Arras. Superior, moving, and realistic memoir, includes a wrenching description of how Moore was severely injured by mustard gas.

723. Marson, Thomas B. *Scarlet and Khaki*. London: Cape, 1930. 226pp., illustrated.

Autobiography, about half on World War I. The author, a Boer War veteran and polo rider, joined the 3rd County of London Yeomanry in 1914 and was commissioned a second lieutenant in 1915, and went to Gallipoli in July of that year. In early 1917 he joined R.F.C. No. 56 Squadron as a recording officer, and in December of that year he went to the United States to supervise technical supply and training. Rather stuffy and disappointingly sparse on Gallipoli, but provides a good record of the activities of No. 56 Squadron in 1917.

724. Martin, Bernard. *Poor Bloody Infantry: A Subaltern on the Western Front 1916–1917*. London: John Murray, 1987. 174pp., illustrated.

Memoir, August 1914–November 1918. Martin was a second lieutenant in the North Staffordshire Regiment. He participated in the Somme and was badly wounded on the first day of Passchendaele. A lively memoir made from an extended tape recording, with a memorable description of Martin's wounding.

725. Masefield, John. *John Masefield's Letters From the Front 1915–1917*. Edited by Peter Vansittart. London: Constable, 1984. 307pp.

Letters, March 1915–May 1917. The well-known author and poet Masefield served after February 1915 as a medical orderly in the British Red Cross, and subsequently tried to form a mobile hospital unit on the Western Front. He spent the first half of 1916 on a propaganda tour in the United States. His letters are evocative and reflective but also patriotic and anti-German. See also *Letters to Margaret Bridges, 1915–1919* (1984).

726. Mather, William D. *Muckydonia, 1917–1917, Being the Adventures of a One-Time Pioneer in Macedonia and Bulgaria During the First World War*. Ilfracombe, Devon: Arthur H. Stockwell, 1979. 254pp.,

illustrated.

Diary/memoir, January 1917–February 1919. Mather served as a private in the 3/4th York and Lancaster Regiment, later joining the Oxfordshire and Buckinghamshire Light Infantry. An amusingly cynical diary of a troublemaker, showing the tedium of life on the Salonika Front. Ironically, in old age Mather looked back on the war as a "wonderful experience."

727. Maxwell, Francis Aylmer. *Frank Maxwell: A Memoir and Some Letters*. London: J. Murray, 1921. 228pp., illustrated.

Biography/letters, 1914–1917. Brigadier General Maxwell, who had won the Victoria Cross during the Boer War, was killed in action in September 1917.

728. Maxwell, William Babington. Time Gathered: An Autobiography. London: Hutchinson, 1937. 357pp., illustrated.

Autobiography, includes extended section on the author's service as a transport officer on the Western Front, including the Somme.

729. May, Ernest. *Signal Corporal: The Story of the 2nd London Irish Rifles (2/18th Battalion London Regiment) 1914–1918*. London: Johnson, 1972. 179pp., illustrated.

Essentially a unit history of this formation, which fought in France, Salonika, and Palestine.

730. Maybury, Harold. *The Years of Remembrance: "Ich Dien."* Warrington: John Walker & Co., 1924. 166pp.

731. Maze, Paul. *A Frenchman in Khaki*. London: William Heinemann, 1934. 353pp.

Maze, an English-educated Frenchman and artist, served (unofficially) with his friend Winston Churchill in the Royal Scots Greys and in liaison and reconnaissance work for the French army.

732. Meade, Patrick. *Born to Trouble*. New York: G.P. Putnam's Sons, 1939. 406pp.

Autobiography, about 50pp. on World War I, when Meade served as an officer in the Irish Guards in France 1914–1918, and then at Murmansk in 1919.

733. Meager, George. *My Airship Flights, 1915–1930.* London: Kimber, 1970. 239pp.

Meager joined the Royal Naval Air Service in 1915 and was attached to the Airship Section. He flew a variety of airships from the English coast until 1917, when he went to Italy in order to serve on Adriatic patrols. He flew an Italian airship from Rome to England in 1918. Fascinating story of a colorful career.

734. Meinertzhagen, Richard. *Army Diary 1898–1926.* Edinburgh: Oliver and Boyd, 1960. 301pp., illustrated.

Diary includes a large section devoted to August 1914–November 1918, during which period the author served as an intelligence officer in the campaign in German East Africa until 1917, when he went to Palestine. Includes excellent descriptions of the Battle of Tanga in 1914 and other battles, with very good maps and illustrations.

735. Mellersh, H. E. L. *Schoolboy into War.* London: Kimber, 1978. 200pp., illustrated.

Memoir, 1914–1918. Mellersh went to France in April 1916 as a lieutenant in the 2nd Battalion, East Lancashire Regiment, and was wounded three times in the next two years during fighting on the Somme and in the Salient. Much of the book is taken up with Mellersh's memories of training in 1915, but it also includes some candid passages on how he coped throughout his life with memories of the war's horrors. He nevertheless remained convinced that he had done the right thing by joining up.

736. Miles, Hallie Eustace. *Untold Tales of War-time London: A Personal Diary.* London: Cecil Palmer, 1930. 173pp.

Civilian reminiscences of life on the home front.

737. Mills, Fred. *Great Uncle Fred's War: An Illustrated Diary, 1917–1920.* Edited by Alan Pryor and Jennifer K. Woods. Whitstable: Pryor Publications, 1985. 97pp., illustrated.

Diary, April 1917–January 1920, of a sapper in 570 (Devon) Army Troop Company of the Royal Engineers, who did construction work in Egypt. Mundane but nicely illustrated.

738. Mitchell, Francis. *Tank Warfare: The Story of the Tanks in the Great*

War. London: T. Nelson and Sons, 1933. 312pp., illustrated.

History/memoir, 1914–1918. The author served as a tank commander in the 1st Tank Battalion, and won the M.C. in April 1918 during the first recorded tank to tank duel of history. He describes every major tank battle of the war, including his own experiences when he participated.

739. Money, Robert R. *Flying and Soldiering*. London: Ivor Nicholson & Watson, 1936. 320pp.

Memoir, June 1915–1928. Money joined R.F.C. No. 12 Squadron in 1915 as an observer in B.E.2c and other aircraft. He flew on some night bombing missions before being shot down and captured in September 1916, and spent the rest of the war in a prison camp. Not terribly eventful, but with some interesting details on air observation work.

740. Montague, Charles Edward. *Disenchantment*. London: Chatto & Windus, 1922. 220pp.

Memoir, 1914–1918. Montague, a journalist for the Manchester *Guardian*, was forty-seven years old when he joined up in 1914, and served as a sergeant in the 24th Battalion, Royal Fusiliers, and as a captain in the intelligence service. This book is less a memoir than a collection of essays detailing how men became disenchanted with the war. It is a very important early exposition on what later came to be called "disillusionment."

741. Montgomery, D. H. *Down the Flare Path*. London: J. Hamilton, 1937. 144pp., illustrated.

An account of aerial combat.

742. Moore, Aubrey. *A Son of the Rectory: from Leicestershire to the Somme*. Gloucester: A. Sutton, 1982. 160pp., illustrated.

Autobiography, about 40pp. on World War I, when Moore served as a lieutenant in the 5th Battalion of the Leicestershire Regiment, 46th Division. Moore went into the trenches near Neuve Chappelle in 1915, and commanded a tunneling company in fighting at Ypres, Lens, and the Somme. Written from memory and vague at times.

743. Moore, Harold William [pseud. Holdar Roome]. *One Man's War, 1914–1918: A Chapter of Autobiography*. London: Mitre, 1968. 157pp.

Memoir in verse, describing the author's experiences on the Somme and wounding at Ypres.

744. Moore, William Geoffrey. *Early Bird*. London: Putnam, 1963. 146pp.

Memoir, 1914–1918. Moore trained in 1914 and joined the Royal Naval Air Service. He flew seaplane patrols in Sopwith Scouts and then flew a B.E.2c over East Africa.

745. More, John. *With Allenby's Crusaders*. London: Heath Cranton, 1923. 232pp., illustrated.

Memoir, 1917–1918. The author served as a captain in the 1/6th Battalion of the Royal Welch Fusiliers, and as a staff officer in the 53rd (Welsh) Division in the Palestine Campaign. Good record of daily life.

746. Morris, John. *Diary of a Soldier, 1918–1919*. Edited by Eirwen Smith. London: Minerva Press, 1994. 50pp.

Account of a Welsh soldier's service during the Russian intervention.

747. Morten, John Clarke. *I Remain, Your Son Jack*. Wilmslow: Sigma, 1993. 194pp., illustrated.

Letters from a soldier in the 7th Manchester Regiment.

748. Mottistone, John Edward Bernard Seely. *Adventure*. London: W. Heinemann, 1930. 326pp., illustrated.

Autobiography, part on World War I. Lord Mottistone was Secretary of State for War in August 1914, when he left the government to take command of the Canadian Cavalry Brigade. He led the counterattack at Moreuil Ridge on March 30, 1918. See also his book about his horse: *My Horse, Warrior* (1934), which contains good illustrations and chapters on the Somme and Cambrai.

749. Mottram, Ralph Hale. *Through the Menin Gate*. London: Chatto & Windus, 1932. 260pp.

Memoir, roughly 1914–1918. A brooding and fragmentary record of some of the author's experiences in France and Flanders. Mottram is better known for his novels forming the *Spanish Farm Trilogy* (1927). See also *Ten Years Ago* (1928).

750. Mottram, R. H., John Easton, and Eric Partridge. *Three Personal*

Records of the War. London: Scholartis Press, 1929. 406pp.

Three somewhat incoherent narratives, the most notable one by Mottram. For Partridge, see entry #133.

751. Mousley, Edward Opotiki. *The Secrets of a Kuttite: An Authentic Story of Kut, Adventures in Captivity and Stamboul Intrigue*. London: John Lane, 1921. 392pp., illustrated.

Captain Mousley describes the siege of Kut, his capture, and subsequent imprisonment in Turkey.

752. Moyne, Walter Edward Guinness, 1st Lord. *Staff Officer: The Diaries of Walter Guinness (first Lord Moyne), 1914–1918*. Edited by Brian Bond and Simon Robbins. London: L. Cooper, 1987. 256pp., illustrated.

Diary, July 1914–November 1918, compiled after war from notes. Moyne served in the 11th Cheshires and as a divisional staff officer at Gallipoli, the Somme, Passchendaele, and throughout 1918.

753. Mügge, Maximilian August. *The War Diary of a Square Peg. With a Dictionary of War Words*. London: G. Routledge, 1920. 224pp.

Memoir, 1914–1918. The author sympathized with Germany, but tried to enlist anyway. A weak heart prevented him from frontline service, and he joined the military police on French docks.

754. Murray, Joseph. *Gallipoli as I Saw It*. London: William Kimber, 1965. 192pp. Sequel: *Call to Arms: from Gallipoli to the Western Front* (1980).

Memoir, 1915–1918. Murray served as a rating in the Hood Battalion of the Royal Naval Division; on Gallipoli he was attached to the Royal Engineers. He was wounded twice in France, and did not return to the front after his last wounding in November 1917. Two excellent, highly recommended memoirs.

755. Nash, Thomas Anthony Havelock. *The Diary of an Unprofessional Soldier*. Chippenham: Picton, 1991. 202pp., illustrated.

The author served as a captain in the 16th Battalion of the Manchesters, on the Somme and elsewhere on the Western Front.

756. Neame, Philip. *Playing with Strife: The Autobiography of a Soldier*.

London: G.G. Harrap, 1947. 352pp., illustrated.

Autobiography, part on World War I. Neame won the Victoria Cross in December 1914 at Neuve Chapelle, as a lieutenant in the 15th Field Company of the Royal Engineers. He went on to become brigade major of the 168th Brigade, 56th London Division, serving on the Somme and in other battles on the Western Front.

757. Needham, Evelyn Jack. *The First Three Months: The Impressions of an Amateur Infantry Subaltern*. London: Gale and Polden, 1936. 113pp., illustrated.

Memoir, August–November 1914. This obscure book by a subaltern of the Northamptonshire Regiment is actually one of the best accounts of the B.E.F. in 1914, including Mons and subsequent encounters up to 1st Ypres.

758. Nettleton, John, *The Anger of the Guns: An Infantry Officer on the Western Front*. London: Kimber, 1979. 206pp., illustrated.

Memoir, January 1916–November 1918. Nettleton served in the 28th London Regiment at Passchendaele and in the 1918 battles. Critical of the high command.

759. Nevill, Wilfred Percy. *Billie: The Nevill Letters, 1914–1916*. Edited by Ruth Elwin Harris. London: Julia MacRae Books, 1991. 222pp., illustrated.

Nevill, a captain in the 1st East Yorkshire Regiment, attached to the 8th East Surrey Regiment, was killed on July 1, 1916, the first day of the Battle of the Somme. He had prepared for the battle by purchasing four footballs for each of his platoons to kick toward the enemy during the advance.

760. Neville, James Edmund Henderson. *The War Letters of a Light Infantryman*. London: Sifton, Praed, 1930. 201pp.

The author served as an officer in France and Russia with the Oxfordshire and Buckinghamshire Light Infantry.

761. Newton, Walt. *The Soul of the Camp: A Derbyman's Odyssey*. London: A.H. Stockwell, 1920. 112pp., illustrated.

Memoir, 1918. Recollections of life in a British military camp in 1918. Uneventful.

762. Nichols, George Herbert Fosdike. *Pushed.* London: Constable, 1930. 336pp.

Memoir, 1918. The author, a journalist, recounts his experiences with the 18th Divisional Artillery in the German March 1918 offensive and the Allied counteroffensive. See also *Pushed and the Return Push* (1919).

763. Nicholson, W. N. *Behind the Lines: An Account of Administrative Staffwork in the British Army, 1914–1918.* London: Jonathan Cape, 1939. 320pp.

Memoir, May 1914–July 1919. Nicholson served throughout the war as a staff officer with the 17th and 51st Divisions. Dull but useful memoir from the point of view of the much-maligned staff.

764. Nickalls, Vivian. *Oars, Wars and Horses.* London: Hurst & Blackett, 1932. 292pp., illustrated.

Autobiography, part on World War I. The author was a rower, sportsman, adventurer, and World War I officer.

765. Noakes, Frederick Elias. *The Distant Drum: The Personal History of a Guardsman in the Great War.* Privately printed, 1952. 241pp.

Memoir, 1914–1918. Noakes tried to enlist several times, but was turned down because of asthma. Ironically, he was then conscripted in 1917 and served as a private in the Coldstream Guards until the end of the war.

766. Noble, Walter. *With a Bristol Fighter Squadron.* London: A. Melrose, 1920. 186pp.

Memoir, January–November 1918, during which period Noble served as an observer in R.F.C. No. 20 Squadron. Introduction by Winston Churchill.

767. O'Connor, Armel. *A Knight in Palestine.* New York: Benziger Brothers, 1923. 98pp.

Catholic memoir of the Palestine campaign.

768. Ogle, Henry. *The Fateful Battle Line: The Great War Journals and Sketches of Captain Henry Ogle, MC.* Edited by Michael Glover. London: Leo Cooper, 1993. 216pp., illustrated.

Diary, 1915–1918. Ogle went to France in 1915 as a private in the 7th

Royal Warwickshire Regiment, and was commissioned in 1918. A trained artist, he carried his paintbox everywhere he went, including the Somme. Recommended.

769. Ogston, Alexander. *Reminiscences of Three Campaigns*. London: Hodder and Stoughton, 1919. 335pp., illustrated.

Autobiography, part on World War I. The author was a military surgeon, and served in the Egyptian War of 1884–85 and the Boer War before going to Serbia and Italy during the First World War. Ogston claims to have had a near-death experience.

770. Oliver, F. S. *The Anvil of War: Letters Between F. S. Oliver & His Brother 1914–1918*. Edited by Stephen Gwynn. London: Macmillan, 1936. 351pp., illustrated.

Letters (almost all from F.S. Oliver rather than his brother in Canada), dating from August 1914 to November 1918. A London businessman, Oliver visited Haig's headquarters in France in September–October 1917; his candid letters include commentary on that visit as well as wartime London and events at the front as reported by the newspapers.

771. Onions, Maude. *A Woman at War: Being Experiences of an Army Signaller in France, 1917–1919–"807" Unit 3, W.A.A.C., L. Signals, A.P.O. 3, France*. Liverpool: Daily Post, 1928. 60pp.

772. Orpen, William. *An Onlooker in France, 1917–1919*. London: Williams and Norgate, 1921. 123pp., illustrated.

Memoir, April 1917–June 1919. A wonderfully illustrated book by Britain's official war artist. The text fades in comparison to Sir William Orpen's artwork.

773. Orr, John Boyd. *As I Recall*. London: Macgibbon and Kee, 1966. 290pp., illustrated.

Autobiography, part on World War I. Orr served in the R.A.M.C. and in the Royal Navy, and was decorated for bravery. He won the Nobel Peace Prize in 1949.

774. Osburn, Arthur. *Unwilling Passenger*. London: Faber and Faber, 1932. 415pp., illustrated.

Memoir, 1914–1915. Osburn was a doctor and a veteran of the South

African War. This book concentrates on the first six months of the war, and is written in an intentionally shocking manner. His accounts of the suffering caused by battle are completely devoid of conventional devices often used to soften their impact. Unfortunately, the author's evident determination to tarnish the high reputation of the soldiers of the old B.E.F., combined with his obvious cynicism, blunt what otherwise might have been a very effective anti-war message.

775. Oswald, Oswald Charles Williamson. *61: How Some Wheels Went Round*. London: H.J. Drane, 1929. 218pp.

Memoir of the 61st Heavy Artillery Group.

776. Owen, Harold Owen. *A Welshman in Mesopotamia*. Edited by David Wyn Davies. Aberystwyth: Gwasg Cambria for E.D. Norman, 1986. 120pp., illustrated.

Letters, August 1915–May 1919. Owen was a second lieutenant in the 6th Battalion, Royal Welch Fusiliers, and served at Gallipoli and in Mesopotamia.

777. Owen, Harry Collinson. *Salonica and After: The Sideshow that Ended the War*. London: Hodder and Stoughton, 1919. 295pp., illustrated.

Memoir, 1915–1918. The author was the editor of the army newspaper *Balkan News* and the official correspondent for the Near East. Apologia for the "easterners."

778. Owen, Wilfred. *Collected Letters*. Edited by Harold Owen and John Bell. London: Oxford University Press, 1967. 629pp., illustrated.

Letters, 1898–October 1918. Owen was commissioned in the 5th (Reserve) Battalion of the Manchester Regiment in June 1916 and went to France at the end of the year, where he joined the 2nd Manchesters. He missed Passchendaele and spent many months with Siegfried Sassoon at Craiglockhart Hospital in England, but was killed in November 1918 after returning to the front. Fascinating letters of one of England's great poets. Printed in a revised edition, *Selected Letters*, in 1985.

779. Packer, Charles. *Return to Salonika*. London: Cassell, 1964. 164pp., illustrated.

Memoir/history, 1915–1918. The author served in the 26th Divisional Ammunition Column. This book mixes personal reminiscences with general observations on the high command and the history of the Salonika campaign.

780. Page, Edward. *Escaping from Germany*. London: A. Melrose, 1919. 387pp.

Memoir, 1914–1918. The author, a private in the Royal Marine Light Infantry, was held at Dulmen, Duisberg, Friedrichsfeld, and Munster.

781. Palmer, Robert Stafford Arthur. *Letters from Mesopotamia in 1915 and January, 1916*. London: Women's Printing Society, 1926. 134pp., illustrated.

Letters of a soldier who was killed at Um El Hannah in January 1916, providing his reflections on the war and the challenges of fighting in Mesopotamia.

782. Parker, Alfred Chevallier. *The Diaries of Parker Pasha: War in the Desert, 1914–1918, Told from the Secret Diaries of Colonel Alfred Chevallier Parker*. Edited by H.V.F. Winstone. London: Quartet Books, 1983.

The author, a nephew of Lord Kitchener, was the governor of Sinai and the military intelligence chief during the Arab Revolt. Provides an interesting contrast to T.E. Lawrence's perspective.

783. Parker, Ernest Walter. *Into Battle, 1914–1918*. London: Longmans, 1964. 98pp.

The author enlisted in 1914, age seventeen, in the 10th Durham Light Infantry. He fought at Loos, and was commissioned in 1916 into the 5th Battalion of the Royal Fusiliers. He ended the war in a military hospital. Introduction by John Terraine.

784. Parker, George. *The Tale of a Boy Soldier*. Brighton: QueenSpark, 2001. 90pp., illustrated.

Memoir, 1914–1917. Parker, a poor Brighton lad, joined the army at the age of fifteen and fought at the Somme and Ypres before being badly wounded and evacuated in 1917. Scarce printing.

785. Paton, Alexander Watson. *Occasional Gunfire: Private War Diary of a Siege Gunner*. London: Bishop-Laggett, 1998. 215pp., illustrated.

Diary, 1915–1918. The author served at Arras, the Somme, and Ypres as a Battery Commander's Assistant in the 118th Siege Battery of the Royal Garrison Artillery. Excellent entries with good illustrations.

786. Peacock, Basil. *Tinker's Mufti; Memoirs of a Parttime Soldier.* London: Seeley, 1974. 214pp., illustrated.

Autobiography, a little under half on World War I. Peacock did not make it to the front until April 1917, as a second lieutenant in the 22nd Battalion, Northumberland Fusiliers. He was captured during the German March 1918 offensive.

787. Pearn, Charles Lukey. *Meet Me at Paddington: The Letters and Diary of Charles Lukey Pearn, 1914 to 1919.* Edited by Daphne Pearn and Alison M. Pearn. Cambridge: Windward Press, 1998. 536pp., illustrated.

788. Peel, R. T., and A. H. MacDonald. *Campaign Reminiscences: 6th Seaforth Highlanders.* Elgin: W.R. Walker, 1923. 61pp.

A series of vignettes reprinted from newspaper articles.

789. Peterkin, Millicent B. *Hospital Barges in France: Correspondence from a Nursing Sister, with the British Expeditionary Force, During World War 1.* Edited by Peter L. High. Abernethy: Chavril Press, 1997. 20pp., illustrated.

Letters, September 1917–December 1918. The focus of this book is not Peterkin's letters but the postmarks on them.

790. Plowman, Max [pseud. Mark VII]. *A Subaltern on the Somme in 1916.* London: J.M. Dent, 1927. 241pp.

Memoir, July 1916–January 1917. Understated and largely unheralded, this is one of the most important memoirs of disillusionment. Plowman joined the territorial field ambulance of the R.A.M.C. in December 1914 and became a subaltern in the 10th West Yorkshire Battalion. He served on the Somme before a shell burst inflicted a concussion and shell shock on him at the beginning of 1917. He convalesced at a branch of Craiglockhart, where Wilfred Owen and Siegfried Sassoon were also treated, until July 1917. In January 1918 he became a religious conscientious objector, and he was expelled from the army three months later. See also *Bridge into Future: Letters of Max Plowman* (1944).

791. Pollard, Alfred Oliver. *Fire-Eater: The Memoirs of a V.C.* London: Hutchinson, 1932. 278pp., illustrated.

Memoir, 1914–1918. Pollard was serving as a second lieutenant in the 1st Battalion of the Honourable Artillery Company when he won the Victoria Cross at Gavrelle, France, in April 1917. Interesting memoir, now difficult to find; Pollard's personality matched the book's title.

792. Price, Hereward Thimbleby. *Boche and Bolshevik: Experiences of an Englishman in the German Army and in Russian Prisons.* London: John Murray, 1919. 247pp.

Memoir, 1914–1918, reprinted from articles that appeared after the end of the war in the *China Illustrated Weekly*. Price, a native Englishman and naturalized German, was forced to join an Alsatian regiment and sent to the Russian front as a private in August 1915. Captured by the Russians, he was held prisoner in Siberia. Interesting observations on Germany, the German army, Russian prison camps, and the Russian Revolution.

793. Price, Julius Mendes. *On the Path of Adventure.* London: John Lane, 1919. 244pp., illustrated.

Memoir, 1914–1918, of an the artist and war correspondent of the *Illustrated London News*.

Prichard, Vernon. *See* Hesketh-Prichard, Vernon.

794. Priestley, J. B. *Margin Released; A Writer's Reminiscences and Reflections.* London: W. Heinemann, 1962. 236pp., illustrated.

Autobiography, a third on World War I. Priestley, a well-known writer and literary critic, went to France in February 1915 with the 10th Duke of Wellington's Regiment, fought at Loos, was wounded in June 1916, and returned to the front with a commission near the end of the war. Priestley professed himself "deeply divided between the tragedy and comedy" of the war.

795. Quigley, Hugh. *Passchendaele and the Somme; A Diary of 1917.* London: Methuen, 1928. 191pp.

Letters, June–November 1917. The author served with the 12th Royal Scots of the 9th Division. His letters are impressionistic, describing sights and emotions associated with his service on the Somme front and in the latter stages of Passchendaele. He also describes his hospital experiences after being wounded in October 1917.

796. R., L. F. *Naval Guns in Flanders, 1914–1915*. London: Constable, 1920. 184pp., illustrated.

Memoir, October 1914–April 1915. The author was a lieutenant in the Royal Navy. This fascinating little memoir describes his service on an armored train from Antwerp and Ypres to La Bassée in France.

797. Ravenscroft, Pelham Donovan. *Unversed in Arms: A Subaltern on the Western Front, the First World War Diary of P.D. Ravenscroft*. Marlborough: Crowood, 1990. 166pp., illustrated.

Diary, November 1915–April 1919. Ravenscroft served in the King's Royal Rifle Corps, mostly as a Lewis Gun Officer in charge of training for that weapon. Largely mundane diary.

798. Rawlinson, Alfred. *Adventures on the Western Front, August 1914 to June 1915*. London: A. Melrose, 1925. 315pp., illustrated. See also: *The Defence of London, 1915–1918* (1923), and *Adventures in the Near East 1918–1922* (1923).

Memoir, August 1914–November 1922. An old-fashioned Victorian adventurer, Lieutenant Colonel "Toby" Rawlinson took his racing car to France, mounted a machine gun on it, and drove staff officers to and from the front, sometimes encountering German cavalry patrols. From 1915 to the spring of 1918 he served with a mobile antiaircraft unit in London. He then fought in Mesopotamia and the Caucasus with the so-called "Dunsterforce" under Major General L.C. Dunsterville. He remained with British forces in the Caucasus after the war until he was captured at the end of 1920, spending almost two years in a Turkish prison. Exciting and readable.

799. Rayner, Harold Leslie. *Letters from France, July 26, 1915 to June 30, 1916*. London: John Bale, Sons & Danielson, 1919. 218pp.

Second Lieutenant Rayner served in the 9th Battalion of the Devonshire Regiment and was killed on the first day of the Somme.

800. Read, Herbert. *In Retreat*. London: The Hogarth Press, 1925. 43pp.

Memoir, March 1918. Read, a poet, leftist intellectual, and noted pacifist after the war, served as a captain in the Yorkshire Regiment. In this short volume he recounts his experiences in the first week of the

German March 1918 offensive, writing in a realistic and highly effective style. See also his book *Ambush* (1930).

801. Read, I. L. *Of Those We Loved.* Bishop, Auckland: Pentland Press, 1994. 518pp., illustrated.

Memoir, August 1914–November 1918. Read enlisted as a private soldier at the beginning of the war and served with the 8th Battalion, Leicestershire Regiment, eventually rising to the rank of sergeant before his commission in 1917 as a lieutenant in the Royal Sussex Regiment. Excellent chapters on his experiences at the Somme, Bazentin, Arras, Gueudecourt, Vermelles, and the Second Battle of the Marne, augmented by the author's original drawings. One of the best memoirs ever published and thus highly recommended.

802. Rees, Robert Tait. *A Schoolmaster at War.* London: Haycock Press, 1935. 123pp., illustrated.

Short and sketchy account by a Lancashire captain, later major. Most useful for the author's experiences as a trench-mortar officer and his participation in Passchendaele and the 1918 German offensive.

803. Reith, John Charles Walsham Reith, Baron. *Wearing Spurs.* London: Hutchinson, 1966. 223pp.

Memoir, August 1914–October 1915. Reith, later Director-General of the BBC, served as a transport officer in the 5th Battalion of the Scottish Rifles and the 1/2nd Highland Field Company of the Royal Engineers before he was severely wounded near Cuinchy in October 1915.

804. Repington, Charles A. *The First World War, 1914–1918: Personal Experiences.* London: Constable, 1920. 2 volumes, 621 and 581pp.

Diary, August 1914–June 1919. Comprehensive political view of the war from the correspondent of the *Times* and the *Morning Post.*

805. Reynardson, Henry Birch. *Mesopotamia, 1914–1915: Extracts from a Regimental Officer's Diary.* London: A. Melrose, 1919. 272pp., illustrated.

The author served in Mesopotamia as a captain in the Oxford & Bucks Light Infantry.

806. Richards, Frank. *Old Soldiers Never Die.* London: Faber and Faber,

1933. 324pp.

Memoir, August 1914–December 1918. Richards was a private in the 2nd Battalion of the Royal Welch Fusiliers, and fought at Mons, Loos, the Somme, Passchendaele, and just about every other engagement on the Western Front. One of the best war memoirs, introduced and reputedly rewritten by Robert Graves.

807. Richardson, James C. *The Living, and the Living Dead.* London: A.H. Stockwell, 1923. 206pp.

"Ruminations, whims, fancies, jokes and philosophies, with a batch of war experiences thrown in after 1914–1918."

808. Rider, R. J. *Reflections on the Battlefield; From Infantryman to Chaplain, 1914–1919.* Edited by Alan C. Robinson. Liverpool: Liverpool University Press, 2001. 272pp.

Memoir, 1914–1918. Episodic memories of a Methodist minister who joined the 14th Royal Warwickshire Regiment as a soldier in October 1914 and became a chaplain to an artillery unit in 1916.

809. Roberts, G. D. *Witness These Letters.* Denbigh: Gee & Son, 1983. 112pp., illustrated.

Letters, 1915–1918, about a soldier's experiences on the Western Front.

810. Roberts, William. *Memories of the War to End War, 1914–18.* London: Privately printed, 1974. 45pp., illustrated.

Memoir, August 1914–October 1919. The author, a Cubist painter and associate of Wyndham Lewis, went to France in August 1916 as a 4.5 howitzer gunner in the 51st Brigade, Royal Field Artillery. He saw action at Arras and in the early battles of 1918 before being commissioned to paint a picture for the Canadian War Memorial Fund that summer. Straightforward record of his war experiences, with little commentary on his paintings.

811. Robertson, William. *From Private to Field-Marshal.* London: Constable, 1921. 396pp., illustrated.

Autobiography, about half on World War I, when Robertson served as Chief of the Imperial General Staff. Important source for British wartime politics and the Staff, though of course quite biased. See also

Soldiers and Statesmen, 1914–1918 (1926) by the same author.

812. Rochford, Leonard H. *I Chose the Sky*. London: Kimber, 1977. 224pp., illustrated.

Memoir, 1914–1918, of a pilot in No. 3 (Naval) Squadron and in R.F.C. No. 203 Squadron.

813. Rogerson, Sidney. *Last of the Ebb*. London: A. Baker, 1937. 147pp., illustrated.

Memoir, 1918. The author was commissioned in the 2nd West Yorkshire Regiment in 1916 and fought at the Somme before becoming adjutant to General Jack. This memoir concerns his experiences on the Aisne in 1918. See also *Twelve Days* (1933) by the same author, recounting twelve typical days on the Somme in November 1916.

Roome, Holdar. *See* Moore, Harold William.

814. Rorie, David. *A Medico's Luck in the War: Being Reminiscences of R.A.M.C. Work with the 51st (Highland) Division*. Aberdeen: Milne & Hutchison, 1929. 264pp., illustrated.

Memoir, May 1915–November 1918. Colonel Rorie was O.C. of the 1/2nd Highland Field Ambulance and later A.D.M.S. of the 51st Division. Inexplicably, Rorie avoids giving any description of actual hospital work, preferring to record routine events and marches from place to place. Reads like a unit history, with some admittedly funny anecdotes and good illustrations.

815. Ross, Ishobel. *Little Grey Partridge: First World War Diary of Ishobel Ross who Served with the Scottish Women's Hospital's Unit in Serbia*. Aberdeen: Aberdeen University Press, 1988. 93pp., illustrated.

Diary, July 1916–July 1917. Ross served as a cook in a Scottish Women's Hospital unit in the Salonika campaign. Diary suffers from lack of annotation, as many of the cryptic references are unexplained; interesting photographs.

816. Royston, W. Stewart. *The Real Life Story of the Walking Stick King . . . "A Memento."* Warrington: "Examiner," 1919. 16pp.

Brief story of a disabled soldier.

817. Rudkin, Mabel S. *Inside Dover 1914–1918: A Woman's Impressions*. London: Elliot Stock, 1933. 216pp.

Memoir of a civilian's impressions in Dover during four years of war.

818. Russell, Arthur. *The Machine Gunner*. Kineton: The Roundwood Press, 1977. 172pp., illustrated.

Memoir, August 1914–April 1919. Russell served in the 98th Machine Gun Company from February until September 1916, when he transferred to the 13th Machine Gun Company, usually with the 5th Division. He served in the Somme, Vimy Ridge, and Passchendaele, and for a few months in Italy in the winter of 1917–1918 before helping to stem the German 1918 offensive. Russell saw very heavy fighting but led a charmed existence. Despite his disenchantment with the high command he testifies to the innate cheerfulness of the English soldier. See also his book *With the Machine Gun Corps from Grantham to Cologne* (1923).

819. Russell, Henry. *Slaves of the War Lords*. London: Hutchinson, 1928. 287pp.

Memoir, September 1916–March 1918. The author went to France in September 1916 as a private in the 10th Worcesters, and saw action on the Somme, Ancre, and Messines before being wounded on the first day of the German March 1918 offensive. As the title indicates, Russell retained bitter memories of the war.

820. Rutherford, Nathaniel John Crawford. *Soldiering with a Stethoscope*. London: Stanley Paul, 1937. 288pp., illustrated.

Autobiography, about 70pp. on World War I, when Rutherford served as a divisional medical officer in France, Flanders, and Salonika. Good detail on medical work and casualties.

821. St. John, Isabella. *A Journey in War-Time*. London: John Lane, 1919. 192pp.

Unintentionally hilarious tale of how a snobbish English lady went to France in search of her wounded son and ran into endless frustrations from officials and bureaucrats.

822. Saint-Mande, Wilfred. *War, Wine and Women*. London: Cassell, 1931. 555pp. Published in the United States as *Sons of Cain* (1931).

Autobiography, mostly on World War I, when the author served as an infantryman and R.F.C. pilot.

823. Salkeld, Harry. *The Vital Year*. Harpenden: Gospel Standard Trust Publications, 1996. 79pp., illustrated.

Autobiography of a minister, including brief reminiscences of his experiences in World War I.

824. Samson, Charles R. *Fights and Flights*. London: E. Benn, 1930. 372pp.

Memoir, August 1914–November 1918. Samson began the war in armored cars, then flew over Belgium in the R.N.A.S. until February 1915, when he transferred to the Mediterranean. He spent most of 1915 flying over Gallipoli. In May 1916 he took command of the seaplane carrier *Ben-My-Chree*, which operated off Palestine until it was sunk by a submarine in January 1917. He later became commander of the Great Yarmouth air station.

825. Sandes, E. W. C. *Tales of Turkey*. London: John Murray, 1924. 173pp., illustrated.

Major Sandes was captured at Kut with the 6th Indian Division and held prisoner in Turkey.

826. Sandes, Flora. *The Autobiography of a Woman Soldier: A Brief Record of Adventure with the Serbian Army, 1916–1919*. London: H.F. & G. Witherby, 1927. 222pp., illustrated.

Memoir, August 1914–November 1918. Sandes went to Serbia in February 1915 as a nurse in a Red Cross unit, then promptly enlisted in the 2nd Infantry Regiment of the Serbian army. Wounded in 1916, she nevertheless stayed in service until the end of the war, eventually gaining promotion to lieutenant. The verity of her account has been questioned. See also *An English Woman-Sergeant in the Serbian Army* (1916), which describes her experiences in 1915.

827. Sansom, A. J. *Letters from France: Written between June 1915–July 1917*. Edited by Ivy Sansom. London: Andrew Melrose, 192–?. 383pp.

The author, a lieutenant colonel in the 5th Battalion of the Royal Sussex Regiment, and served on the Somme before being killed near Arras in July 1917.

828. Sassoon, Siegfried. *The Complete Memoirs of George Sherston*. London: Faber and Faber, 1937. 804pp. Complete edition of the trilogy composed of *Memoirs of a Fox-Hunting Man* (1928), *Memoirs of an Infantry Officer* (1930), and *Sherston's Progress* (1936).

From May 1915 until his hospitalization in July 1917 Sassoon served in France as a second lieutenant with the 1st and 2nd Battalions of the Royal Welch Fusiliers. From February to July 1918 he served in Palestine and France with the 25th Battalion of the same regiment. This book, one of the most important works of English literature of the twentieth century, has been misused by literary critics who have taken it as a collective manifesto of English veterans of the war. It is more useful to see the book for what it is: The slightly fictionalized memoir of a sensitive, intelligent, and brave individual who was shocked to the core of his soul by the suffering caused by modern war. Sassoon's perceptiveness and deep moral sense make for a highly profound and moving work. See also *Siegfried Sassoon Diaries 1915–1918* (1983).

829. Scott, A. B., et al. *Artillery & Trench Mortar Memories: 32nd Division*. London: Unwin Brothers, 1932. 684pp.

Diaries of Lieutenant A.B. Scott, July 1916–January 1919; Rev. R.E. Grice-Hutchinson, June 1916–October 1919; Major L. Heathcoat-Amory, December 1916–August 1918; and short memoirs of six others, all of the 32nd Divisional Artillery. An invaluable compilation; Grice-Hutchinson's diary is especially lengthy and interesting.

830. Scott, Ralph. *A Soldier's Diary*. London: W. Collins Sons, 1923. 194pp.

Diary, April–November 1918. Scott, whose real name was George Scott Atkinson, served as an officer in the Royal Engineers, mostly in the vicinity of Ypres. Good maps and effective description of British attacks in August 1918, with some less-than-complimentary references to American troops. Scott became increasingly antiwar.

831. Scrivenor, John Brooke. *Brigade Signals*. Oxford: Basil Blackwell, 1932. 176pp.

Memoir of a scientist who was working in Malaya when the war began and returned home to become a brigade signaling officer in the Royal Engineers.

832. Seligman, Vincent Julian. *The Salonica Side-show*. London: G. Allen & Unwin, 1919. 256pp., illustrated.

Easy-going memoirs of a subaltern in the A.S.C. in Salonika.

833. "Senior Subaltern." *A Vision of No Man's Land: A True Incident in the Late War*. Edited by J. Stuart Holden. London: Morgan and Scott, 1920. 41pp.

Religious pamphlet, with one episode written by an R.F.A. officer who was later killed as a pilot in August 1918.

Seton, Graham. *See* Hutchison, Graham Seton.

834. Shaw, Frank Hubert. *Knocking Around*. London: Cassell, 1927. 344pp., illustrated.

Autobiography, part on World War I, when Shaw served in the navy.

835. Shead, Samuel George. *With the R.A.S.C. in Palestine: A Lecture Given Before the United Wards Club, April 14, 1920*. London: G.W. Jones, 1920. 47pp., illustrated.

836. Shears, Edward Hornby. *Active-Service Diary, 21 January 1917–1 July 1917*. Liverpool: H. Young, 1919. 85pp., illustrated.

Memorial of a lieutenant in the 1st Battalion of the Irish Guards who was killed near Poperinghe in July 1917.

837. Shephard, Ernest. *A Sergeant-Major's War: from Hill 60 to the Somme*. Edited by Bruce Rosser. Marlborough: Crowood Press, 1987. 157pp., illustrated.

Diary, January 1915–December 1916. Shephard enlisted in 1909 and went to France as a sergeant of the 1st Battalion, the Dorset Regiment, in January 1915. In November 1916 he was commissioned a second lieutenant in the 5th Battalion of the same regiment, and was killed in action in January 1917. Excellent diary, well annotated and especially useful on Ypres in 1915 and the Somme in 1916.

838. Shephard, Gordon. *Memoirs of Brigadier-General Gordon Shephard, D.S.O., M.C.* Edited by Shane Leslie. London: Privately printed, 1924. 233pp., illustrated.

Shephard took command of the 1st Brigade Wing, R.F.C., before he was killed in a flying accident in January 1918.

839. Siepmann, Hal. *Echo of the Guns: Recollections of an Artillery Officer, 1914–1918*. Edited by H.R. Siepmann. London: Hale, 1987. 191pp., illustrated.

Diaries/letters and postwar articles of Hal Siepmann, edited by his son Harry. Hal enlisted in the Royal Field Artillery in the summer of 1915, went briefly to Egypt, arrived in France in early 1916, and went to Italy in 1917. Extraordinarily detailed account of artillery work, including an entire chapter describing the function and accuracy of an 18-pounder gun.

840. Slack, Cecil Moorhouse. *Grandfather's Adventures in the Great War, 1914–1918*. Ilfracombe, Devon: Arthur H. Stockwell, 1977. 284pp., illustrated.

Letters/memoir, September 1914–November 1918. Excellent letters of a lieutenant in the 4th Battalion of the East Yorkshire Regiment. His complete letters and diaries have been placed in the public domain and are now available on the Internet.

841. Slim, William. *Unofficial History*. London: Cassell, 1959. 242pp.

Autobiography, with short sections on Slim's service as an officer in the Royal Warwickshire Regiment at Gallipoli, where he was badly wounded, and in Mesopotamia during World War I. He is better known for his service in World War II.

842. Smethurst, Horace. *One Man's War: 1916–1918*. Bolton: Aurora Publishing, 1995. 64pp.

Memoir, December 1916–June 1918. Smethurst was a trooper in the Household Battalion, 2nd Life Guards, and saw fighting at Arras and Passchendaele before receiving a "Blighty" wound in October 1917.

843. Smith, Aubrey. *Four Years on the Western Front: Being the Experiences of a Ranker in the London Rifle Brigade, 4th, 3rd and 56th Divisions*. London: Odhams Press, 1922. 409pp.

Memoir, 1914–1918. Smith enlisted in the London Rifle Brigade in 1914, and saw action at Ploegsteert and during the gas attack at Ypres in 1915. He then transferred to the transport section of the 1/5th London Regiment and remained there until the end of the war. Surprisingly interesting details on transport work.

844. Smith, H. Raymond. *A Soldier's Diary: Sidelights on the Great War 1914–1918*. Evesham, Worcester: The "Journal" Press, 1940.

Memoir, August 1914–November 1918. Smith enlisted as a private in the 8th Worcesters in August 1914, went to France in March 1915, and served on the Somme before being commissioned a second lieutenant in the Machine Gun Corps and the Rifle Brigade. He saw further action at Passchendaele and Cambrai.

845. Smith, Lesley. *Four Years Out of Life*. London: Philip Allan, 1931. 302pp., illustrated.

Memoirs of a nurse on the Western Front.

846. Smith, Richard Skilbeck. *A Subaltern in Macedonia and Judæa, 1916–17*. London: The Mitre Press, 1930. 183pp., illustrated.

Memoir, December 1915–1918. Smith served as an officer in the Middlesex Regiment in Egypt before joining the 1st Leinsters of the 10th Division and going to Salonika in July 1916. In the summer of 1917 his unit went to Palestine. Interesting commentary on Irish soldiers, but mostly dry and mundane.

847. Smith, Victor. *Diary of a Young Civil Servant in Westminster, 1914–1918*. London: The Co-Operative Printing Soc., 1927. 224pp.

848. Solomon, Solomon J. *Strategic Camouflage*. London: John Murray, 1920. 62pp.

The author, a painter, advised the British army on camouflage in France, and found German methods to be far superior.

849. Sommers, Cecil. *Temporary Crusaders*. London: John Lane, 1919. 143pp.

Diary, November 1917–June 1918. Author was a junior officer in a "dismounted yeomanry unit turned into a de-kilted Highland battalion," serving in Egypt and Palestine. Indistinguishable from wartime propaganda accounts.

850. Sorley, Charles Hamilton. *The Collected Letters of Charles Hamilton Sorley*. Edited by Jean Moorcroft Wilson. London: Woolf, 1990. 310pp., illustrated.

Letters, December 1911–October 1915. Sorley's promising career as a writer was cut short when, as a lieutenant in the 7th Suffolks, he was killed by a sniper in October 1915. See also *The Letters of Charles Sorley, with a Chapter of Biography* (1919).

851. Sotheby, Lionel. *Lionel Sotheby's Great War: Diaries and Letters from the Western Front*. Athens, Ohio: Ohio University Press, 1997. 148pp., illustrated.

Diary/letters, December 1914–October 1915. Sotheby, a second lieutenant in the 1st Battalion of the Black Watch, was killed during the Battle of Loos in September 1915. His diaries are particularly candid, detailed, and moving.

852. Soutar, Andrew. *With Ironside in North Russia*. London: Hutchinson, 1940. 250pp., illustrated.

Memoir, roughly 1918–1919. Soutar was a war correspondent of the London *Times*. Observant not just of the work of the Allied high command but also of the common soldiers and the plight of the Russian peasantry. Ardently anti-Soviet.

853. Spears, Edward. *Liaison, 1914: A Narrative of the Great Retreat*. London: W. Heinemann, 1930. 597pp., illustrated.

Memoir, August–September 1914. Spears served as the liaison officer between the B.E.F. and the French Fifth Army during the retreat from Mons. The most important and complete account of the war's first month.

854. Spicer, Lancelot Dykes. *Letters from France 1915–1918*. London: Robert York, 1979. 131pp., illustrated.

Letters, September 1915–November 1918. The author served as a temporary lieutenant and temporary captain in the 9th King's Own Yorkshire Light Infantry from 1915 until 1917, when he became an adjutant in the 10th (Service) Battalion of the same regiment. He became brigade major to the 64th Infantry Brigade in 1918.

855. Spotter. *"Bird Up": A Tale of Wartime Archie. Absorbing Incidents in the Trail of the Anti-Aircraft Forces*. London: Alexander-Oursley, 1930. 317pp.

856. Stansgate, William Wedgwood Benn, Viscount. *In the Side Shows*. London: Hodder and Stoughton, 1919. 310pp., illustrated.

Memoir, August 1914–November 1918. The author was commissioned at the beginning of the war in the Middlesex Yeomanry, and served with it in Egypt and Gallipoli. Most of this book is, however, concerned with his subsequent service in the R.N.A.S., and in various official and unofficial duties over Mesopotamia, the Eastern Mediterranean, and the Adriatic.

857. Stephen, Rosamond. *An Englishwoman in Belfast: Rosamond Stephen's Record of the Great War*. Edited by Oonagh Walsh. Cork: Cork University Press, 2000. 94pp.

Memoir, 1914–1918. Stephen describes the war effort in Belfast and its impact on her attempts to reconcile Protestants and Catholics.

858. Steuart, Robert Henry Joseph. *March, Kind Comrade*. London: Sheed & Ward, 1931. 261pp., illustrated.

Humane memoirs of a Jesuit priest who served for three years as an army chaplain. Includes a moving description of the execution of a deserter.

859. Stevenson, Betty. *Betty Stevenson, Y.M.C.A., Croix de Guerre avec Palme: Sept. 3, 1896–May 30, 1918*. London: Longmans, Green, 1920. 295pp.

Memorial record of a young Y.M.C.A. volunteer who was killed in an air raid in May 1918.

860. Still, John. *A Prisoner in Turkey*. London: John Lane, 1920. 250pp.

The author was an officer in the 6th East Yorkshires of the 11th Division when he was captured at Gallipoli in August 1915. He describes the bad conditions he endured and the Armenian massacres in an imprisonment that lasted over three years. He wrote poetry and concealed it in his walking stick; the Turks declared him insane.

861. Stinton, Harry. *Harry's War: Experiences in the "Suicide Club" in World War One*. Edited by Virginia Mayo. London: Brassey's, 2002. 224pp., illustrated.

Memoir, 1915–1917. Stinton, a private in the 1/7th London Regiment, served as a bomber at Loos and the Somme before being wounded at Messines Ridge in June 1917. Fascinating illustrations from original watercolors not discovered until after the author's death.

862. Stoker, Henry Hew Gordon Dacre. *Straws in the Wind.* London: Herbert Jenkins, 1925. 315pp.

Stoker commanded the Australian submarine *AE2* when it passed the Dardanelles to the Sea of Marmora in April 1915. He was forced to rise and captured, but his exploit made him a hero. He remained in prison for the rest of the war.

863. Stokes, Louis. *A Dear and Noble Boy: The Life and Letters of Louis Stokes, 1897–1916.* London: Leo Cooper,1995. 190pp., illustrated.

Stokes held a commission in the 2nd Royal Marine Light Infantry when he was killed at Beaumont Hamel in November 1916. Moving, nicely illustrated letters.

864. Stone, Christopher. *From Vimy Ridge to the Rhine: The Great War Letters of Christopher Stone.* Edited by G.D. Sheffield and G.I.S. Inglis. Marlborough: Crowood, 1989. 192pp., illustrated.

Stone enlisted as a private soldier in the 16th Battalion Middlesex Regiment in September 1914, and eventually gained a commission in the 22nd Battalion, Royal Fusiliers. See also *B.B.* by same author (1919).

865. Strange, Henry George Latimer. *Never a Dull Moment.* Toronto: Macmillan, 1941. 373pp., illustrated.

Memoir, roughly 1914–1918. Strange, a second lieutenant in the Royal Engineers, was involved in the development of various experimental projects, including the Livens Projector, which he tested on the front lines.

866. Strange, Louis A. *Recollections of an Airman.* London: Hamilton, 1933. 224pp.

Memoir, August 1914–1919. Strange served in R.F.C. Squadron Nos. 5, 6, 23, and 12 before he took command of the 51st and 80th wings. Includes a chapter on the Australian squadrons that served under his command.

867. Stuart-Wortley, Rothesay. *Letters From a Flying Officer.* London: Humphrey Milford, 1928. 207pp.

The author served in the Hampshire Yeomanry from 1914 until 1917, when he joined R.F.C. Squadron No. 22, flying Bristol fighters. He recorded six victories, took command of No. 44 Squadron in England, and then took over No. 88 Squadron in September 1918.

868. Swinton, Ernest D. *Eyewitness: Being Personal Reminiscences of Certain Phases of the Great War, Including the Genesis of the Tank.* London: Hodder and Stoughton, 1932. 321pp., illustrated.

Memoir, August 1914–July 1918. Swinton served as an official correspondent to the B.E.F. and on liaison service in the United States. Overly self-important, but with some interesting comments on the birth of mechanized warfare.

869. Sykes, Frederick H. *From Many Angles: An Autobiography.* London: G.G. Harrap, 1942. 592pp.

Autobiography, only part on World War I, but an important source for the administrative history of the Royal Flying Corps. Sykes commanded the military wing of the R.F.C. at the beginning of the war and went on to Chief of the Air Staff.

870. Tait, James. *Hull to the Somme: The Diary of Pte. James Tait, 10th Battn. East Yorkshire Regt., 24th November 1915 to 30th June 1916.* Hull: Malet Lambert High School, 1982. 51pp., illustrated.

Tait enlisted in April 1915 at age fifteen and served in Egypt and France before his parents obtained his release due to his youth. He enlisted in the Durham Light Infantry in 1917, returned to France the next year, and survived the war.

871. Tawney, R. H. *The Attack, and Other Papers.* London: George Allen & Unwin, 1953. 194pp.

Collected essays, the first of which describes Tawney's experiences in the 22nd Manchester Regiment and his wounding at Fricourt on the first day of the Battle of the Somme.

872. Tayler, Henrietta. *A Scottish Nurse at Work: Being a Record of what One Semi-trained Nurse has been Privileged to See and Do During Four and a Half Years of War.* London: John Lane, 1920. 156pp., illustrated.

The author served as a nurse in Belgium, France, and Italy.

873. Taylor, F. A. J. *The Bottom of the Barrel.* London: Regency Press, 1978. 174pp., illustrated.

The author tried to enlist in the R.F.C. in September 1917 but was rejected and joined the 19th Battalion, London Regiment, instead. He went to Flanders in April 1918 with the 2nd Battalion, Worcestershire

Regiment, and stayed at the front through the last battles of 1918.

874. Taylor, George William. *The Boy with the Guns*. London: John Lane, 1919. 197pp., illustrated.

Letters/memoir/biography, 1914–1918, of a lieutenant in the 67th Brigade of the Royal Field Artillery who fought at Salonika in 1916 and at Messines in June 1917, and who died of mustard gas poisoning in November 1917. Includes a moving introduction by his grandfather.

875. Teichman, Oskar. *The Diary of a Yeomanry M.O.: Egypt, Gallipoli, Palestine and Italy*. London: Fisher Unwin, 1921. 283pp.

Teichman, a medical officer in the R.A.M.C., was attached to the Worcestershire Yeomanry in 1914 and followed it through campaigns in Egypt, Gallipoli, Sinai, and Palestine. In June 1918 he was posted to the 22nd Brigade and served with it in Italy during the last month of the war.

876. Tennant, John E. *In the Clouds Above Baghdad: Being the Record of an Air Commander*. London: C. Palmer, 1920. 289pp., illustrated.

Memoir, 1916–1918, by the lieutenant colonel commanding the R.F.C. in Mesopotamia before the last offensive there. He was shot down and held prisoner for a few days before escaping.

877. Tennant, Norman. *A Saturday Night Soldier's War, 1913–1918*. Waddesdon, Buckinghamshire: Kylin Press, 1983. 122pp., illustrated.

Diary of a member of the 11th West Riding Howitzer Battery, including his experiences on the Somme.

878. Tennent, R. Josephine. *Red Herrings of 1918*. Tunbridge Wells: Midas Books, 1980. 114pp., illustrated.

An account of first aid work in the Nursing Yeomanry.

879. Thomas, Alan Ernest Wentworth. *A Life Apart*. London: Gollancz, 1968. 160pp., illustrated.

The author, later a novelist, recounts his experiences in the 6th Battalion of the Royal West Kent Regiment on the Somme and elsewhere on the Western Front.

880. Thomas, Edward. *Diary of Edward Thomas, 1 January–8 April, 1917*. Edited by R. George Thomas. Pembroke Dock, Wales: Dock Leaves

Press, 1971. 32pp.

Sparse diary. Thomas was one of the war's many tragic figures. A young poet, critic, and essayist, he enlisted in the 28th London Regiment (Artists' Rifles) in July 1915, and was commissioned in the Royal Garrison Artillery in August 1916. He was killed at Arras on April 9, 1917.

881. Thompson, Edward John. *The Leicestershires Beyond Baghdad.* London: Epworth Press, 1919. 156pp.

The author was a chaplain attached to the Leicester Regiment. He light-heartedly describes their advance up the Tigris River after capture of Baghdad, with particular interest in nature and archaeology.

882. Thomson, Basil. *Queer People.* London: Hodder and Stoughton, 1922. 320pp., illustrated. Published in the United States in 1923 under the title *My Experiences at Scotland Yard.*

Memoir, 1913–1921. Thomson, head of the Criminal Investigation Department and overseer of Special Branch at Scotland Yard, describes his efforts during and after the war to fend off German spies, Irish nationalists, British labor leaders, and communists.

883. Thorburn, A. D. *Amateur Gunners; The Adventures of an Amateur Soldier in France, Salonica and Palestine in the Royal Field Artillery, Recording Some of the Exploits of the 2/22nd County of London Howitzer Battery R.F.A. on Active Service* Liverpool: W. Potter, 1933. 199pp., illustrated.

Memoir/unit history, 1916–1918. The author's unit fought in France in 1916, in Salonika and Palestine, and then returned to France for the final battles of 1918.

884. Thornhill, Christopher James. *Taking Tanganyika: Experiences of an Intelligence Officer, 1914–1918.* London: S. Paul, 1937. 288pp., illustrated.

Nicely written account of a "typical East African settler soldier" during the East African campaign, with emphasis on daily experiences rather than strategy and tactics.

885. Thurstan, Violetta. *The Hounds of War Unleashed.* St. Ives, Cornwall: United Writers Publications, 1978. 93pp., illustrated.

Memoir of a nurse in Belgium and Russia. See also her book *Field Hospital and Flying Column* (1915).

886. Thwaites, Norman Graham. *Velvet and Vinegar*. London: Grayson & Grayson, 1932. 283pp.

Memoirs of a journalist who became one of the most important British intelligence officers in the United States after 1916. Particularly interesting with respect to the Anglo-American response to the Russian Revolution.

887. Tomlinson, Albert E. *From Emmanuel to the Somme: The War Writings of A.E. Tomlinson, 1892–1968*. Cambridge: Lutterworth Press, 1997. 190pp.

Collected essays and letters of a prominent poet, including Tomlinson's hitherto unpublished memoir of his experiences at the front.

888. Townsend, Philip Brereton. *Eye in the Sky 1918: Recollections of a World War One Pilot on Artillery and Infantry Co-operation Duties*. Knaresborough: P.B. Townsend, 1986. 40pp., illustrated.

Townsend served as a stretcher bearer in the 135th Field Ambulance, R.A.M.C., before transferring to the R.F.C. in November 1917. He flew mainly photo reconnaissance missions, and was commissioned in August 1918.

889. Townshend, Charles Vere Ferrers. *My Campaign in Mesopotamia*. London: T. Butterworth, 1920. 400pp., illustrated.

Memoir, October, 1914–November, 1918. Major General Townshend, commanding the 6th (Poona) Indian Division, surrendered his force at the end of the legendary siege of Kut-al-Amara in April 1916. He was a prisoner for the rest of the war. Naturally, most of this memoir centers on Townshend's part in the war in Mesopotamia.

890. Trafford, Edward Henry. *Love and War: A London Terrier's Tale of 1915–16*. Edited by Peter Trafford. Bristol: Peter Trafford, 1994. 160pp., illustrated.

Letters, 1915–1916. Private Trafford joined the 20th Battalion of the London Regiment in 1914, went to France in March 1915 and saw action at Loos and the Hohenzollern Redoubt before being wounded at High Wood, the Somme, in September 1916. He was then invalided home and never returned to the front.

891. Trevelyan, G. M. *Scenes from Italy's War*. London: T.C. & E.C. Jack, 1919. 240pp., illustrated.

Memoir, June 1915–November 1918. Trevelyan, commander of a British Red Cross unit in Italy from September 1915 to the end of the war, writes mostly in general terms of Italy at war with occasional reference to his personal experiences.

892. "Trooper." *The Four Horsemen Ride*. London: P. Davies, 1935. 211pp., illustrated. Foreword by Hubert Gough.

893. Tucker, John F. *Johnny Get Your Gun: A Personal Narrative of the Somme, Ypres, and Arras*. London: W. Kimber, 1978. 207pp., illustrated.

Tucker enlisted in the 13th Battalion of the London Regiment (Kensington Battalion), arrived in France in August 1915, and fought at the Somme and elsewhere on the Western Front. The trenches destroyed his idealism, but he claimed to remain patriotic.

894. Tucker, William Albert. *The Lousier War*. London: New English Library, 1974. 125pp.

Memoir, 1914–1918. Tucker joined the army at age seventeen and entered the 15th Battalion, Royal Welch Fusiliers, only to be captured by the Germans. The title refers to his troubles with lice and other vermin in the poorly managed German prison camps.

895. Tuohy, Ferdinand. *The Crater of Mars*. London: William Heinemann, 1929. 325pp.

See also *Occupied 1918–1930: A Postscript to the Western Front* (1931) by the same author.

896. Turle, George Herbert. *A Soldier's Diary: R.Q.M.S. Turle, G.H., 1917: The Battle for Mesopotamia (1914–1918)*. Feltham: G.F. Turle, 1998, illustrated.

897. Turner, Frank. *Turner's War*. Braunton: Merlin, 1983. 42pp.

898. Tyndale-Biscoe, Julian. *Gunner Subaltern: Letters Written by a Young Man to His Father During the Great War*. London: Cooper, 1971.

192pp., illustrated.

Fascinating letters of a lieutenant in a battery of 18–pounder guns, R.H.A., on the Western Front, including the Somme.

899. Urquhart, John Dallas. *News from the Front, World War One*. Victoria, B.C., Canada: Dorothy M. Marryatt, 1991. 63pp.

Articles/letters, May 1917–April 1918. Urquhart, a journalist for the *Northern Scot*, was a private and signaler in the Royal Scots when he was killed in April 1918. Sparse.

900. Vaughan, Edwin Campion. *Some Desperate Glory: The World War I Diary of a British Officer, 1917*. London: F. Warne, 1981. 232pp.

Diary, January–August 1917. Focuses on the battle of Passchendaele, or 3rd Ypres in August 1917, and is one of the best available accounts of that battle. Vaughan was a second lieutenant in the 1/8th Warwickshire Regiment. A powerful diary that traces Vaughan's development as a young officer and gradual acceptance by his men, and culminates in gripping passages that recount his experiences at Passchendaele.

901. Villiers, Algernon Hyde. *Letters and Papers of Algernon Hyde Villiers, with a Memoir [by] Henry Graham*. London: Society for Promoting Christian Knowledge, 1919. 199pp.

Villiers, a lieutenant in the Lothians and Border Horse Regiment, attached to the 121st Company of the Machine Gun Corps, was killed in November 1917.

902. Vivian, Alfred Percival George. *The Phantom Brigade; or, The Contemptible Adventures*. London: E. Benn, 1930. 255pp.

Memoir, 1914. The author fought at Mons and Le Cateau as a lance corporal of 4th Middlesex Regiment, 3rd Division. Fascinating story of the war's first battles.

903. Voigt, Fritz August. *Combed Out*. London: Swarthmore Press, 1920. 162pp.

Memoir, 1914–1918. Voigt was conscripted into the army in 1916 and served for the rest of the war in the Royal Garrison Artillery. His increasing pacifism got him into a great deal of trouble; and it forms the core of this book.

904. Voss, Vivian (Roger Vee). *Flying Minnows*. London: J. Hamilton, 1935.

Memoir, 1917–1918. The author trained in Canada and then flew Bristol fighters over the Western Front in R.F.C. Squadron Nos. 48 and 88. The 1977 edition replaces pseudonyms with actual names.

905. Wade, Aubrey. *The War of the Guns: Western Front, 1917 & 1918*. London: B.T. Batsford, 1936. 142pp., illustrated.

Memoir, 1917–1918. Wade went to France in late 1916 as a signaler in the territorial horse artillery, and fought at Passchendaele and on the Somme in 1918. Exciting, realistic, and extremely well written. Reprinted in 1959 as *Gunner on the Western Front*.

906. Walker, Dora M. *With the Lost Generation, 1915–1919, from a V.A.D.'s Diary*. Hull: A. Brown & Sons, 1970. 36pp., illustrated.

Memoir based on letters, 1914–1918. Walker served as a nurse at various hospitals in Belgium and France, including No. 9 Red Cross Hospital at Calais and No. 22 Casualty Clearing Station at St. Omer and elsewhere. Short but with good illustrations and observations on hospital work.

907. Walkington, M. L. *Twice in a Lifetime*. London: Samson Books, 1980. 221pp., illustrated.

Memoir, August 1914–November 1918. Walkington enlisted in the Queen's Westminster Rifles in August 1914, went into the trenches near Lille in November 1914, was gazetted a second lieutenant in the Lincolnshire Regiment in November 1915, and transferred to the Machine Gun Corps in July 1916. He saw action at Fricourt, Passchendaele, and on the Somme in 1918.

908. Walpole, Hugh. *Extracts from a Diary*. Glasgow: R. Maclehose, 1934. 68pp.

Walpole, an extremely prolific novelist, was working in Russia as a journalist when the war began, and he volunteered to work with the Russian Red Cross. Only 100 copies of this work were printed, for the author's friends.

909. Walshe, Douglas. *With the Serbs in Macedonia*. London: John Lane, 1920. 278pp., illustrated.

Memoir, June 1916–January 1919. Walshe served with 708 Company M.T., A.S.C., a light ammunition and supply unit of Ford vans attached to the Serbian army in Macedonia. Lighthearted account with lots of local color.

910. Ward, J. E. *Messages: The Trench Diaries of L/Cpl (later Sgt) J.E. Ward, April to August 1915*. Bradford: Bradford Mechanics Institute, 2001. 82pp.

The author served as a signaler in the 1/6th Battalion of the West Yorkshire Regiment. Diaries of daily life in the Ypres and Neuve Chapelle sectors.

911. Ward, John. *With the "Die-Hards" in Siberia*. London: Cassell, 1920. 278pp., illustrated.

Memoir, November 1917–June 1919. Ward was colonel of the 25th Battalion of the Middlesex Regiment. A contentious but important book, violently anti-Bolshevik but also highly critical of American and Japanese policy in Siberia.

912. Ware, Gwen. "*A Rose in Picardy*": *The Diaries of Gwen Ware, 1916–1918*. Farnham: Farnham District & Museum Society, 1984. 43pp.

Diary of a nurse on the Western Front.

913. Warren, Frank. *Honour Satisfied: A Dorset Rifleman at War, 1916–18*. Edited by Anthony Bird. Swindon: Crowood, 1990. 109pp., illustrated.

Diary, October 1916–March 1918. Warren served on the Somme and elsewhere on the Western Front as a lieutenant in the 20th King's Royal Rifle Corps. Excellent description of events on the Somme Canal and at Mericourt.

914. Waterhouse, Francis A. *Journey Without End: An Autobiography*. London: S. Paul, 1940. 252pp., illustrated.

915. Watson, William Henry Lowe. *A Company of Tanks*. London: William Blackwood, 1920. 296pp., illustrated.

Memoir, 1916–1918. Watson was captain of a company of the XI Corps Cycle Battalion in September 1916, when he saw tanks for the first time on the Somme. He applied for the Tank Corps, was accepted, and saw action in the armored attack at Bullecourt in April 1917. Very well written and exciting.

916. Waugh, Alec. *The Early Years of Alec Waugh*. London: Cassell, 1962. 313pp., illustrated.

Autobiography, part on World War I. Waugh served on coastal duty in a provisional battalion in 1914–15, but did not go to the front until August 1917, as a lieutenant in the 233rd Machine Gun Company attached to the 3rd Division. He saw action at Passchendaele but was captured during the March 1918 offensive, and spent the rest of the war in prison. See also *The Prisoners of Mainz* (1919) describing his captivity in Germany.

917. Wavell, Archibald Percival. *The Good Soldier*. London: Macmillan, 1948. 214pp.

A collection of essays, articles, and lectures, with passing reference to Wavell's experiences during World War I, when he fought at Ypres as a brigade major and lost an eye. He then went on to join Allenby's 20th Corps staff in Palestine.

918. Wedderburn-Maxwell, John. *Young Contemptible*. Weybridge: J. Wedderburn-Maxwell, 1982. 38pp., illustrated.

The author served in the artillery.

919. Weldon, L. B. *"Hard Lying." Eastern Mediterranean, 1914–1919*. London: Jenkins, 1925. 246pp., illustrated.

The author commanded the prize ship *Anne* off Gallipoli and Egypt, tending French seaplanes. He also engaged in secret service work in Egypt, of which he became Surveyor-General after the war. Includes uncomplimentary references to T.E. Lawrence.

920. West, Francis Charles Bartholomew. *Frank West, Lt. Col. 4th South Midland Brigade (How.) R.F.A., a Record of the Great War, 1914–1916*. Privately published, 1921. 111pp.

Various papers of West, who was killed in September 1916. A rare publication.

921. Westropp, L. H. M. *The Memoirs of Colonel L. H. M. Westropp, D.L.: Being His Experiences in World Wars I and II, Together with Some*

Other Matters: for the Westropp Family Records. London: Regency Press, 1970. 467pp.

922. Wheatley, Dennis. *The Time Has Come: The Memoirs of Dennis Wheatley.* Volume 2, *Officer and Temporary Gentleman, 1914–1919.* London: Hutchinson, 1978. 254pp., illustrated.

Wheatley served as a lieutenant in the 2/1st City of London Royal Field Artillery, and after August 1917 on the staff of the 36th Division. Rambling, cynical, and ultimately unpleasant account by a well-known novelist, dripping with contempt for Wheatley's fellow officers but evincing little sympathy for his men. See also *Saturday with Bricks, and Other Days under Shell-Fire* (1961), by the same author.

923. Wheeler, Robert Eric Mortimer. *Still Digging; Interleaves from an Antiquary's Notebook.* London: M. Joseph, 1955. 236pp., illustrated.

Autobiography, with one chapter on World War I. The author was an archaeologist but served in the artillery during the war. His chapter on that conflict covers an attack on August 21, 1918, and two incidents in 1917.

924. White, Arthur Preston. *No Easy Hopes or Lies: The Letters of Lt. Arthur Preston White, 1st Battalion, Northamptonshire Regiment, 1914–1918.* Edited by Michael Hammerson. London: London Stamp Exchange, 1991. 264pp. illustrated.

Includes White's experiences on the Somme.

925. Whitsed, Juliet de Key. *Come to the Cook-House Door!: A V.A.D. in Salonika.* London: H. Joseph, 1932. 185pp.

926. Willcocks, James. *With the Indians in France.* London: Constable, 1920. 406pp., illustrated.

From the diary of Willcocks, who commanded the Indian Corps in Flanders. Much like a unit history, with detailed reference to the service of each unit.

927. Willey, Basil. *Spots of Time: A Retrospect of the Years 1897–1920.* London: Chatto & Windus, 1965. 249pp.

Autobiography, about 100pp. on World War I, when Willey served as an officer in the 18th West Yorkshire Regiment (the "Bradford Pals"). Willey went to France in January 1917 but either did not participate in any major battles or chose to say little about them.

928. Williamson, Benedict. *"Happy Days" in France & Flanders: with the 47th and 49th Divisions*. London: Harding & More, 1921. 196pp.

Catholic chaplain's memoir of service with the British army on the Western Front.

929. Williamson, Henry. *The Wet Flanders Plain*. London: Faber and Faber, 1929. 147pp.

Memoir, roughly 1914–1918. Williamson served as a private in the 5th Battalion, City of London Regiment, London Rifle Brigade from the beginning of the war to April, 1915, when he was commissioned a second lieutenant in the Bedfordshire Regiment. He transferred to 208 Company, Machine Gun Corps as a transport officer in June 1916, becoming a full lieutenant in November of that year. In October 1917 he joined the 3rd Battalion of the Bedfordshire Regiment, remaining on home defense for the rest of the war. In this unique and intimate memoir, one of the best produced by a British soldier, Williamson wanders the battlefields of Flanders, remembering life at the front and ruminating on the meaning of the war for himself and for Europe. See also *A Patriot's Progress: Henry Williamson and the First World War* (Sutton, 1998), a biography by Anne Williamson that reproduces many of Henry Williamson's letters and diaries.

930. Wilson, Jessie Millar. *Aunt J: Jessie Millar Wilson M.B.E.; Wartime Memories of a Lady Y.M.C.A. Volunteer in France, 1915–1918*. Ilkley: J.E. Duncan, 1999. 96pp., illustrated.

Wilson went to France in July 1915 and served at Hut 15, Harfleurs, until the Armistice.

931. Wilson, Robert Henry. *Palestine 1917*. Tunbridge Wells: Costello, 1987. 192pp., illustrated.

The author volunteered in the Royal Berkshire Yeomanry but transferred to the Royal Gloucestershire Hussars Yeomanry in 1916. He fought in the Battle of Romani and the raid on Rafa, was wounded, and returned in time for the Gaza battles. He was one of the first British officers to enter Damascus.

932. Wintringham, J.W. *With the Lincolnshire Yeomanry in Egypt and*

Palestine, 1914–1918. Grimsby: Lincolnshire Life, 1979. 84pp., illustrated.

933. Wollocombe, Frank. *In the Trenches with the 9th Devons: Frank Wollocombe's War Diary*. Bath: R.H. Wollocombe, 1994. 126pp., illustrated.

934. Worden, Alan Fletcher. *"Yes Daddy, But There Has Been Another War Since Then."* London: P.R. Macmillan, 1961. 91pp.

935. Wright, Harry. *The Memoirs of Sergeant Harry Wright: A Personal Account of the Raid on Zeebrugge and His Experiences as a Prisoner of War*. Edited by D. A. Oakley. Portsmouth: Royal Marines Historical Society, 1990. 80pp., illustrated.

936. Wright, Stanley Sherman. *Of that Fellowship: The Tragedy, Humour and Pathos of Gallipoli*. London: A.H. Stockwell, 1931. 128pp.

937. Yeats-Brown, Francis. *Caught by the Turks*. London: Edward Arnold, 1919. 220pp. Revised edition: *Bloody Years: Plot and Counter-plot by the Golden Horn* (1932).

The author was shot down over Baghdad in November 1915, captured by the Turks, and eventually escaped.

938. Young, Desmond. *Try Anything Twice*. London: H. Hamilton, 1963. 368pp., illustrated.

Autobiography, part on World War I, when Young—later author of a best-selling biography of Erwin Rommel—was wounded at Ypres in 1915.

939. Young, Filson. *With the Battle Cruisers*. London: Cassell, 1921. 295pp., illustrated.

Memoir, 1914–1915. Colorful memoir by a journalist who managed to get a commission as a lieutenant on Admiral Beatty's flagship and thus participated in Dogger Bank, but not Jutland. Includes interesting descriptions of both Beatty and Lord Fisher.

940. Young, Sir Hubert. *The Independent Arab*. London: John Murray, 1933. 344pp.

Memoir, 1913–1921. Young was adjutant of the 116th Mahrattas at the beginning of the war, and spent the following years in a variety of staff and political positions throughout the Middle East and Mesopotamia. He came into repeated contact with T.E. Lawrence and joined the Desert Mounted Corps as a captain in September 1918. An important source for study of Lawrence and military-political affairs in the Middle East.

Chapter 7

Italy

941. D'Aquila, Vincenzo. *Bodyguard Unseen: A True Autobiography.* New York: R.R. Smith, 1931. 279pp., illustrated.

Memoir of an Italian native's journey from New York to fight in the Alps.

942. De Carlo, Camillo. *The Flying Spy.* Translated by Maria Sermolino. New York: E.P. Dutton, 1919. 402pp. Italian edition: *La Spia Volante* (1919).

Propaganda account of how spies were dropped behind enemy lines and what they did after they got there.

943. Lussu, Emilio. *Sardinian Brigade.* New York: A. A. Knopf, 1939. Translated by Marion Rawson. 274pp. Italian edition: *Un Anno Sull'altipiano* (1930).

Memoir, 1916–1917. Semi-fictionalized account of Lussu's service with the Sassari Brigade in the Alps; the only major Italian war memoir published in English.

944. Monelli, Paolo. *Toes Up: A Chronicle of Gay and Doleful Adventures, of Alpini and Mules and Wine.* Translated by Orlo Williams. London: Duckworth, 1930. 224pp., illustrated. Italian edition: *La Scarpe al Sole: Cronaca di Gaie e di Tristi Avventure d'Alpini, di Muli e di Vino* (1921).

Tales of the Alpini fighting against Austria in the Alps.

945. Mussolini, Benito. *My Diary, 1915–1917.* Translated by Rita Wellman. Boston: Small, Maynard, 1925. 195pp., illustrated. Italian version: *Il Mio Diario di Guerra* (1923).

The Italian dictator's classic account of his wartime service, and probably largely fictional. Important all the same.

946. Viglino, Camillo. *Memoirs of Lt. Camillo Viglino: Italian Air Force, 1915–1916.* Translated by Camilla Viglino Hurwitz and Victor Viglino. Victoria, B.C., Canada: Trafford, 2001. 121pp., illustrated.

Chapter 8

Russia

947. Babel, Isaac. *Red Cavalry*. Translated by Nadia Helstein. New York: Knopf, 1929. 213pp. Russian edition: *Konarmiia* (1928).

A Bolshevik revolutionary's account of the campaign against Poland in 1920.

948. Benckendorff, Constantine. *Half a Life: The Reminiscences of a Russian Gentleman*. London: Richards Press, 1954. 319pp., illustrated.

Memoirs of a commander in the Russian Imperial Navy who went on to serve in the Soviet Navy.

949. Bezobrazov, Vladimir Mikhailovich. *Diary of the Commander of the Russian Imperial Guard, 1914–1917*. Translated by Marvin Lyons. Boynton Beach, Fla.: Dramco, 1994.

950. Boleslavsky, Richard, and Helen Woodward. *Way of the Lancer*. New York: The Literary Guild, 1932. 316pp.

Memoir, autumn 1916–about 1920. Boleslavsky was a lieutenant in the Polish Lancers. Grim story of the collapse of the Russian army, revolution, and atrocities in the Russian Civil War. The sequel is *Lances Down* (1932).

951. Botcharsky, Sophie. *They Knew How to Die: Being a Narrative of the Personal Experiences of a Red Cross Sister on the Russian Front*. London: Peter Davies, 1931. 311pp.

Memoir, August 1914–February 1917. Semi-fictionalized but interesting account of the travails of nursing during battles on the Eastern Front.

952. Brusilov, Aleksiei Aleksieevich. *A Soldier's Note-Book, 1914–1918*.

London: Macmillan, 1930. 340pp.

Memoir, August 1914–July 1917. Brusilov commanded the Russian Eighth Army on the Austrian Front in 1914 and then led the famed Brusilov Offensive of June–August 1916. More intimate than most staff memoirs, expressing contempt for the Czar and many of Brusilov's fellow officers.

953. Dadeshkeliani, Ekaterina Aleksandrovna. *Princess in Uniform*. Translated by Arthur J. Ashton. London: G. Bell and Sons, 1934. 301pp., illustrated.

The author's parents were Princess Eristavi and Prince Alexander of Georgia. During the war she joined the 4th Tartar regiment and drove ambulances on the Austrian Front before being wounded in 1916.

954. Iogolevitch, Paul. *The Young Russian Corporal: The Story of the Youngest Veteran of the War*. New York: Harper, 1919. 327pp., illustrated.

Memoir, July 1914–1919. Iogolevitch, a Jewish musician, enlisted at age thirteen to prove that his ethnicity was no obstacle to his patriotism, and served as a mounted messenger before joining the 3rd Dragoons. He was captured, cruelly mistreated by the Germans, and escaped; after the Russian Revolution he fled across Siberia to the United States. Rather silly tale, probably at least partly fabricated.

955. Kournakoff, Sergei Nicholas. *Savage Squadrons*. New York: Hale, Cushman & Flint, 1935. 360pp., illustrated.

Memoir, 1916–1917. Account of the author's Cossack service in the Circassian Horse Regiment before and during the revolution.

956. Littauer, Vladimir S. *Russian Hussar: A Story of the Imperial Cavalry, 1911–1920*. London: J. A. Allen, 1965. 295pp.

Memoir. This book follows Littauer from training through his wartime service in the Sumsky Hussars, in various battles as a captain on the Eastern Front, and his final escape via Siberia and Japan to the United States. Readable and intriguing.

957. Lobanov-Rostovsky. *The Grinding Mill: Reminiscences of War and Revolution in Russia, 1913–1920*. New York: Macmillan, 1935. 387pp.

Based on diaries that the author kept during fighting on the Eastern

Front and on the Macedonian Front after 1917. He also served as an interpreter for Anton Denikin, who commanded the South-Western Army Group during the war and led a White army in the Civil War.

958. Rodzianko, Paul. *Tattered Banners: An Autobiography*. London: Seely, Service, 1939. 287pp., illustrated.

Memoir of an officer in the guards who fought in the war, dealing partly with the death of the Czar.

959. Sabsay, Nahum. *A Moment of History; A Russian Soldier in the First World War*. Caldwell, Idaho: Privately printed, 1960. 346pp., illustrated. See also *The Lure* (1968) by the same author.

Sabsay served in the Russian and Belgian armies during the war and commanded a Jewish self-defense unit during the Civil War.

960. Sikorsky, Igor I. *The Story of the Winged-S: An Autobiography*. New York: Dodd, Mead, 1938. 266pp.

By a pioneering aircraft designer who developed the helicopter.

961. Tschebotarioff, Gregory. *Russia, My Native Land: A U.S. Engineer Reminisces and Looks at the Present*. New York: McGraw-Hill, 1964. 384pp., illustrated.

Autobiography. The author served during the war as an officer in a Don Cossack artillery unit, fled to the United States after the revolution, and visited on exchange as an engineer in the 1950s.

962. White, Dmitri Fedotoff. *Survival Through War and Revolution in Russia*. Philadelphia: University of Pennsylvania Press, 1939. 395pp.

Memoir, 1910–1921. At the start of the war White was a watch-lieutenant on the old cruiser *Rossiia* of the Baltic Fleet. Early in 1915 he was transferred to the Russian embassy in Washington, D.C., where he remained until mid-1916, when he returned to join the destroyer *Strashnyi* in the Baltic. The remaining two-thirds of the book concern the February 1917 Revolution, diplomacy, and the Russian Civil War

963. Yurlova, Marina. *Cossack Girl*. London: Cassell, 1934. 312pp., illustrated.

Memoir, 1915–1919. A girl's reminiscences of life in the Caucasus and Siberia during the war.

Chapter 9

South Africa

964. Alport, Arthur Cecil. *The Lighter Side of the War: Experiences of a Civilian in Uniform*. London: Hutchinson, 1934. 290pp., illustrated.

The author was a major in the R.A.M.C., and served in South Africa, Salonika, and France.

965. Cloete, Stuart. *A Victorian Son: An Autobiography, 1897–1922*. London: Collins, 1972. 319pp.

Autobiography, most on World War I. A popular author. Born in Paris but Boer heritage, served in WWI as an officer with Yorkshire Light Infantry and Coldstream Guards, twice wounded.

966. Haussmann, Leon. *Corporal Haussmann Goes to War: Armed with Motor-Cycle and Camera*. Kenilworth, S.A.: C. Martin, 2000. 58pp., illustrated.

Beautifully illustrated book about a young soldier who served as a dispatch rider during the fighting in central and eastern Africa from 1915 to 1917.

967. Levyns, J. E. P. *The Disciplines of War: Memories of the War of 1914–18*. New York: Vantage Press, 1984. 173pp., illustrated.

Memoir, 1914–1918. Levyns served in the South African Scottish, South African Brigade, 9th Division, on the Western Front. He later joined R.A.F. Squadron No. 102, a night bombing squadron. Especially interesting on his experiences in the air.

968. Payne, Adam. *Blow, Blow the Winds of Change*. Johannesburg: PENS, 1989. 142pp., illustrated.

969. Reitz, Denys. *Trekking On*. London: Faber and Faber, 1933. 351pp.

Autobiography, part on World War I, when the author participated in the 1914–1915 South African rebellion, and went to East Africa and Europe. See also *Afrikander* (1933).

970. Shackleton, Charles Walter. *East African Experiences, 1916, from the Diary of a South African Infantryman in the German East African Campaign*. Durban: The Knox Pub. Co., 1940. 123pp., illustrated.

Memoir, 1916. The author, who has been called the "South African Bairnsfather," served as a private in the 3rd South African Brigade. Lively writing and cartoons do a good job of recreating the hardships and diversions of campaigning in Africa.

971. Wade, Brian. *Peace, War, and Afterwards, 1914 to 1919: A Young Man's Letters Written Chiefly to His Mother*. Halifax: Sentinel Projects, 1996. 117pp., illustrated.

Wade, a South African, went to England at the beginning of the war and was commissioned in the 7th Battalion of the London Regiment. As a member of a transport section he saw action at Ypres and the Somme.

972. Walpole, Valentine. *The Men in the Line: Sketches and Impressions, Western Front, 1916–18*. Cape Town: Juta, 1929. 96pp.

973. Walsh, Cyril. *Letters Home: A Compilation of Letters and Diary Extracts from a South African Infantryman in the First World War*. Edited by Peter and Betty Walsh. Victoria, B.C., Canada: Peter Walsh, 2001. 200pp., illustrated.

Letters/diary, February 1917–March 1919. Walsh served as a private in the 2nd South African Infantry Regiment in France and Flanders. Skimpy diary, censored letters reveal little about Walsh's service.

974. Warwick, George William. *We Band of Brothers: Reminiscences from the 1st S. A. Infantry Brigade in the 1914–18 War*. Cape Town: Howard Timmins, 1962. 211pp., illustrated.

Memoir based on diary, August 1914–September 1917. Warwick was a lance-corporal in the 4th South African Infantry Regiment (South African Scottish), and served in Egypt from January to April 1916 before going to France. He was posted at Armentières before joining in the Battle of the Somme, where he was wounded; he also fought at Arras and Passchendaele, where he was severely wounded. Very good account, includes memories of postwar visit to battlefields.

Chapter 10

Turkey

975. Dayal, Har. *Forty-four Months in Germany and Turkey, February 1915 to October 1918; A Record of Personal Impressions*. London: P.S. King & Son, 1920. 103pp.

976. Fasih, Mehmed. *Lone Pine (Bloody Ridge) Diary of Lt. Mehmed Fasih, 5th Imperial Ottoman Army, Gallipoli, 1915: The Campaign as Viewed from Ottoman Trenches*. Edited by Hasan Basri Danisman. Beyoglu, Istanbul: Denizler Kitabevi, 2001. 210pp.

977. Kusçubasi, Esref Sencer. *The Turkish Battle at Khaybar*. Translated by Philip H. Stoddard and H. Basri Danisman. Khadikoy-Istanbul: Arba, 1999. 296pp., illustrated.

978. Nogales y Mendez, Rafael de. *Four Years Beneath the Crescent*. Translated by Muna Lee. New York: Charles Scribner's Sons, 1926. 416pp.

Memoir, 1914–1918. The author, a Spaniard, was Inspector-General of the Turkish Forces in Armenia and Military Governor of Sinai. His memoir contains observations on the Sinai campaign as well as testimony on the Armenian massacres.

979. Ölçen, Mehmet Arif. *Vetluga Memoir: A Turkish Prisoner of War in Russia, 1916–18*. Translated and edited by Gary Leiser. Gainsville: University Press of Florida, 1995. 246pp., illustrated.

Memoir, February 1916–August 1918. Arif was a lieutenant in the 30th Division, fighting in the Caucasus before being captured at Erzurum in February 1916. He spent the next two years a prisoner at Varnavino in Russia east of Moscow.

Chapter 11

United States

980. Abels, Charles H. *The Last of the Fighting Four*. New York: Vantage Press, 1968. 173pp., illustrated.

Memoir written in third person, 1898–1959. Covers Abels's service as a private on the Mexican border in 1916–17 with the 35th Infantry Regiment, and in France with the 18th Infantry Regiment, 1st Division. Largely anecdotal, but describes fighting at Cantigny, Soissons (where Abels was a runner), St. Mihiel, and Argonne Forest. Abels ended the war as a sergeant.

981. Adams, Sam N. *The Forgotten Army: The Experiences of Private Sam: Vladivostok, Siberia, 1918–1919.* Nashville, Tenn.: Parthenon Press, 1977. 148pp., illustrated.

Memoir written in third person, 1917–about 1920. Adams remained behind in Texas as a member of a supply company when his division, the 90th, left for France. He then sailed with the supply company for Vladivostok, Siberia. Anecdotal, frustrating lack of dates, but good illustrations.

982. Albertine, Connell. *The Yankee Doughboy*. Boston: Branden Press, 1968. 306pp., illustrated.

Memoir, April 1917–April 1919. Author was a private in the 104th Infantry Regiment, 26th Division, and was orderly to chaplain Fr. John B. de Valles. He served during February 1918 on the Lorraine front, July in Belleau Wood, September in the St. Mihiel salient, and November in Meuse-Argonne. Extremely detailed, probably transcribed from diary, includes striking account of Meuse-Argonne and the last hour before the Armistice.

983. Albertson, Ralph. *Fighting Without a War: An Account of Military Intervention in North Russia.* New York: Harcourt, Brace and Howe, 1920. 138pp., illustrated.

Memoir, November 1918–September 1919. The author, who served with the Y.M.C.A. at Archangel, is harshly critical of the British officers who commanded the expedition. Good illustrations.

984. Alexander, Robert. *Memories of the World War, 1917–1918.* New York: Macmillan, 1931. 309pp.

Memoir, November 1917–May 1919. Alexander was Inspector General of the Lines of Communication from November 1917 to February 1918, when he was appointed brigadier general and commander of the 41st (1st Depot) Division. In August 1918 he commanded the 63rd Infantry Brigade before being promoted to major general at the end of the month and placed in command of the 77th Division. Dry and thoroughly professional, but good on the activities of the 77th Division in the last months of the war.

985. Allen, Henry T. *My Rhineland Journal.* Boston: Houghton Mifflin, 1923. 593pp., illustrated.

Diary, June 1918–February 1923. Allen commanded the American occupying contingent on the Rhine. His journal mostly concerns politics but sheds some light on military affairs.

986. Allen, Hervey. *Toward the Flame: A War Diary.* New York: George H. Doran, 1926. 250pp. Revised second edition, New York: Farrar & Rinehart, 1934.

Memoir, July–August 1918. Allen was a lieutenant in the 111th Infantry Regiment, 28th Division. One of the best American memoirs, this realistic and slightly cynical book records six weeks of the Aisne-Marne battles north of Château-Thierry. The last few chapters on the destruction of the American bridgehead at Fismette are some of the most powerful and unsettling pages ever written in a war memoir.

987. Allen, Minne Elisabeth, and Edward Allen. Translated and edited by Julius W. Allen. *Tenderness and Turmoil: Letters to a German Mother, 1914–1920.* Santa Ana, Calif.: Seven Locks Press, 1998. 283pp., illustrated.

Letters, September 1914–March 1920, from a young American and his German bride in Ann Arbor, Michigan, to her mother in Germany. Mostly of local and family interest, but sheds some light on the American home front.

988. Anderson, Jesse A. *A Doughboy in the American Expeditionary Forces, Siberia: The Diary of Corporal Jesse A. Anderson, 1918–1919.* Berkeley, Calif.: William A. Anderson, 1983. 95pp., illustrated.

Diary, August 1918–November 1919. Anderson was a corporal with the 146th Ordnance Depot Company, arriving in Vladivostok in September 1918. In June 1919 he served as a guard on Red Cross Train No. 15, which carried supplies to the Ural Mountains and returned to Vladivostok in September of that year. Fairly sparse diary supplemented by dozens of interesting photographs.

989. Andrews, Paul Shipman. *Guns of the A.E.F.: Being the Journal of Captain Paul Shipman Andrews, Operations Officer, 151st Artillery Brigade, American Expeditionary Forces, France, 1918.* Syracuse, N.Y.: Lyman Bros., Inc., 1920. 161pp., illustrated.

Diary, July 1918–April 1919. The author's brigade was a part of the 76th Division. Detailed account of staff work and life behind the lines enlivened with rumors and anecdotes.

990. Archibald, Norman. *Heaven High, Hell Deep, 1917–1918.* New York: Albert & Charles Boni, 1935. 350pp., illustrated.

Memoir in novel form, April 1917–November 1918. Author trained on Nieuport November 1917–April 1918; also flew Sopwith Camels. Commissioned lieutenant June 1918, joined 95th Squadron, First Pursuit Group, flying Spads, in July 1918. Stirring account of air combat. Captured September 1918; extended account of mistreatment in captivity.

991. Ashford, Bailey K. *A Soldier in Science: The Autobiography of Bailey K. Ashford.* New York: William Morrow and Company, 1934. 425pp., illustrated.

Memoir of Ashford's life from birth to the 1930s; about 125 pages deal with the war. Ashford, a renowned doctor and scientist before the war, sailed for France as colonel and Medical Chief of the 1st Division in June 1917. After several months he left the 1st Division to oversee the creation of the School for War for American officers at Langres. In this capacity he visited and evaluated British and French military hospitals throughout France, and this memoir provides a useful critical analysis of Allied military medicine during the war.

992. Atwood, John H. *What I Saw of the War: Notes of My Trip Through England and France in the Autumn of 1918*. Privately printed, 1919. 208pp., illustrated.

Memoir/diary, August–November, 1918. Atwood went abroad to investigate the American Air Service for Senator James A. Reed of Missouri. He provides interesting observations on his visits to the Graham-White, Handley-Page, Ford Junction, and other aircraft factories. Also a civilian's view of wartime London and Paris, and battlefields and air bases in France.

993. Baker, C. Earl. *Doughboy's Diary*. Shippensburg, Pa.: Burd Street Press, 1998. 138pp., illustrated.

Memoir, spring 1916–May 1919. Baker was a corporal in the 112th Regiment, 28th Division. Excellent memoir, realistically depicting combat in the Aisne-Marne offensive of July–August 1918, including at Fismette (compare with Hervey Allen's *Toward the Flame*), and in the Argonne. Gritty and patriotic.

994. Baker, George R. *Heroes and Angels. Diary: A Medic Remembers World War I, France and Belgium: 1917–1919*. Baltimore, Md.: Gateway Press, 1999. 146pp., illustrated.

Diary, April 1917–April 1919. Private Baker served as an orderly and surgical assistant in Base Hospital No. 12, sponsored by Northwestern University and based in Camiers, France. Tended mainly British army wounded. Diary has more on air raids and furloughs than hospital work.

995. Baker, Horace L. *Argonne Days: Experiences of a World War Private on the Meuse-Argonne Front, Compiled From His Diary*. Aberdeen, Miss.: Aberdeen Weekly, 1927. 122pp.

Memoir, September–November 1918. Baker was a private in the 128th Infantry Regiment, 32nd Division. Unpolished but honest account of the Meuse-Argonne offensive, with some striking depictions of combat.

996. Baldwin, Marian. *Canteening Overseas, 1917–1919*. New York: Macmillan, 1920. 200pp., illustrated.

Letters, June 1917–June 1919. Typically cheerful letters about

Y.M.C.A. work in various parts of France, filled with "thrilling" air raids, plucky wounded *poilus*, and "splendid" Americans marching to the front; the Germans play the role of "bestial and heartless brutes."

997. Barber, Thomas H. *Along the Road.* New York: Dodd, Mead and Company, 1924. 141pp.

Memoir, September–October 1918. Barber was a captain of pioneer infantry, apparently attached to the 79th Division though the unit is unnamed. His unit spent this period repairing roads behind the Meuse-Argonne advance of 26 September from Esnes to Montfaucon. A minor classic, wryly humorous but realistically exposing the shortcomings of some American troops and the incompetence with which transport and supply was handled during the offensive.

998. Barclay, Harold. *A Doctor in France, 1917–1919: The Diary of Harold Barclay.* New York: Privately printed, 1923. 176pp., illustrated.

Diary, June 1917–January 1919. Barclay served as a captain and major of the Roosevelt Hospital Unit until May 1918, and as medical consultant of the 42nd Division until September 1918. The diary records little of Barclay's service near the front.

999. Barkley, John Lewis. *No Hard Feelings!* New York: Cosmopolitan Book Corporation, 1930. 327pp., illustrated.

Memoir, summer 1917–spring 1919. Author was private first class in 4th Infantry Regiment, 3rd Division, promoted to corporal near end of war. Entered fighting in May 1918 at Château-Thierry. Served as a member of a semi-autonomous "intelligence" unit, sniping and raiding. Recipient of Congressional Medal of Honor for conduct in defensive action near Cunel, France, 7 October 1918. Barkley portrays his unit as an unusually rough and dangerous set of men, and depicts their exploits with relish and possible exaggeration.

1000. Barrington, Harold P. *The Great Adventure: A World War I Soldier's Diary.* Edina, Minn.: Beaver's Pond Press, 2000. 186pp., illustrated.

Diary, March 1916–May 1919. Barrington enlisted in May 1917 and served as an M.P. in the 32nd Division in France. A rare, candid account from the M.P.'s point of view; merits more than the fifty copies printed.

1001. Bartley, Albert Lea. *Tales of the World War*. Dallas: Clyde C. Cockrell Co., 1935. 172pp.

Memoir, summer 1917–June 1919. Bartley, a Texas farm boy, was a private first class in an automatic rifle squad; although he does not name his unit he was clearly in the 90th Division. This unvarnished but highly recommended memoir includes the St. Mihiel and Meuse-Argonne battles, with some memorable pages on what it was like to go over the top.

1002. Bayne, J. Breckenridge. *Bugs and Bullets: A Doctor's Story*. New York: Richard R. Smith, 1944. 256pp., illustrated.

Memoir, August 1916–summer 1919. Author was a Maryland doctor who volunteered for service with the Allies and ended up in Bucharest, Romania, in November 1916, serving as a surgeon with a British hospital unit. When his British colleagues evacuated the city before the Germans captured it a few weeks later, Bayne elected to remain behind, and single-handedly ran makeshift hospitals under the worst of conditions. He nearly died in the course of fighting cholera and typhus epidemics. Unusually detailed descriptions of wounds, illnesses, and operations.

1003. Beal, Howard W. *The Letters of Major Howard W. Beal, Headquarters, First Division, Medical Department, Killed in Action July 18, 1918*. Paris: J.R.E. Guild, 1926. 74pp.

Letters, July 1917–July 1918. Beal, a surgeon with the 1st Division, was killed by an aerial bomb. His letters to his wife, written mostly from Field Hospital 13 and the 6th Field Artillery, are of moderate interest.

1004. Biddle, Charles John. *The Way of the Eagle*. New York: Charles Scribner's Sons, 1919. 297pp., illustrated.

Letters, April 1917–December 1918. Author was a corporal and sergeant with the French Escadrille N. 73 from July to December 1917, becoming a captain in the 103rd Aero Squadron (Lafayette Escadrille) in February 1918, then being appointed commanding officer of the 13th Aero Squadron in June, and of the 4th Pursuit Group in October 1918. In training he flew a Blériot monoplane, a Nieuport, and a Spad; in his combat assignments he flew Spads. Long and very detailed letters, with excellent accounts of air combat.

1005. Bingham, Hiram. *An Explorer in the Air Service*. New Haven: Yale University Press, 1920. 260pp., illustrated.

Memoir, late 1916–March 1919. Lieutenant Colonel Bingham served in staff positions with Aviation Headquarters and the Chief of the Air Service until August 1918, when he took command of the 3rd Aviation Instruction Centre at Issoudun, France. This memoir is mainly about flight training, with good illustrations and technical information about flying and types of aircraft.

1006. Bittle, Celestine Nicholas Charles. *Soldiering for Cross and Flag: Impressions of a War Chaplain.* Milwaukee, Wis.: Bruce Publishing Co., 1929. 331pp., illustrated.

Memoir, August 1918–June 1919. Bittle was a first lieutenant and Catholic chaplain attached to the Motor Transport Reconstruction Park at Verneuil, France, ministering to mechanics, influenza victims, and about 2,000 German prisoners. A pious narrative including a trip to Lourdes but nothing about the front lines, which Bittle never saw.

1007. Blackford, Charles Minor. *Torpedoboat Sailor.* Annapolis: United States Naval Institute, 1968. 156pp., illustrated.

Memoir, August 1916–late 1918. Blackford was a sailor on the torpedoboat destroyers *Paulding* and *McDougal*, which patrolled the Atlantic. Lighthearted story of a common sailor's life on shipboard and shore leave, with occasional reference to encounters with submarines.

1008. Blake, Katherine. *Some Letters Written to Maude Gray and Marian Wickes 1917–1918.* New York: Scribner Press, 1920. 202pp.

Letters, November 1917–November 1918. Blake served in a Paris hospital and at Fortoiseau, apparently with the Y.M.C.A. Her letters say very little about her own volunteer work, and contain mainly incredibly naive commentary on political and military affairs.

1009. Blankenhorn, Heber. *Adventures in Propaganda: Letters from an Intelligence Officer in France.* Boston, Houghton Mifflin, 1919. 167pp., illustrated.

Letters, July–November 1918. Author was a captain in the Military Intelligence Division, whose primary task was to distribute Allied propaganda to the Germans. These censored and edited letters from Blankenhorn to his wife contain few surprises; illustrations include some interesting samples of German and Allied propaganda.

1010. Blodgett, Richard Ashley. *Life and Letters of Richard Ashley Blodgett, First Lieutenant, United States Air Service*. Boston: MacDonald & Evans, 192–?. 181pp., illustrated.

Biography/Letters, May 1917–May 1918. Blodgett drove ammunition trucks in France from May 1917 until he was commissioned a lieutenant near the end of that year. He then flew for the 94th and 95th Aero Squadrons until he was killed in action in May 1918.

1011. Blumenstein, Christian. *Whiz Bang!* Buffalo, N.Y.: Privately printed, 1927. 36pp., illustrated.

1012. Borden, Mary. *The Forbidden Zone*. London: W. Heinemann, 1929. 211pp., illustrated.

Borden, an American novelist, heiress, and wife of Major General Sir Edward Spears, was a war nurse with the French army, 1914–1918. This is a collection of impressionistic sketches, stories, and poems based on the author's experiences with suffering French soldiers and civilians in various hospitals.

1013. Borden, Raymond D., and Prosper Buranelli. *Maggie of the Suicide Fleet*. Garden City, N.Y.: Doubleday, Doran, 1930. 278pp., illustrated.

Rewritten by Buranelli in memoir style from Borden's log of 1917–1918. Lieutenant Borden was gunnery officer on the *Margaret*, Submarine Patrol 527. A humorous account of the barely seaworthy craft's adventures, including cartoon illustrations by Herbert Roth, who also served on the ship.

1014. Bowerman, Jr., Guy Emerson. *The Compensations of War: The Diary of an Ambulance Driver during the Great War*. Austin: University of Texas Press, 1983. 178pp.

Diary, June 1917–November 1918. Bowerman was a member of S.S.U. 585 attached to the 128th French Infantry Division, which fought near Villers-Cotterêts during the German March 1918 offensive. Interesting and extensive diary, one of the best by an American ambulance driver.

1015. Braddan, William S. *Under Fire with the 370th Infantry (8th I.N.G.) A.E.F.* W.S. Braddan, n.d., circa 1919. 109pp., illustrated.

Memoir/letters, July 1917–November 1918. Braddan was captain and chaplain of the 370th Infantry Regiment, 93rd Division, an African

American unit. Privately printed and therefore rare, but invaluable firsthand account of this historic and highly decorated regiment.

1016. Brannen, Carl Andrew. *Over There: A Marine in the Great War*. College Station: Texas A & M University Press, 1996. 167pp., illustrated.

Memoir, February 1918–September 1919. Brannen was a private in the 6th Marine Regiment, 2nd Division, fighting in Belleau Wood, the St. Mihiel salient, and the Meuse-Argonne offensive. His memoir makes up only about 50 pages of the book, which is padded with excessive annotation and the musings of Brannen's son. Some harrowing memories of combat, however.

1017. Brooks, Alden. *As I Saw It*. New York: Alfred A. Knopf, 1929, 1930; published in 1929 by H. Jonquières in Paris as *Battle in 1918: Seen by an American in the French Army*. 328pp., illustrated.

Memoir, December 1917–November 1918. Brooks was a lieutenant in the 2nd Group, 81st Regiment of Heavy Artillery of the French army, equipped with 145mm long guns. In March 1918 his unit was attached to the 65th English Artillery Brigade of the British 5th Army trying to stem the German offensive near Saint Quentin. Brooks also witnessed at first hand American fighting at Château-Thierry and Belleau Wood in May–June 1918 and the September Meuse-Argonne offensive. Sober but harshly critical of the American high command, Brooks gives good detail on heavy artillery work and an interesting perspective on Anglo-French relations as well as European views on American participation.

1018. Brown, Hilton U., Sr., ed. *Hilton U. Brown, Jr., One of Three Brothers in Artillery: Letters and Verses Assembled by Hilton U. Brown, Sr.* Indianapolis: United Typothetae of American School of Printing, 1920. 162pp., illustrated.

Hilton U. Brown, Jr., was a second lieutenant in Battery D, 7th Field Artillery, 1st Division. He served during the winter of 1917–1918 near Toul, then in the St. Mihiel and Argonne battles, and was killed in action a week before the end of the war. The censored letters, May 1917–October 1918, make up about half the book and are of limited interest.

1019. Brown, William. *The Adventures of an American Doughboy*. Tacoma: Smith-Kinney, 1919. 77pp., illustrated.

Memoir, March 1917–June 1919. Author was private in 9th Infantry

Regiment, 2nd Division. Served near Château-Thierry, Soissons, and St. Mihiel battles, July–October 1918, then nearly died from influenza. Refreshingly naive account by a common soldier, some striking depictions of combat.

1020. Broyles, Watkins A. *Soldier, Doctor, Doctor: The Memoirs of Dr. Watkins A. Broyles, M.D.* Bethany, Mo.: Bethany Printing Company, 1981. 179pp., illustrated.

Autobiography, with about 50pp. on WWI, when Broyles was a lieutenant in the 355th Infantry Regiment, 89th Division. Good on St. Mihiel, the Meuse-Argonne, and Broyles's experiences after being wounded.

1021. Bryan, Arthur Darst. *Oceans of Love: A Collection of World War I Letters*. N.P. Hammer, 1996. Unpaginated, illustrated.

Letters, December 1917–May 1919. Bryan served in the headquarters company of the 150th Field Artillery, 42nd Division. Mundane, unremarkable letters, but well illustrated.

1022. Buck, Beaumont B. *Memories of Peace and War*. San Antonio, Tex.: Naylor Company, 1935. 284pp., illustrated.

Autobiography, only partially dealing with World War I, when Buck commanded the 28th Infantry Regiment and 2nd Brigade of the 1st Division. He was promoted to major general in August 1918. Fairly candid and told from a more personal perspective than many staff memoirs.

1023. Buell, Charles Townshend. *The Great World War and the Americans on the Field of Battle*. Newark, Ohio: Charles T. Buell & Co., 1924. 105pp., illustrated.

Written as a companion to the *Great War Memorial*, with a history of the war and other material, as well as a section recounting Buell's personal experiences. Author's rank and unit not given, served in St. Mihiel and Meuse-Argonne battles. Illustrated with interesting drawings by a veteran.

1024. Bullard, Robert Lee. *Personalities and Reminiscences of the War*. Garden City, N.Y.: Doubleday, Page, 1925. 347pp.

Memoir, April 1916–May 1919. Major General Bullard took command of the 1st Division in December 1917 and led it at Cantigny in May 1918. He subsequently commanded the III Corps at the Aisne-Marne and Meuse-Argonne offensives, and ended the war in command of the Second Army. Includes a chapter on Bullard's "nightmare" experiences with the 92nd Division of African American soldiers.

1025. Burdick, Joel Wakeman. *Lorraine: 1918*. New Haven: Yale University Press, 1919. 88pp., illustrated.

Letters, April–November 1918. These censored letters from Burdick, a captain in the Red Cross, to his wife contain little of interest.

1026. Burns, Charles Henry. *Shadows of the Argonne. First World War: The Story and Letters of Lieutenant Charles Burns*. Edited by Robert M. Jackson. Hampton, N.H.: R.M. Jackson, Jr., 1994. 165pp., illustrated.

Fragmentary letters, summer 1917–late 1918, and making up only 28pp. of entire book. Burns was a lieutenant in the 6th Infantry Regiment, 5th Division, and was killed by a minenwerfer in the Argonne in October 1918.

1027. Burton, Caspar Henry. *Letters of Caspar Henry Burton, Jr.* Edited by Spence Burton. Cambridge, Mass.: Riverside Press, 1921. 404pp., illustrated.

Biography, with war letters covering July 1915–February 1919. Burton, from Cincinnati, enlisted as a lieutenant in the British Red Cross in July 1915, serving in the Hector Munro Ambulance Corps on the Yser River front. In October 1915 he enlisted as a private in the 29th Royal Fusiliers, but remained in Britain until he went to France in December 1916 as a second lieutenant in the 4th King's (Liverpool) Regiment. He fought at the Somme, Ancre, Arras, and Bullecourt before being badly wounded in May 1917. He returned for a brief stint in 1918 with the headquarters of the U.S. 2nd Army Corps, but died from his old war wounds in March 1920. Valuable, extensive letters.

1028. Butler, Charles E. *The Yanks are Coming*. New York: Vantage Press, 1963. 143pp.

Novelized memoir, 1917–1919, told in the third person, with the author renamed "Baxter." Butler served as a lieutenant and captain in the 28th Infantry Regiment, 1st Division. An exciting war story that is probably at least partially fiction.

1029. Butler, Charles Terry. *A Civilian in Uniform*. Ojai, Calif.: Butler,

1975. 399pp., illustrated. Privately printed for the author's relatives.

Autobiography, war chapters covering May 1916–May 1919. Butler was an assistant surgeon at Hospital Militaire V.R. 76, Ris-Orangis, near Paris from May 1916 to January 1917, and then served with Evacuation Hospital No. 3 behind the American front lines for the remainder of the war. Includes detailed accounts of war wounds and medical work.

1030. Cade, John Brother. *Twenty-Two Months with "Uncle Sam," Being the Experiences and Observations of a Negro Student Who Volunteered for Military Service Against the Central Powers from June, 1917 to April, 1919.* Atlanta, Ga.: Robinson-Cofer, 1929. 128pp., illustrated.

Memoir, June 1917–April 1919. Cade, later a professor of history at Paine College in Georgia, was a second lieutenant in the 366th Regiment, 92nd Division. Thoughtful and realistic account of the 92nd Division's battles against racism and the German army.

1031. Calhoun, Emile M. *"For We're All Just Back From Hell": World War I: The Diary of Pvt. Emile M. Calhoun, 353rd Infantry Medical Corps 89th Division.* Edited by Michael C. Joseph. Independence, Mo.: Two Trails Publishing, 1999. 204pp., illustrated.

Diary, April 1918–June 1919. Calhoun, a decidedly reluctant soldier, served as a battlefield medic in St. Mihiel and Meuse-Argonne battles; his unit joined German occupation force. Some very moving entries, showing strains and dangers endured by medics.

1032. Callaway, A. B. *With Packs and Rifles: A Story of the World War.* Boston: Meador Pub. Company, 1939. 270pp.

Memoir, April 1918–June 1919. Author was private, then corporal in 353rd Infantry Regiment, 89th Division. Written from Callaway's diary and partly fictionalized, but apparently no more so than most memoirs. Low-key and engaging, with good descriptions of St. Mihiel and German occupation.

1033. Callender, Alvin Andrew. *War in an Open Cockpit: The Wartime Letters of Captain Alvin Andrew Callender, R.A.F.* Edited by Gordon W. Callender, Jr., and Gordon W. Callender, Sr. West Roxbury, Mass.: World War I Aero Publishers, 1978. 108pp., illustrated.

Letters, June 1917–October 1918. Callender was an American serving with Squadron No. 32 of the R.F.C., flying an S.E. 5a over the Western

Front from May 1918 until 30 October, when he was killed in action. Censored, sketchy, but surprisingly interesting letters, with good annotation and maps.

1034. Campbell, Douglas. *Let's Go Where the Action Is! The Wartime Experiences of Douglas Campbell*. Edited by Jack R. Eder. Knightstown, Ind.: JaaRE Pub., 1984. 97pp., illustrated.

Letters, July 1917–January 1919. Campbell trained in a Curtiss Jenny in the United States and a Nieuport at Issoudun, France, before being assigned to the 94th Aero Squadron as a lieutenant. He scored six victories before being wounded and reassigned to the United States in July 1918. The letters are heavily censored and sketchy, but contain some vivid accounts of combat. Well illustrated.

1035. Campbell, Jack. *Jack Campbell's War Diary, 1918–1919*. Verona, Va.: McClure Printing Company, 1982. 48pp., illustrated.

Diary, May 1918–February 1919. Campbell, a sergeant in the 18th Division, never saw front line service due to illness, and his diary is of limited interest.

1036. Campbell, Peyton Randolph. *The Diary-Letters of Sergt. Peyton Randolph Campbell*. Buffalo: Pratt and Lambert, 1919. 142pp., illustrated.

Letters in diary form, April–August 1918. Campbell ranked from private to sergeant in the 306th Machine Gun Battalion, 77th Division, and was killed in action near Fismes on 4 September 1918. His censored letters are mostly about training and the reserves, with not much on the front lines.

1037. Carstairs, Carroll. *A Generation Missing*. London: William Heinemann, 1930. 208pp.

Memoir, 1914–1919. Carstairs, an American, served as a junior officer in the British 3rd Grenadier Guards and was badly wounded a week before the end of the war. Impressionistic but very effective antiwar memoir. Bitter foreword by Osbert Sitwell, who served in the same unit.

1038. Carter, Eliot Avery. *Lanes of Memory: An Autobiography*. Edited by Emory S. Basford. Boston: Thomas Todd Co., 1963. 344pp., illustrated.

Autobiography, about a third of which relates to the war. Carter served as a second and first lieutenant in the 103rd Infantry Regiment, 26th Division, and was at the front from February 1918. Worthwhile for Carter's description of September 1918 St. Mihiel battles.

1039. Carter, William Arthur. *The Tale of a Devil Dog*. Washington, D.C.: Canteen Press, 1920. 91pp., illustrated.

Gripping memoir of a marine's experiences in 1918.

1040. Casey, Robert Joseph. *The Cannoneers Have Hairy Ears: A Diary of the Front Lines*. New York: J.H. Sears, 1927. 337pp.

Diary, August–November 1918, of a U.S. Field Artillery unit—75mm guns—attached to the 33rd Division. One of the best American artillery accounts.

1041. Catlin, Albertus Wright. "*With the Help of God and a Few Marines*." Garden City, N.Y.: Doubleday, Page, 1919. 425pp., illustrated.

Memoir, April 1917–November 1918. Catlin, who as a major had won the Congressional Medal of Honor at Vera Cruz in April 1914, was colonel in command of the 6th Marine Regiment, 2nd Division, at Belleau Wood in June 1918, where he was shot through the right lung. He became a brigadier general a month later. Patriotic memoir with an excellent account of Belleau Wood.

1042. Center, Charles. *Things Usually Left Unsaid*. Quincy, Ill.: 1927. 203pp.

Memoir, March 1917–May 1919. Center wandered from unit to unit in the United States and France, gaining promotion from lieutenant colonel to colonel, and serving in various staff and administrative positions with the 33rd and 1st Divisions, among others. His memoir holds little of interest.

1043. Chamberlin, Joseph Edgar. *The Only Thing for a Man to Do: The Story of Raymond Chamberlin, Private, 102d Machine Gun Battalion U.S.A.* Boston: Privately printed, 1921. 99pp.

Biography, with letters and diaries, October 1917–September 1918. Chamberlin was killed in September 1918 while his unit, a part of the 26th Division, lay in the Troyon sector. Excerpts hint at a diary that would be valuable if printed complete.

1044. Chambers, Hilary Ranald, Jr. *United States Submarine Chasers in the Mediterranean, Adriatic and the Attack on Durazzo*. New York: Knickerbocker Press, 1920. 91pp.

Memoir, March–November 1918. Lieutenant Chambers commanded submarine chasers No. 128 and No. 215. More descriptive than personal, but recounts some exciting experiences in the lesser-known naval war in the Adriatic.

1045. Chapman, Charles Wesley. *Letters of Second Lieutenant Charles Wesley Chapman, Jr., December 19, 1894–May 3, 1918*. Waterloo, Iowa: 1919. 146pp., illustrated.

Letters, May 1917–May 1918. Chapman was killed in action near Toul in May 1918 while serving with the 94th Aero Squadron. Most letters document his training experiences.

1046. Christian, Royal A. *Roy's Trip to the Battlefields of Europe: Being the Diary of Royal A. Christian, Confidential Messenger to Colonel Moorhead C. Kennedy, Deputy Director-General of Transportation, American Expeditionary Forces in the World War*. Chambersburg, Pa.: Press of J.R. Kerr, 192–?. 157pp.

Memoir, October 1917–December 1918. Little about the front lines in this book, but it is an uncommon and honest account from an African American perspective.

1047. Clark, Coleman Tileston. *Soldier Letters, Coleman Tileston Clark ... Salter Storrs Clark, Jr. ... : Their Stories in Extracts from Their Letters and Diaries*. New York: L. Middleditch Co., 1919. 174pp., illustrated.

1048. Clarke, Carolyn W. *"Evacuation 114" as Seen from Within*. Boston: Hudson Print Co., 1919. 71pp., illustrated.

Memoir, June 1918–January 1919. Clarke was a nurse's aide with Evacuation Hospital 114, stationed at Jouy-sur-Morin, Château-Thierry, Toul, and Fleury-sur-Aire near Verdun. Short but candid.

1049. Clarke, William F. *Over There with O'Ryan's Roughnecks; Reminiscences of a Private 1st Class who Served in the 27th U.S. Division with the British Forces in Belgium and France*. Seattle: Superior Publishing Company, 1968. 176pp., illustrated.

Memoir, August 1917–March 1919. Clarke was the gunner in a

platoon of the 104th Machine Gun Battalion, 27th Division. The 27th was one of two American divisions under British command, and Clarke therefore served near Ypres in August–September 1918 and in the U.S./Australian assault on the Hindenburg Line on 27 September. Often rambling but with amusing reflections on the relative merits of British and Australian soldiers and good illustrations. Includes an extended description of the author's return to the old battlefields in 1953.

1050. Clover, Greayer. *A Stop at Suzanne's and Lower Flights.* New York: George H. Doran, 1919. 265pp., illustrated.

A collection of vignettes by, letters from, and tributes to Clover, a volunteer truck driver for the French army in 1917 who transferred to the air service and was killed in a training accident in August 1918.

1051. Codman, Charles R. *Contact.* Boston: Little, Brown and Company, 1937. 248pp.

Memoir, November 1917–1919. Lieutenant Codman flew a Breguet 14 bomber for the 96th Aero Squadron until he was shot down and captured in September 1918. The second half of this book describes his experiences as a POW, which he shared with James Norman Hall (q.v.). Well-written and exciting, one of the classic aviation memoirs.

1052. Cohen, Louis. *A Story for the Young and Old.* New York: Pageant Press, 1962. 119pp.

Memoir, May 1914–Summer 1917. Unremarkable tale of an American civilian in Poland, Russia, and Holland during the war.

1053. Coolidge, Hamilton. *Letters of an American Airman.* Boston: Privately printed, 1919. 231pp., illustrated.

Letters, July 1917–October 1918. Coolidge served as a lieutenant and captain in the 94th Aero Squadron until a direct hit from German flak killed him at the end of October 1918. Censored but otherwise unedited letters, some good passages on combat.

1054. Coolidge, John Gardner. *A War Diary in Paris, 1914–1917.* Cambridge: Riverside Press, 1931. 283pp.

Diary, August 1914–October 1917. Coolidge was appointed special agent to the U.S. embassy in Paris in November 1914. Useful perspective on Paris in wartime.

1055. Corning, Walter D. *The Yanks Crusade: A Book of Reminiscences*. Chicago: Privately printed, 1927. 84pp., illustrated.

Memoir, June 1917–spring 1919. Corning served, apparently as a private, with the 131st Infantry, 33rd Division. Crudely printed and illustrated, but with some interesting vignettes of the British, Australian, and French troops who fought alongside this division. Includes July 4th attack on Beaumont-Hamel, Meuse-Argonne, and occupation of Germany.

1056. Cowan, Robert G., and Roger M. Baty. *Foibles, Fun, Flukes, Facts of Life in World War I, San Francisco, Oakland, and France, Los Angeles*. Glendale, Calif.: Arthur H. Clark, 1985. 111pp., illustrated.

Autobiography, with brief diary, May 1918–May 1919, describing Cowan's experiences in France with Park Battery A, Army Artillery Park, 1st Army.

1057. Crane-Gartz, Kate. *A Woman and War*. Long Beach, Calif.: Mary Craig Sinclair, 1928. 184pp.

The first 72pp. contain the 1927–28 letters of Kate Crane-Gartz, a Socialist politician and antiwar activist; the rest of the book prints the February 1916–January 1919 letters of her son, Captain Crane-Gartz. Gartz served as an ambulance driver in A.F.S., S.S.U. 8 until August 1916, when he returned to the United States as a dirigible flight instructor. He went back to France as a naval aviator in October 1918. Gartz's wartime experiences convince him that "the more I see of men the more I realize that they *must* be ruled by an iron hand and that Bolshevism will *not* go."

1058. Crocker, Charles Thomas. *Tom's Letters: American Expeditionary Force, France—1917*. Privately printed, 1956. 91pp., illustrated.

Letters, October 1917–May 1919. Moderately interesting letters of a first lieutenant flying Spads in the 94th Aero Squadron; some descriptions of combat.

1059. Cronk, Earle Tabor, and Les Leatherman. *The Leatherman-Cronk Story of Two Innocents Abroad in the 21st Engineers, Light Railway, World War One*. Richmond, Va.: Privately printed, 1963. 136pp.

Memoir (prepared from rewritten diaries of Cronk and Leatherman), October 1917–July 1919. The authors were privates, working on railways behind the lines in the St. Mihiel and Meuse-Argonne sectors, sometimes under fire. Printed on a shoestring but surprisingly good content.

1060. Crosby, Henry Grew. *War Letters*. Paris: Black Sun Press, 1932. 312pp.

Letters, July 1917–February 1919. Crosby served in A.F.S. ambulance, S.S.U. 641, supporting the French 158th, 120th, and 17th Divisions on various fronts. Invariably optimistic.

1061. Crowe, James Richard. *Pat Crowe, Aviator: Skylark Views and Letters from France, Including the Story of "Jacqueline."* New York: N.L. Brown, 1919. 220pp.

Edited letters, December 1917–September 1918. Crowe trained in the United States and France and was commissioned a second lieutenant in July 1918, but he died in a training accident before he was assigned to the front. Literate but unexceptional.

1062. cummings, e. e. *The Enormous Room*. New York: Boni & Liveright, 1922. 271pp.

Classic, literate, highly idiosyncratic memoir of the author's experiences while interned in a French internment camp in 1918. More notable as a work of literature than as an account of World War I.

1063. Cupples, William H. *My Helpful Angel Flew With Me*. Hicksville, N.Y.: Exposition Press, 1975. 94pp., illustrated.

Memoir, April 1917–November 1918. Minor but engaging memoir of training at Tours and Issoudun. Cupples also served a brief stint in the 22nd Pursuit Squadron without seeing combat.

1064. Curtiss, Elmer H. *Going and Coming as a Doughboy*. Palo Alto, Calif., Press of F. A. Stuart, 1920. 39pp.

Memoir, November 1917–March 1919. Curtiss was a private with the 161st Infantry, 41st Division, and the 102nd Infantry, 26th Division. He fought in several engagements before being sent to the hospital with a leg injury in October 1918. Surprisingly matter-of-fact reminiscences.

1065. Cushing, Harvey. *From a Surgeon's Journal, 1915–1918*. Boston: Little, Brown, 1936. 534pp., illustrated.

Diary, March 1915–February 1919. Extremely detailed and well-annotated diary of Dr. Cushing's service throughout France during the war, with a Harvard unit of the American Ambulance at Neuilly in 1915, with the B.E.F. in Flanders in 1916–1917, as director of American Base

Hospital No. 5 in 1917–1918, and as senior consultant in neurosurgery with the A.E.F. Medical Headquarters after July 1918. An indispensable guide to wartime medical work.

1066. Cutchins, John A. *An Amateur Diplomat in the World War.* Richmond, Va.: The Commanders Committee, American Legion, 1938. 227pp., illustrated.

Memoir, June 1916–July 1919. Lieutenant Colonel Cutchins served, among other posts, as a staff officer with the British 12th Division and the American 29th Division, as well as working with the Army General Staff College. His memoir gives a fairly honest perspective on staff work, and also describes some scenes at or near the front.

1067. Cutler, G. Ripley. *Of Battles Long Ago: Memoirs of an American Ambulance Driver in World War I.* Hicksville, N.Y.: Exposition Press, 1979. 280pp., illustrated.

Letters and diaries covering March 1917–February 1919, rewritten into narrative by Cutler's nephew, Charles H. Knickerbocker. Cutler joined the A.F.S. in December 1916, serving near Verdun in S.S.U. 18, and then transferred to U.S.A.A.S. section 642. He was wounded by a shell in February 1918, but continued to serve on various U.S. Army fronts until the end of the war. Nicely illustrated, with good content despite being rewritten.

1068. Dawes, Charles Gates. *A Journal of the Great War.* 2 vols. Boston: Houghton Mifflin, 1921. 344 and 283pp., illustrated.

Volume 1 contains a diary dating August 1917–August 1919; volume 2 consists of an appendix containing postwar reports of American supply officers. Dawes was Chief of Supply Procurement for the A.E.F., and the American member of the Military Board of Allied Supply. Indispensable for research into the American supply system.

1069. Day, Kirkland Hart. *Camion Cartoons.* Boston: Marshall Jones Company, 1919. 120pp., illustrated.

Letters, October 1918–January 1919. Day served with the Reserve Mallet, a camion unit of five-ton trucks. Unexceptional letters and Bairnsfather-style cartoons.

1070. Deckard, Percy Edward. *List of Officers Who Served With the 371st*

Infantry and Headquarters, 186th Infantry Brigade During the World War; And also My Experience in the World War, with Memoirs of France and Service in the Medical Department of 371st Infantry. Allegany, N.Y.: The Allegany Citizen, 1929. 127pp.

Deckard's regiment was part of the 93rd Division; he was a first lieutenant and surgeon from November 1917–January 1919. His "memoirs" make up only about 20pp. of the total, and are of little interest.

1071. Derby, Richard. *"Wade In, Sanitary!": The Story of a Division Surgeon in France*. New York: G.P. Putnam's Sons, 1919. 260pp., illustrated.

Memoir, December 1917–January 1919. Lieutenant Colonel Derby, a brother-in-law of Theodore Roosevelt's children, was Division Surgeon of the 2nd Division. His memoir, alternately dry and vivid with many statistics and details of surgical procedures, includes a lengthy diatribe against pacifism.

1072. Detzer, Karl. *True Tales of the D.C.I.* Indianapolis: Bobbs-Merrill Co., 1925. 343pp.

Memoir, 1918–1919. Detzer was a captain in the Division of Criminal Investigation, and helped to police the American embarkation area at Le Mans, France, after the Armistice. Lurid true crime stories.

1073. Devan, Scoville T. *Overseas Letters from a Y Secretary*. Columbus, Ohio: Privately printed, 1919. 77pp., illustrated.

Letters, October 1917–October 1918. As a Y.M.C.A. secretary, Devan catered to the 26th and 82nd Divisions near Château-Thierry.

1074. Dickman, Joseph Theodore. *The Great Crusade: A Narrative of the World War*. New York: D. Appleton and Company, 1927. 313pp., illustrated.

Memoir, April 1917–July 1919. Major General Dickman commanded the 3rd Division at Château-Thierry, the IV Corps in the St. Mihiel Offensive, and the I Corps in the Meuse-Argonne Offensive. He ended the war in command of the Third Army, continuing through the occupation of Germany in 1919. Dickman writes mainly about troop movements and has little to say on his personal experiences.

1075. Dittmar, Gustav Charles. *The Big Adventure*. Dallas, Tex.: Hicks

Printing Company, 1943. 285pp.

Memoir in diary form, June 1918–May 1919. Dittmar was a second lieutenant in the 360th Infantry Regiment, 90th Division. Confident, patriotic, but realistic depiction, including St. Mihiel battles. Dittmar was badly wounded in early November and sent to Base Hospital 28 at Limoges, then joined the German occupation force. He writes of the war: "As much as I hate it I wouldn't be out of it for anything."

1076. Duffy, Francis Patrick. *Father Duffy's Story*. New York: George H. Doran, 1919. 382pp., illustrated.

Diary/memoir, June 1917–April 1919. Duffy was chaplain of the 165th Infantry, 42nd Division. An exciting account by the legendary chaplain, recounting his exploits in St. Mihiel, the Argonne, and elsewhere.

1077. Dunton, Gardner. *The Letters of a World War I Pilot in the Army Air Corps, December 1917 to January 1919*. Manhattan, Kans.: Aerospace Historian, 1977. 230pp.

Unedited typescript transcription of letters, 1917–1918. Dunton, a second lieutenant, trained in Texas and Oklahoma from December 1917 to June 1918, when he become an instructor in aerial gunnery in Michigan. He never made it to France. Of value to researchers only.

1078. DuPuy, Charles M. *A Machine Gunner's Notes, France 1918*. Pittsburgh: Reed & Witting Company, 1920. 143pp., illustrated.

Memoir, September 1915–November 1918. DuPuy was a major in the 316th Infantry Regiment, 79th Division, until December 1917, when he was transferred to the 311th Machine Gun Battalion as its commanding officer. This interesting memoir describes how DuPuy whipped his battalion into shape during training and then commanded it during the Meuse-Argonne offensive. Good illustrations.

1079. Edwards, Frederick Trevenen. *Fort Sheridan to Montfaucon; The War Letters of Frederick Trevenen Edwards*. DeLand, Fla.: Elizabeth Satterthwait, 1954. 296pp.

Letters, May 1917–September 1920. Edwards was a first lieutenant in the 18th Field Artillery, 3rd Division, and was in action from July to October 1918 at Château-Thierry, St. Mihiel, and the Argonne. An only son, he was mortally wounded at Montfaucon on October 5, and this book includes a moving introduction by his father. Good letters, though comparatively few are about combat.

1080. Ellinwood, Ralph E. *Behind the German Lines, a Narrative of the Everyday Life of an American Prisoner of War*. New York: Knickerbocker Press, 1920. 162pp.

1081. Elliott, Stuart E. *Wooden Crates & Gallant Pilots*. Philadelphia: Dorrance & Company, 1974. 275pp., illustrated.

Memoir, April 1917–November 1918. Elliott trained in a Curtiss Jenny at Kelly Field in the United States, and in Caudrons and Nieuports at Tours and Issoudun in France. After becoming a lieutenant, he flew various planes, including Salmsons and D.H. 4s, and piloted a Spad 13 with the 13th Aero Squadron of the 2nd Pursuit Group. This is a must for aviation enthusiasts, as Elliott goes into detail about qualities and defects of each plane, but it deals more with training than combat.

1082. Ely, Dinsmore. *Dinsmore Ely, One Who Served*. Chicago: A.C. McClurg & Co., 1919. 215pp., illustrated.

Diary and letters, June 1917–April 1918. Ely, a second lieutenant, flew with a French escadrille in the Toul and Montdidier sectors during the first few months of 1918 before being killed in action in April 1918. Patriotic, but mostly about flight training.

1083. Emmett, Chris. *Give 'Way to the Right: Serving with the A.E.F. in France During the World War*. San Antonio, Tex.: The Naylor Company, 1934. 302pp., illustrated.

Memoir, April 1917–early 1919. Author was a private, then corporal in the 359th Infantry Regiment, 90th Division. Involved in September 1918 St. Mihiel battles, where he was lightly gassed. One of the better American memoirs, providing a straightforward and believable narrative of a common soldier's experiences from basic training to combat. Notable also for recording the Doughboys' songs, and for the author's racism.

1084. Ettinger, Albert M., and A. Churchill Ettinger *A Doughboy with the Fighting 69th: A Remembrance of World War I*. Shippensburg, Pa.: White Mane Publishing Company, 1992. 286pp., illustrated.

Memoir, 1915–April 1919. Ettinger was a motorcycle dispatch rider in the 165th (formerly 69th) Regiment of the 42nd Division. This memoir was transcribed from tape recordings, and is episodic and disjointed, with tales of combat and of famous members of the regiment, such as Father Duffy.

1085. Evans, Frank E. *Daddy Pat of the Marines: Being His Letters from France to His Son Townie*. New York: Frederick A. Stokes, 1919. 153pp., illustrated.

Letters, November 1917–June 1918, written from Evans, Adjutant of the 6th Marines, 2nd Division, to his six-year-old son. Printed in large type with cartoons. An unconventional rendition of war experiences, including the Argonne, from soldier to child.

1086. Evarts, Jeremiah Maxwell. *Cantigny, a Corner of the War*. Privately printed, 1938. 96pp.

Memoir, April–July 1918. Evarts was a captain in the 18th Infantry Regiment, 1st Division. This book consists of a series of artfully written vignettes about military life and combat while the regiment was stationed at Cantigny, near Montdidier in France. Some chapters are very good, and merit comparison with Hervey Allen's *Toward the Flame*.

1087. Ferguson, John B. *Through the War with a Y Man*. Privately printed, 1919. 269pp., illustrated.

Memoir, September 1917–January 1919. Pious, patriotic account of Y.M.C.A. service, attached to the 32nd Division in France. Good illustrations.

1088. Finney, Ben. *Once a Marine—Always a Marine*. New York: Crown Publishers, 1977. 128pp., illustrated.

Autobiography, with about 30pp. on World War I, 1917–1918. Finney was an enlisted soldier in the 5th Marine Regiment, 2nd Division, and was badly gassed three days before the Armistice. Aside from some memories of training at Paris Island and scraps about combat at Soissons and St. Mihiel, Finney's account is anecdotal and disappointingly sparse.

1089. Fitch, Willis Stetson. *Wings in the Night* Boston: Marshall Jones Company, 1938. 302pp., illustrated.

Memoir, March 1917–November 1918. Fitch served as a first lieutenant in the Italian 10th Caproni Squadron on the Alpine front, flying big Caproni bombers. Fascinating, readable memoir of unconventional air service.

1090. Florence, Lella Secor. *Lella Secor: A Diary in Letters, 1915–1922.* Edited by Barbara Moench Florence. New York: Burt Franklin & Company, 1978. 295pp., illustrated.

Letters, December 1915–June 1923. Secor was a New York feminist and peace activist; this diary provides a good overview of her activities before and after the war. See also her *The Ford Peace Ship and After* (1935).

1091. Foote, Katherine. *88 Bis and V.I.H.: Letters from Two Hospitals by an American V.A.D.* Boston: The Atlantic Monthly Press, 1919. 104pp.

Letters, January 1917–March 1918. Author served at Hospital "88 Bis," French 9th Army Corps at Tours from January to March 1917, then at Vernon Institute Hospital near Chester, England, 76th Detachment, Cheshire County Division, British Red Cross. Useful, with good detail on hospital work, home front privations, and the wounded.

1092. Foulois, Benjamin D., with Carroll V. Glines. *From the Wright Brothers to the Astronauts: The Memoirs of Major General Benjamin D. Foulois.* New York: McGraw-Hill, 1968. 306pp., illustrated.

Autobiography, with about 45pp. on World War I. Brigadier General Foulois became Chief of Air Service for the U.S. Army in November 1917. Despite his important responsibilities in the organization of American aviation, Foulois here provides only a sparse account of his wartime activities.

1093. Gallagher, Bernard J. *The Cellars of Marcelcave: A Yank Doctor in the B.E.F.* Edited by Christopher Gallagher and Mary E. Malloy. Shippensburg, Pa.: Burd Street Press, 1998. 268pp., illustrated.

Memoir, 1915–1918, edited and partially rewritten by the author's grandson from an older original. Gallagher volunteered for medical service with the British army and joined the Gloucesters on the Somme. A superior medical memoir, even if it is hard to distinguish the author's writings from his grandson's.

1094. Gallagher, David B. *The Battle of Bolts and Nuts in the Sector of Cognac Hill.* Fort Worth, Tex.: Gallagher-Crosby Co., 1931. 175pp.

Memoir, April 1917–April 1919. Gallagher was a sergeant in the 17th

Engineers (Railway), which served behind the lines in France. Semi-satirical and uneventful.

1095. Gansser, Emil B. *On the Battle Fields of France in 1918*. Grand Rapids, Mich.: Emil B. and Robert L. Gansser, 1958. 166pp.

Memoir, June–November 1918. Gansser was a captain in the 126th Infantry Regiment, 32nd Division, and saw action in the Aisne-Marne and Meuse-Argonne battles, among other engagements. Somewhat clumsily rendered in novel format, but nevertheless exciting and worth reading.

1096. Gates, Percival T. *An American Pilot in the Skies of France: The Diaries and Letters of Lt. Percival T. Gates, 1917–1918*. Edited by David K. Vaughan. Dayton, Ohio: Wright State University Press, 1991. 209pp., illustrated.

Diaries/letters, January 1918–January 1919. Gates underwent intensive flight training at Issoudun and elsewhere in France and then flew Spads with the 185th and 27th Aero Squadrons. Excellent annotation; most material is about training, but with a few descriptions of combat.

1097. Genet, Edmond Charles Clinton. *An American for Lafayette: The Diaries of E.C.C. Genet, Lafayette Escadrille*. Edited by Walt Brown, Jr. Charlottesville: University Press of Virginia, 1981. 224pp., illustrated.

Diaries, October 1915–April 1917. The diary begins with the last days of Genet's service in the Foreign Legion on the Champagne front, and ends just before his death as a corporal with the Lafayette Escadrille in April 1917, the first American killed after the U.S. Declaration of War. One of only two surviving diaries from this celebrated unit, and includes Genet's 1917 flight log.

1098. George, Herbert. *A Farrier in Arms*. New York: Pageant Press, 1953. 236pp., illustrated.

Memoir, March 1917–April 1919. This disjointed and badly written book is told from the point of view of Clayborn Baxter, a farrier in the 165th Field Hospital, 117th Sanitary Train, attached to the 42nd Division. Herbert George apparently rewrote Baxter's oral account. Includes rear-area perspectives on St. Mihiel and Meuse-Argonne. Revised as *The Challenge of War* (1966).

1099. Gilchrist, John W. Stuart. *An Aerial Observer in World War I.*

Richmond, Va.: Privately printed, 1966. 134pp., illustrated.

Memoir, May 1917–November 1918. Gilchrist was briefly a second lieutenant in the 322nd Infantry Regiment, 81st Division, before transferring out of the infantry to become an aerial observer in November 1917. He flew in a Salmson 2A2 for the 104th Aero Squadron over St. Mihiel. Rough but useful account of an underappreciated service.

1100. Gleeson, Joseph J. *A Soldier's Story: A Daily Account of World War I.* Oakmont, Pa.: M.S. Gleeson, 1999. 88pp., illustrated.

Diary, January 1918–March 1919. Gleeson was a sergeant in the 12th Field Artillery, 2nd Division, and saw battle at Château-Thierry, St. Mihiel, and the Aisne-Marne and Meuse Argonne offensives. A sparse but careful daily record.

1101. Gow, Kenneth. *Letters of a Soldier.* New York: Herbert B. Covert, 1920. 457pp., illustrated.

Letters, June 1916–October 1918. Remarkably detailed letters describe Gow's service on the Mexican border and then as a first lieutenant in the 107th Infantry Regiment, 27th Division, until his death in action in October 1918. Best on the Meuse-Argonne offensive.

1102. Greeman, Edward. *Grandpa's War: The French Adventures of a World War I Ambulance Driver.* New York: Writers and Readers Publishing, 1992. 240pp., illustrated.

Memoir, roughly 1916–1919. Greeman was a private with S.S.U. 592 of the U.S.A.A.S., attached to French and British units. The rambling, disjointed chapters of this book were originally humorous stories Greeman wrote as letters to his son after the war. Strongly antiwar.

1103. Green, Julian. *Autobiography.* Vol. 2, *The War at Sixteen.* Translated by Euan Cameron. New York: Marion Boyars, 1993. 207pp.

Memoir, 1917–1919. Green was an American raised in Paris, and originally wrote this book in French. He served in 1917 as an ambulance driver in the American Field Service, mostly in the Argonne region, and then as an officer in the French artillery during the occupation of Germany. This deeply religious memoir deals only partially with the war.

1104. Greene, Warwick. *Letters of Warwick Greene, 1915–1928.* Edited by Richard W. Hale. Boston: Houghton Mifflin, 1931. 310pp.

Collected letters, with 90pp. of war letters covering May 1915–February 1919. Greene did relief work in New York and Paris for the American Red Cross in 1917, then served as a major in supply for the air service in 1918. Sketchy, of only slight interest.

1105. Gregg, William Cephas. *Three Months in France*. New York: Knickerbocker Press, 1919. 230pp., illustrated.

Memoir, January–April 1918. Gregg was a secretary in the Y.M.C.A. His memoir is dry and largely uninteresting, except perhaps for his defense of Y.M.C.A. methods against the disdain of the Doughboys.

1106. Grider, John MacGavock. *War Birds: Diary of an Unknown Aviator*. New York: George H. Doran, 1926. 277pp., illustrated.

Diary, September 1917–August 1918. An aviation classic, unattributed in the original edition but later disclosed to have been the diary of Grider edited and supplemented by his friend Elliott White Springs. Grider, a first lieutenant, trained in Oxford during the winter of 1917–18, went to the front with the 85th Squadron of the R.F.C. in March 1918, and was killed in action in June 1918. *Above the Bright Blue Sky: More About the War Birds* (1928), by Springs, is apparently fictionalized. See also *Marse John Goes to War* (1933), by the same author.

1107. Groessl, Quiren M. *"Big Boy": A Diary of World War I*. Privately printed, 1981. 122pp., illustrated.

Diary, February 1918–January 1919. Private Groessl began the war as a member of the 32nd Division, but was reassigned to the 28th Infantry Regiment, 1st Division, in March 1918. On May 27th a German raiding party captured Groessl; in a daring escape he was badly wounded, and spent the rest of the war in hospitals.

1108. Gulberg, Martin Gus. *A War Diary: into this Story is Woven an Experience of Two Years' Service in the World War with the 75th Company, 6th Regiment, United States Marines*. Chicago: Drake Press, 1927. 50pp.

Memoir, May 1917–May 1919. Gulberg, a private, fought at Château-Thierry, and in the Aisne-Marne and Meuse-Argonne battles, and was wounded in July 1918. Brief but vivid, with extensive depictions of combat.

1109. Guttersen, Granville. *Granville: Tales and Tail Spins from a Flyer's Diary*. New York: Abingdon Press, 1919. 176pp., illustrated.

Letters/diary, January 1918–January 1919. Guttersen remained a second lieutenant in training at Ellington Field and San Leon Aerial Gunnery School, Texas, throughout the war. Unremarkable.

1110. Hagood, Johnson. *The Services of Supply: A Memoir of the Great War*. Boston: Houghton Mifflin, 1927. 403pp., illustrated.

Memoir, April 1917–November 1918. Colonel Hagood was placed in command of the 7th Regiment of the Coast Artillery Corps (railway guns) in July 1917, serving near Soissons in September 1917 until he was appointed to command the Advance Section, Line of Communications the following month. Hagood ended the war as a brigadier general and Chief of Staff of the Services of Supply, which he had helped to create. Personal but technically detailed account of logistics in the A.E.F.

1111. Hall, Bert, and John J. Niles. *One Man's War: The Story of the Lafayette Escadrille*. New York: Henry Holt, 1929. 353pp., illustrated.

Memoir, 1910–May 1918. Hall served during the last months of 1914 as a private in the French Foreign Legion, seeing heavy fighting in the vicinity of Rheims. Most of this memoir concerns Hall's subsequent service as a lieutenant and pilot in the Lafayette Escadrille. One of the best aviation memoirs, and an invaluable record of a famous unit.

1112. Hall, James Norman. *Flying with Chaucer*. Boston: Houghton Mifflin Company, 1930. 56pp.

Memoir, summer-winter 1918. Hall, who later co-authored *Mutiny on the Bounty* (1932) with fellow pilot Charles Nordhoff, served as a private in the 9th Battalion Royal Fusiliers from August 1914 to December 1915 (see his book *Kitchener's Mob*, published in 1916). From October 1916 to May 1918 he served as a corporal, sergeant, and captain in the Lafayette Escadrille, 103rd and 94th Aero Squadrons (see his book *High Adventure*, 1918). Hall was shot down behind enemy lines and captured in May 1918. This book is a whimsical account of his months in a German prison camp and subsequent release. See also *My Island Home: An Autobiography* (1952) by the same author.

1113. Hall, Melvin A. *Journey to the End of An Era*. New York: Charles Scribner's Sons, 1947. 438pp.

Autobiography, part on World War I, when Hall commanded the 1st Observation and 1st Night Reconnaissance Groups.

1114. Halsey, William F., and Joseph Bryan III. *Admiral Halsey's Story.* New York: McGraw-Hill, 1947. 310pp., illustrated.

Autobiography, mostly about World War II but with some reminiscences of Halsey's command of the destroyers USS *Benham* and USS *Shaw* during World War I.

1115. Halyburton, Edgar, and Ralph Gall. *Shoot and Be Damned.* New York: Covici Friede, 1932. 452pp.

Memoir, October 1917–December 1920. Halyburton was a sergeant in the 16th Infantry Regiment, 1st Division. German troops captured him during a trench raid in November 1917, and he remained a POW for the rest of the war. A self-described hard-boiled sergeant who killed one of his own men during a fight, Halyburton gruesomely describes his life in prisoner of war camps, and records extensive German mistreatment of Allied prisoners.

1116. Hanson, William. *World War I: I Was There.* Gerald, Mo.: Patrice Press, 1982. 115pp., illustrated.

Memoir, January 1917–November 1919. Hanson served from January 1917 as a doctor with the British Red Cross and later the R.A.M.C., mostly at Dartford War Hospital for POWs in Kent. From June 1918 he was a doctor attached to the U.S. 79th Division, serving in the St. Mihiel and Meuse-Argonne offensives. Interesting and readable.

1117. Harbord, James G. *Leaves from a War Diary.* New York: Dodd, Mead, 1925. 407pp., illustrated.

Diary at least partially rewritten as a memoir, May 1917–November 1918. Harbord was a lieutenant colonel and Pershing's Chief of Staff until May 1918, when he was promoted to brigadier general and placed in command of the 4th Marine Brigade of the 2nd Division. He commanded the brigade at Belleau Wood in June, and as a major general led the 2nd Division at Soissons in July. Later that month he was placed in command of the Service of Supplies, a post he held to the end of the war. An unusually intimate and useful view from the top. See also Harbord's *The American Army in France 1917–1919* (1936).

1118. Harden, Elmer Stetson. *An American Poilu*. Boston: Little, Brown and Company, 1919. 244pp.

Letters, July 1917–November 1918. Harden served as an enlisted soldier in the 47th and 412th French infantry regiments, mostly near Verdun, until he was badly wounded in July 1918. His letters, intelligent and sensitively written, exude optimistic patriotism at first; but as the war progresses Harden becomes increasingly disillusioned. Graphic depictions of battle and hospitalization.

1119. Harris, Harvey L. *The War as I Saw It: 1918 Letters of a Tank Corps Lieutenant*. St. Paul, Minn.: Pogo Press, 1998. 155pp., illustrated.

Letters, March 1918–January 1919. Harris served as a second lieutenant in the artillery, with various rear area duties, until July 1918 when he was commissioned a first lieutenant in the 345th Tank Battalion commanded by Colonel George S. Patton. Harris saw action in the St. Mihiel and Meuse-Argonne battles as driver of a Renault light tank, and never lost his perception of war as a sort of game. Interesting references to Patton.

1120. Harrison, Carter Henry. *With the American Red Cross in France, 1918–1919*. Chicago: Ralph Fletch Seymour, 1947. 341pp., illustrated.

Memoir, March 1917–May 1919. Harrison, a captain in the American Red Cross, writes about his activities in Toul, Verdun, and Metz, and notes the failures of the Y.M.C.A. Good illustrations.

1121. Hart, Archibald Stephen. *Company K of Yesterday*. New York: Vantage Press, 1969. 152pp.

Memoir, April 1917–November 1918. Hart was an enlisted soldier in the 142nd Infantry Regiment, 36th Division, and fought in the Meuse-Argonne. Humorous and readable.

1122. Harvey, Bartle M. *Me and Bad Eye and Slim: The Diary of a Buck Private*. Monrovia, Calif.: The Press of Charles F. Davis, 1932. 239pp., illustrated.

Diary, May 1918–July 1919. Harvey, a private and corporal in the 22nd Ammunition Train, spent his time driving ammunition trucks well behind the front lines. His "diary" is written for laughs.

1123. Haslett, Elmer. *Luck on the Wing: Thirteen Stories of a Sky Spy*.

New York: E.P. Dutton, 1920. 303pp., illustrated.

Memoir, 1917–November 1918. Major Haslett transferred out of the infantry in September 1917 to become an aerial observer, serving with several French squadrons and eventually ending up with the First Army Observation Wing at St. Mihiel and the Argonne. He was shot down and captured at the end of September 1918. Witty and readable.

1124. Hatler, M. Waldo. *The M. Waldo Hatler Story*. Neosho, Mo.: Ozarkana Book Press, 1968. 220pp.

Autobiography/biography, a little under half dealing with the war. Hatler was a sergeant in the 356th Infantry Regiment of the 89th Division, and won the Congressional Medal of Honor on November 8, 1918 by swimming the Meuse River near Pouilly, France. This book contains some good passages but is disappointingly disorganized.

1125. Heinrichs, Waldo Huntley. *First to the Front: The Aerial Adventures of 1st Lt. Waldo Heinrichs and the 95th Aero Squadron, 1917–1918*. Edited by Charles Woolley. Atlgen, Pa.: Schiffer Military History, 1999. 244pp., illustrated.

Diary, July 1917–December 1918. Heinrichs trained at Issoudun on Blériots and Nieuports, and flew a Nieuport 28 and Spad XIII at the front from February 1918, scoring two victories before being shot down and captured that September. Beautifully illustrated, with exciting, readable and detailed diary entries. Recommended despite heavy padding by the editor.

1126. Hemrick, Levi E. *Once a Marine*. New York: Carlton Press, 1968. 194pp.

Memoir, 1917–1918, of Hemrick's Marine service, including training at Paris Island.

1127. Herbert, Craig S. *Eyes of the Army: A Story About the Observation Balloon Service of World War I*. Lafayette Hill, Pa.: C.S. Herbert, 1986. 300pp., illustrated.

Memoir, April 1917–July 1919. Herbert trained as a private at Fort Omaha, Nebraska, then went to France as a member of the 2nd Balloon Company, serving in the Toul, Aisne-Marne, St. Mihiel, and Meuse-Argonne sectors. This desktop publication reads like a unit history at times but includes some valuable information on the balloon service.

1128. Herring, Ray DeWitt. *Trifling With War*. Boston: Meador Pub. Co., 1934. 379pp.

Memoir, September 1917–July 1919. Herring served as a private and second gunner in an unnamed machine gun unit. Convincingly antiwar, dedicated "to the Maimed and the Dead who went to the Cross for the mob that did not understand."

1129. Herzog, Stanley J. *The Fightin' Yanks; A Book of Plain Facts, Written with the Intention of Perpetuating the Deeds of the Boys of Battery F, 103d Field Artillery, 26th or Yankee Division*. Stamford, Conn.: Cunningham Printers, 1922. 116pp., illustrated.

Memoir, March 1917–April 1919. Herzog served as an enlisted man in the Toul, Aisne-Marne, St. Mihiel, and Meuse-Argonne sectors. This small, unembellished, but fascinating memoir deserves a reprint.

1130. Hightower, Thomas W. *My Experience as a Soldier During the "World War."* Privately printed, 1919. 95pp.

Diary, July 1918–July 1919. Hightower, an African American cook, teacher, and minister, describes his experiences from Camp Gordon, Georgia, to service in France and his return home.

1131. Hilton, H. W. *War Over Half a Century Ago*. Brownsville, Tex.: Springman-King, 1971. 560pp., illustrated.

Memoir, April 1917–1919. Hilton was a private in the 111th Infantry Regiment, 28th Division, and saw heavy fighting in the Aisne-Marne and Meuse-Argonne battles. A direct, powerful account, very well illustrated, including several of the author's original battlefield sketches.

1132. Hinrichs, Ernest. *Listening In: Intercepting German Trench Communications in World War I*. Edited by Ernest H. Hinrichs, Jr. Shippensburg, Pa.: White Mane, 1996. 148pp., illustrated.

Memoir, 1917–1918. Fascinating description of Hinrichs' experiences as a listening station intercept operator in the trenches, particularly during the Meuse-Argonne offensive.

1133. Hoar, Walter George. *The Leaves Have Fallen*. Shell Lake, Wis.: White Birch Printing Company, 1977. 272pp., illustrated.

Memoir, covering World War I, February 1918–April 1919, and World War II. Hoar was a private in the 127th Field Hospital, attached to the 32nd Division. This book contains fragments of Hoar's memories and notes, heavily supplemented by secondary accounts of the war drawn from other sources.

1134. Hoffman, Robert C. *I Remember the Last War*. York, Pa.: Strength & Health Pub. Co., 1940. 320pp., illustrated.

Memoir, 1917–August 1918. Hoffman was a lieutenant in the 111th Infantry Regiment, 28th Division. After the war he became a professional weightlifter and physical fitness expert. This bitterly antiwar account is one of the better American memoirs, replete with vivid and extensive accounts of combat in the Aisne-Marne offensive in the summer of 1918. Like Hervey Allen in *Toward the Flame* (q.v.), Hoffman concludes with the German flamethrower attack on the American bridgehead at Fismette.

1135. Hogan, Martin Joseph. *The Shamrock Battalion of the Rainbow; A Story of the "Fighting Sixty-Ninth."* New York: D. Appleton, 1919. 280pp.

Memoir, July 1917–December 1918. Hogan was a corporal in the 165th Infantry Regiment, 42nd Division. He fought in the Château-Thierry and Meuse Argonne battles, was gassed and hospitalized twice, and then suffered a final debilitating wound in the hand near the war's end. Vigorous, exciting accounts of combat; a good early memoir.

1136. Holden, Frank A. *War Memories*. Athens, Ga.: Athens Book Company, 1922. 215pp., illustrated.

Memoir, April 1917–March 1919. Holden was a second lieutenant in the 328th Infantry Regiment, 82nd Division. He participated briefly in the St. Mihiel offensive of September 1918, then moved on to battle in the Argonne Forest before being hospitalized due to illness. Honest but unremarkable.

1137. Holt, W. Stull. *The Great War at Home and Abroad: World War I Diaries and Letters of W. Stull Holt*. Edited by Maclyn P. Burg and Thomas J. Pressly. Manhattan, Kans.: Sunflower University Press, 1999. 328pp., illustrated.

Diaries/letters, March 1917–July 1919. Holt served as an ambulance driver with A.A.F.S. Section 1 until September 1917, when he joined the 20th Aero Squadron of the 1st Daylight Bombardment Group as an observer and bombardier in D.H. 4 aircraft. Extensive diary entries and excellent illustrations.

1138. Hubbard, Samuel T. *Memoirs of a Staff Officer, 1917–1919.* Tuckahoe, N.Y.: Cardinal Associates, Inc., 1959. 299pp.

Memoir, May 1917–January 1919. Major Hubbard was appointed chief of the Battle Order Section of the A.E.F. in July 1917. In 1918 he served as a liaison officer and as an observer with the 2nd Division; at the end of the war he helped to organize the army intelligence school at Langres. Crudely printed but with some valuable information on staff work.

1139. Hughes, George Forbes, and Gerard Hastings Hughes. *Flying for the Air Service: The Hughes Brothers in World War I.* Edited by David K. Vaughan. Bowling Green, Ohio: Bowling Green State University Popular Press, 1998. 222pp., illustrated.

Letters, with accompanying narrative later added by Gerard Hughes, March 1917–January 1919. Captain George Hughes served in the 12th Aero Squadron, flying Renault AR-1 and Salmson observation planes in March–July 1918, then transferred to the 258th Aero Squadron, again flying the Salmson. Lieutenant Gerard Hughes remained as a flying instructor in Texas for most of the war and never saw front-line service. Interesting letters, well-annotated, though George, who suffered a nervous breakdown due to combat stress, wrote little about his flights over the front.

1140. Hungerford, Edward. *With the Doughboy in France: A Few Chapters of an American Effort.* New York: Macmillan, 1920. 291pp.

Pedestrian account of service in the American Red Cross.

1141. Hunt, Harry Frank. *Letters Home: The True Story of Lt. Harry Frank Hunt, Veterinary Reserve Corps, American Expeditionary Forces, World War I.* Tuscon, Ariz.: Daphne Pub., 1998. 108pp., illustrated.

Letters/diary, November 1917–February 1919. Hunt, a second lieutenant, saw little of the front lines and died in an accident after the end of the war. Mostly of family interest.

1142. Hunton, Addie W. and Kathryn M. Johnson. *Two Colored Women with the American Expeditionary Forces.* Brooklyn, N.Y.: Brooklyn Eagle Press, 1920. 256pp., illustrated.

Memoir, roughly 1918–1919. The authors served in the Y.M.C.A. throughout France. Rare positive view (considering the racism of many American memoirs) of the African American contribution in World War I. With gentle irony the authors contrast the hurdles that they and African American soldiers had to face with the democratic idealism of American propaganda. Accounts are also taken from soldiers of the 92nd Division.

1143. Husband, Joseph. *A Year in the Navy*. Boston: Houghton Mifflin, 1919. 180pp.

Memoir, January 1918–May 1919. Husband was a junior officer at the Great Lakes Naval Training Station on Lake Michigan, and then served on the destroyer *Benham* and other ships. Uneventful.

1144. Irvin, Francis L., and W.P. Taylor. *Francis L. "Spike" Irvin's War Diary and the History of the 148th Aero Squadron Aviation Section*. Manhattan, Kans.: Aerospace Historian, 1974. 128pp. plus appendixes, illustrated.

Irvin's diary, February 1918–April 1919, makes up only 26pp. of the total, and is scant. He was an administrative sergeant major attached to squadron headquarters.

1145. Irwin, George Junkin. *War Letters, 1917–'19, of Professor George Junkin Irwin*. Edited by Charles W. Turner. Verona, Va.: McClure Press, 1976. 131pp., illustrated.

Unremarkable account of the author's experiences in the ambulance service.

1146. Isaacs, Edouard Victor. *Prisoner of the U-90*. Boston: Houghton Mifflin, 1919. 185pp., illustrated.

Memoir, May–October 1918. Isaacs was a navy first lieutenant on the USS *President Lincoln*, a converted Hamburg-American liner serving as a troopship. He was captured on May 31 when the ship, returning from France, was sunk by the submarine *U-90*. Isaacs provides some interesting details of life in a German submarine, along with his internment and escape to Switzerland in October. Patriotic and anti-German.

1147. Jacks, Leo Vincent. *Service Record: by an Artilleryman*. New York: Charles Scribner's Sons, 1928. 303pp.

Memoir, spring 1918–June 1919. Jacks enlisted in the 119th Field

Artillery, 32nd Division, and served in the Aisne-Marne, Oise, and Meuse-Argonne sectors. First-rate memoir, extremely well written and exciting.

1148. Jackson, Edgar B. *Fall Out to the Right of the Road!* Verona, Va.: McClure Press, 1973. 506pp., illustrated.

Memoir, roughly 1917–1918. Jackson served as a corporal in the 329th Infantry Regiment, 83rd Division, and the 110th Infantry Regiment, 28th Division. He fought in the Argonne, where he was wounded in September 1918, and remained hospitalized for the rest of the war. Massive and novelized, with fictional dialogue and some realistic depictions of combat.

1149. Jackson, Warren R. *His Time in Hell: A Texas Marine in France: The World War I Memoir of Warren R. Jackson.* Edited by George B. Clark. Novato, Calif.: Presidio Press, 2001. 249pp., illustrated.

Memoir, June 1917–August 1919. Jackson served as a corporal with the 6th Marines, 2nd Division, in most of the A.E.F.'s major battles. Exciting and readable, with helpful editing that clarifies text originally written in 1930.

1150. Janis, Elsie. *The Big Show: My Six Months with the American Expeditionary Forces.* New York: Cosmopolitan Book Corporation, 1919. 227pp., illustrated.

Memoir, 1918. Janis was a popular music hall entertainer who became known as "sweetheart of the Doughboys" for her shows in France in 1918. The frontispiece, showing Janis posing merrily in "a very smart little French trench," should be sufficient warning of the book's content.

1151. Jelke, Ferdinand Frazier. *Letters from a Liaison Officer.* Chicago: Press of G.F. McKiernan, 1919. 166pp.

Letters, August 1917–February 1919. Jelke enlisted in the 5th Marine Regiment in July 1917 but transferred to the Paris War Risk Bureau in November 1917. In the spring of 1918 he was commissioned a second lieutenant and served thereafter as a liaison officer to the French 5th Army Corps. Some useful observations on French military administration.

1152. Jones, E. Powis. *From the Side Lines.* Privately printed, 1925. 49pp.

1153. Jordan, Walker Harrison. *With "Old Eph" in the Army (not a history) a Simple Treatise on the Human Side of the Colored Soldier*. Baltimore: H.E. Houck & Co., 1919. 53pp., illustrated.

Memoir, June 1918–March 1919. Jordan served in the headquarters company of the 351st Field Artillery, 92nd Division. Equal parts unit history and memoir, but a rare account of a black artillery unit. Several pages describe Jordan's experiences on the front lines near Metz.

1154. Judy, Will. *A Soldier's Diary: A Day-to-Day Record in the World War*. Chicago: Judy Publishing Co., 1930. 216pp., illustrated.

Diary, August 1917–June 1919. Judy was a field clerk at the headquarters of the 33rd Division. His wittiness and the good illustrations relieve the general monotony of the diary entries.

1155. Kean, Robert Winthrop. *Dear Marraine, 1917–1919*. Livingston, N.J., 1969. 289pp., illustrated.

Memoir/letters, April 1917–November 1919. Kean was a lieutenant in the 15th Field Artillery, 2nd Division, and served on a battery of 75s at Château-Thierry, Vaux, and Soissons. From October 1918 he did some intelligence work at A.E.F. Headquarters at Chaumont and then joined the Army Intelligence School at Langres. Well-illustrated, with excellent detail throughout on training, combat, and intelligence work.

1156. Kellogg, Doris. *Canteening Under Two Flags: Letters of Doris Kellogg*. East Aurora, N.Y.: The Roycrofters, n.d., apparently printed about 1920. 198pp., illustrated.

Letters, April–November 1918. Kellogg went to France as a mechanic, but finding little call for her skills she switched to canteen work for the Red Cross near hospitals in Paris and Chantilly. Surprisingly candid letters with respect to American and French wounded.

1157. Kendall, Harry. *A New York Actor on the Western Front: Giving an Account of Many Hitherto Unrecorded Incidents and Unusual Actions that Took Place During the Great Conflict*. Boston: The Christopher Publishing House, 1932. 134pp., illustrated.

Memoir, 1915–November 1918. Kendall served in the British 1st King Edward's Horse as a trooper until he was commissioned an officer in August 1917. He saw fighting at Vimy Ridge, St. Quentin, and throughout Flanders until he was badly wounded at Cambrai in November

1917. He remained in a hospital for the rest of the war. An intriguing account of life in the British cavalry, elegantly written and honest. Kendall dwells at length on executions for cowardice, which shocked him.

1158. Kennedy, Laurence Sarsfield. *War Letters of Laurence Sarsfield Kennedy*. New York, 1932. 223pp.

Letters, December 1917–June 1919. Kennedy served as an enlisted soldier in a machine gun company of the 308th Infantry Regiment, 77th Division, before being commissioned a second lieutenant and transferring to the 5th Machine Gun Battalion, 2nd Division, in July 1918. He fought at St. Mihiel and elsewhere, but his letters are largely routine and omit most of his combat experiences.

1159. Kilham, Eleanor B. *Letters from France, 1915–1919*. Salem, Mass.: Privately printed, 1941. 81pp.

Letters, May 1915–January 1919. Routine, patriotic letters from a woman doctor in France.

1160. Kimmel, Stanley. *Crucifixion*. New York: Gothic Publishing, 1922. 96pp.

Undated letters, apparently 1917. Kimmel served in an unnamed ambulance unit. Atmospheric letters interlaced with antiwar polemics.

1161. Kindall, Sylvian G. *American Soldiers in Siberia*. New York: Richard R. Smith, 1945. 251pp.

Memoir, August 1918–January 1920. Kindall was a lieutenant in the 27th Infantry Regiment that was stationed in Siberia during the period covered by this memoir. Writing during World War II, Kindall is pro-Soviet and anti-Japanese, but on the whole this is an exciting, realistic, and detailed account of the American intervention.

1162. King, David Wooster. *L.M. 8046: The War Diary of a Legionnaire*. London: Arrowsmith, 1929. 212pp.

Memoir, August 1914–January 1919. King joined the 135th Regiment of the French Foreign Legion in November 1914, and fought in the 1915 Champagne offensive, and at Verdun and the Somme in 1916. He transferred to the American Army near the end of the war and served in the counterespionage section at Chaumont. Colorful and engrossing, especially for 1915–16.

1163. Kinney, Curtis, and Dale M. Titler. *I Flew a Camel.* Philadelphia: Dorrance, 1972. 122pp., illustrated.

Memoir, 1917–1918. The author joined the R.F.C. in 1917 and trained on Curtiss Jennys in the United States and England. He was posted to the Sopwith Camel-equipped No. 3 Squadron in March 1918 and wounded in August of that year.

1164. Knapp, Shepherd. *On the Edge of the Storm: The Story of a Year in France.* Worcester, Mass.: Commonwealth Press, 1921. 79pp.

Letters, August 1917–July 1918. Knapp was a Y.M.C.A. worker at several locations in France; his letters are mundane and mostly uninteresting.

1165. Kramer, Harold Morton. *With Seeing Eyes: The Unusual Story of an Observant Thinker at the Front.* Boston: Lothrop, Lee & Shepard, 1919. 397pp., illustrated.

Memoir, February 1917–September 1918. Patriotic account by a former soldier and minor author who served in the Y.M.C.A. in France. Some interesting observations on Franco-American relations.

1166. Kurtz, Leonard Paul. *Beyond No Man's Land.* Buffalo, N.Y.: Foster & Stewart, 1937. 151pp., illustrated.

Memoir, May 1918–May 1919. Kurtz was on detached service with the intelligence section of the 312th Infantry Regiment, 78th Division. He saw fighting at St. Mihiel and the Meuse-Argonne before being captured a few days before the end of the war. Reads like a unit history at times, but has some vivid episodes of combat.

1167. Lahm, Frank Purdy. *The World War I Diary of Col. Frank P. Lahm, Air Service, A.E.F.* Edited by Albert F. Simpson. Maxwell A.F.B., Ala.: Historical Research Division, Aerospace Studies Institute, 1970. 271pp., illustrated.

Diary, August 1917–August 1919. Captain Lahm commanded the Balloon School at Omaha, Nebraska from May to June 1917, when he was promoted to major. In the autumn of 1917 he inspected British and French balloon units and operations, and in October 1917 he was placed in charge of the balloon activities of the A.E.F. He was promoted to colonel, and commanded the air service of the 2nd Army from October 1918. Well-illustrated and annotated, useful for research in the American balloon and air services.

1168. Lambert, William. *Combat Report.* London: William Kimber, 1973. 224pp., illustrated.

Memoir, May 1917–September 1919. Lambert, an American, joined the R.F.C. in June 1917 and was eventually posted to No. 24 Squadron. He flew his first patrol in April 1918 and, flying an S.E.5a, scored nineteen victories before being forced to quit because of ill health in August. Good illustrations and stirring accounts of combat.

1169. Langer, William L. *Gas and Flame in World War I.* New York: Alfred A. Knopf, 1965. 121pp.

Originally published in 1919 as *With "E" of the First Gas*, now extremely rare. Part unit history, part memoir, November 1917–February 1919. Langer was a sergeant with the 30th Engineers, which became the 1st Gas Regiment, Chemical Warfare Service. He served with a Stokes mortar unit in the St. Mihiel salient and Argonne Forest from September to November 1918. Despite the title, this book contains very little information on chemical warfare.

1170. Langille, Leslie. *Men of the Rainbow.* Chicago: O'Sullivan Publishing House, 1933. 203pp.

Memoir, April 1917–May 1919. Langille served as an enlisted man with Battery B of the 149th Field Artillery, 42nd Division. Superior, readable memoir revealing the hardships and camaraderie of artillery service in the Champagne, Château-Thierry, St. Mihiel, and Argonne. Langille also muses at length on war, patriotism, religion, and why men fight.

1171. Lawrence, Joseph Douglas. *Fighting Soldier: The AEF in 1918.* Boulder, Colo.: Colorado Associated University Press, 1985. 165pp., illustrated.

Memoir, July 1918–May 1919. Lawrence served in the 118th Infantry Regiment, 30th Division, experiencing trench warfare near Ypres in August 1918. He then went through officers' training at Langres, and on his graduation as a second lieutenant at the beginning of October was transferred to the 113th Infantry Regiment, 29th Division. A ruthlessly realistic book, with a particularly memorable description of fighting in the Meuse-Argonne, October–November 1918.

1172. Leach, George E. *War Diary*. Minneapolis, Minn.: Pioneer Printers, 1923. 205pp., illustrated.

Diary, September 1917–May 1919. Leach was colonel of the 151st Field Artillery, 42nd Division. Unadorned diary, sparse in places, but good for July–September 1918.

1173. Leach, Maud Shipley. *Hill 7; A Life Sketch of George Elliott Shipley*. Chicago: Willett, Clark & Company, 1935. 380pp., illustrated.

This biography and tribute includes letters from Shipley dating from July 1916 to September 1918. A second lieutenant, he served with the 304th Sanitary Train of the 79th Division until October, 1918, when he transferred to the 4th Infantry, 3rd Division. He was killed in action shortly afterwards.

1174. Leach, William James. *Poems and War Letters*. Peoria, Ill.: Manual Arts Press, 1922. 209pp.

Letters cover March–October 1918. Leach, a Methodist preacher, served in the Y.M.C.A., mostly in sectors controlled by the 2nd Division. Pious letters contain some interesting behind the lines observations.

1175. Lee, Benjamin. *Benjamin Lee, 2d: A Record Gathered from Letters, Note-books, and Narratives of Friends*. Boston: Cornhill, 1920. 333pp., illustrated.

Biography, with letters and notebook extracts dating April 1917–October 1918. Lee was an ensign and aviator in the Naval Reserve Flying Corps, serving on the English Channel patrol in a seaplane before being killed in an accident at the end of October 1918. He never saw combat, but letters describe some particulars of his training and patrols.

1176. Lee, Roger Irving. *Letters from Roger I. Lee, Lt. Colonel, U.S. Army Medical Corps, 1917–1918*. Brookline, Mass.: Privately printed, 1962. 377pp., illustrated.

Letters, May 1917–January 1919. Lee was a major with the Harvard unit, Base Hospital No. 5. Unannotated letters refer mainly to personal matters, politics, and propaganda, with very little about hospital work.

1177. Lejeune, John Archer. *The Reminiscences of a Marine*. Philadelphia: Dorrance, 1930. 488pp., illustrated.

Autobiography, about half on World War I, 1917–1918. Brigadier

General Lejeune went to France in June 1918 and took command of the 2nd Division the next month. His memoir is one of the best written by an American general of World War I.

1178. Leland, Claude Granger. *From Shell Hole to Château with Company I; Personal Recollections of a Line Officer of the 107th U.S. Infantry, 27th Division, in France, 1918*. New York: Society of Ninth Company Veterans, 7th Regiment, New York National Guard, 1950. 303pp., illustrated.

Memoir, May–November 1918. Leland was a captain; his unit fought attached to the British army in Flanders. Nicely illustrated, meticulous account, with very good sketch maps and diagrams. Highly recommended; readable and useful for research.

1179. Lettau, Joseph L. *In Italy with the 332nd Infantry*. Youngstown, Ohio: J.L. Lettau, 1921. 76pp., illustrated.

Memoir, September 1917–May 1919. Lettau was a battalion sergeant major in his unit, which formed part of the 83rd Division. Rare but sparse account of one of the few American units to fight on the Italian front.

1180. Levell, Robert O. *"War on the Ocean": A Sailor's Souvenir*. Newcastle, Ind.: 1937. 56pp., illustrated.

Memoir, May 1917–May 1919. Levell was a seaman first class on several ships, including the destroyer *Benham*, and spent much of his time stationed at Naval Base No. 6 off Queenstown, Ireland. Uneventful.

1181. Libby, Frederick. *Horses Don't Fly*. New York: Arcade, 2000. 274pp., illustrated.

Stirring story of the first American ace. He served in the ambulance corps before entering the Royal Flying Corps, and served in Squadron Nos. 11, 23, 25, and 43, eventually scoring twenty-four victories in F.E.2b, D.H.4, and other aircraft. He never flew in combat for the United States.

1182. Liggett, Hunter. *A.E.F.: Ten Years Ago in France*. New York: Dodd, Mead and Company, 1927–28. 335pp., illustrated.

Edited republication of articles originally printed in the *Saturday Evening Post*, April–July 1927. Memoir, roughly 1917–1918. Liggett was a major general commanding the 41st Division to January 1918, the 1st

Army Corps to October 1918, and then the First Army to the end of the war. This memoir, supplementing *Commanding an American Army* (see below), provides an extended argument for the decisiveness of the American military contribution to victory.

1183. Liggett, Hunter. *Commanding an American Army: Recollections of the World War*. Boston: Houghton Mifflin, 1925. 207pp., illustrated.

Liggett commanded the 41st Division from August 1917 until January 1918, when he took command of the 1st Army Corps. He led it at Cantigny, Belleau Wood, and the Aisne-Marne, and took over the First Army in October 1918. Interesting staff memoir.

1184. Lindner, Clarence R. *Private Lindner's Letters: Censored and Uncensored*. San Francisco: Gladys Lindner, 1939. 126pp., illustrated.

Letters, June 1918–March 1919. Lindner served in the 113th Field Artillery, 30th Division. He saw fighting at St. Mihiel and in the Meuse-Argonne, but makes almost no references to combat in his letters. Primarily of family interest.

1185. Little, Arthur W. *From Harlem to the Rhine: The Story of New York's Colored Volunteers*. New York: Covici Friede, 1936. 382pp., illustrated.

Memoir, April 1917–February 1919. Little served as captain, adjutant, and major in the African American 369th Infantry Regiment of the 93rd Division. A white officer, Little is condescending but sympathetic to the troops of his unit, who served with distinction at the front under French command from April 1918 until the end of the war.

1186. Loeblein, John M. *Memoirs of Kelly Field, 1917–1918*. Manhattan, Kans.: Aerospace Historian, 1974. 59pp.

Loeblein was an assistant engineer officer in charge of the airplane repair shops at Kelly Field, Texas. His memoirs consist of a series of unrelated anecdotes about Kelly Field. Useful for research only.

1187. Lowry, Howard Haines. *Letters to Tweeters: A Memorial to Howard Haines Lowry and Margaret Erwin Holt Lowry*. Westport, Conn.: Eidolon Press, 1980. 180pp., illustrated.

Letters, July 1918–April 1925. Lowry, a Quaker in the Y.M.C.A., reached France just days before the Armistice. His letters contain thoughtful musings on war and demobilization, but are otherwise unremarkable.

1188. Lukens, Edward C. *A Blue Ridge Memoir*. Baltimore: Sun Print, 1922. 152pp., illustrated.

Memoir, May–December 1918. Superior memoir of a lieutenant in the 320th Infantry Regiment, 80th Division, including memories of service with the British in Flanders and in the Meuse-Argonne offensive.

1189. Lynch, John William. *Princess Patricia's Canadian Light Infantry, 1917–1919*. Hicksville, N.Y.: Exposition Press, 1976. 208pp.

Memoir, 1916–1919. Lynch, an American citizen, lied about his age to enlist in Canada, and became a signaler in Princess Patricia's Canadian Light Infantry. He fought at Amiens and Arras before being badly wounded at Cambrai. Excellent memoir, absorbing and readable.

1190. McBride, Herbert. *A Rifleman Went to War*. Onslow County, N.C.: Small-Arms Techincal Publishing Company, 1935. 398pp.

Memoir, September 1915–April 1917. Semi-technical study of the author's experiences as a sniper with the Canadian Corps in France and Belgium, describing the rifle's use in sniping and the duties of the soldier using it.

1191. McCarthy, George T. *The Greater Love*. Chicago: Extension Press, 1920. 161pp., illustrated.

Memoir, April–December 1918. McCarthy, a Catholic priest, became senior chaplain of the 7th Division, and saw some front-line service in the Meuse-Argonne, where he was wounded. He is pious and optimistic, but sparing in his depiction of service at the front.

1192. McCarthy, T. F. *A Year at Camp Gordon*. Wilkes-Barre, Pa.: T.F. McCarthy, 1920. 156pp.

Memoir, June 1918–April 1919. McCarthy was a welfare worker at Camp Gordon, Georgia. Aside from some sketchy references to the 82nd Division and army racism, his memoir is unremarkable.

1193. McClure, M. McKinley. *Hey! Major, Look Who's Here*. Philadelphia: Dorrance, 1972. 92pp.

Memoir, April 1917–May 1919. McClure enlisted underage at fifteen, and served as a private in a Boston coastal defense unit before transferring to the 12th Field Artillery, 2nd Division. He participated in most of the A.E.F.'s major battles, sometimes as a forward observer. A good artillery memoir, vivid in parts.

1194. McCollough, John Milton. *We Flew With One Wing*. Philadelphia: Dorrance, 1977. 50pp.

Autobiography, with details on the author's experiences with the 168th Aero Squadron in World War I.

1195. McCormick, Robert R. *The Army of 1918*. New York: Harcourt, Brace and Howe, 1920. 276pp.

Memoir, May 1917–November 1918. McCormick, later publisher of the *Chicago Tribune*, and author of *With the Russian Army* (1915) about his experiences on the Eastern Front, served as lieutenant colonel of the 122nd Field Artillery Regiment, 33rd Division, then as colonel in command of the 5th Field Artillery Regiment, 1st Division. Most of this book consists of general thoughts on the army and the war, though some of McCormick's own experiences are included.

1196. McElroy, John Lee. *War Diary of John Lee McElroy, 1st Lieut. 315th Field Artillery, 155th Brigade*. Camden, N.J.: Haddon Press, 1929. 50pp., illustrated.

Diary, September 1918–February 1919. McElroy's unit was attached to the 80th Division, serving in St. Mihiel and the Meuse-Argonne before he was hospitalized due to illness in early November. Excellent, unedited diary of artillery service.

1197. McHenry, Herbert L. *As a Private Saw It: My Memories of the First Division, World War I*. Indiana, Pa.: A.G. Halldin, 1988. 174pp., illustrated.

Memoir, May 1918–September 1919. McHenry was drafted in May 1918 and served as a private in the 16th Infantry Regiment, 1st Division, at St. Mihiel and the Meuse-Argonne. He had positive memories of his service despite having been drafted; extended depictions of combat, and of the occupation of Germany.

1198. Mackin, Elton. *Suddenly We Didn't Want to Die: Memoirs of a World War I Marine*. Novato, Calif.: Presidio Press, 1993. 264pp.

Memoir, June–November 1918. Mackin was a private in the 5th Marine Regiment, 2nd Division, serving for most of the time as a runner. He saw bitter fighting in Belleau Wood, the Aisne-Marne offensive, and the St. Mihiel salient, as well as the bloody attack on Mont Blanc of 4 October and the Meuse River crossing of 10–11 November. Mackin was decorated, but also wounded and suffered the lingering effects of shell shock for years to come. An important book that brilliantly evokes the enlisted marine's point of view.

1199. McLaughlin, Joseph M. *Behind the Lines in France*. St. Cloud, Fla.: Double-D, 1970. 25pp.

Memoir, 1918–1919. Vague recollections of the author's service in the 54th Artillery, C.A.C., mostly after the Armistice.

1200. MacLeish, Kenneth. *Kenneth: A Collection of Letters*. Chicago: Privately printed, 1919. 131pp.

The author flew with No. 213 Squadron of the British R.A.F., and was killed in October 1918. Reprinted as *The Price of Honor* (1991).

1201. MacNider, Hanford. *The A.E.F. of a Conscientious Subaltern*. Mason City, Iowa: Klipto, 1924. 62pp., illustrated.

Memoir, 1917–1918. MacNider was a lieutenant in the 9th Infantry Regiment, 2nd Division. This short memoir provides vignettes of fighting near Soissons and St. Mihiel.

1202. Manley, Milford N. *The World War I Letters of Private Milford N. Manley*. Edited by Robert N. Manley and Elaine Manley McKee. Lincoln, Neb.: Dageforde Pub., 1995. 134pp., illustrated.

Letters, August 1918–June 1919. Manley served in ambulance units U.S.A.A.S. 617 and 650, but did not leave the United States until two days after the Armistice. Good illustrations and annotation.

1203. March, Peyton Conway. *The Nation at War*. Garden City, N.Y.: Doubleday, Doran, 1932. 407pp., illustrated.

Memoir, April 1917–1921. March, Chief of Staff from March 1918, writes critically of Pershing and others in the army high command.

1204. Markle, Clifford Milton. *A Yankee Prisoner in Hunland*. New Haven, Conn.: Whitlock's Book Store, 1920. 52pp., illustrated.

Memoir, April–November 1918. Markle, a medic in the 102nd Infantry Regiment, 26th Division, was captured in April 1918 and spent the rest of the war as a POW at Darmstadt, Germany. Anti-German but realistic.

1205. Marshall, George C. *Memoirs of My Services in the World War, 1917–1918*. Boston: Houghton Mifflin, 1976. 268pp., illustrated.

Memoir, April 1917–November 1918. Marshall served in staff positions in the 1st Division and A.E.F. headquarters, ending the war with the temporary rank of colonel. After the war he was Pershing's aide-de-camp. Not very exciting reading but of historical interest; includes diaries of his visits to the battlefields with Pershing after the war.

1206. Martin, Chester Cy. *Men of the Twentieth*. Manhattan, Kans.: Aerospace Historian, 1974. 102pp.

Unedited typescript memoir, May 1917–May 1919. Martin trained in the United States and with the R.F.C. in France before joining the 20th Aero Squadron as a sergeant and crew chief in August 1918. His squadron was equipped with D.H.4 day bombers. Readable, but useful mainly for historical and technical research.

1207. Maverick, Maury. *A Maverick American*. New York: Covici Friede, 1937. 362pp.

Autobiography, with a few chapters on World War I, when Maverick was a first lieutenant in the 28th Regiment of the 1st Division and fought in St. Mihiel and the Argonne. Cynical but interesting.

1208. Mayo, Katherine. *"That Damn Y"; A Record of Overseas Service*. Boston: Houghton Mifflin, 1920. 432pp., illustrated.

Memoir, 1917–1918. Immense, protracted, and ostensibly objective apologia for the Y.M.C.A. in Europe by a woman who was commissioned to write the organization's war story. Her conclusion: that soldiers disliked the Y.M.C.A. because of their instinctive aversion to welfare!

1209. Meisinger, Clarence LeRoy. *A World War One Soldier's Diary, June 2, 1917 to July 26, 1919*. Edited by A.J. Ostergaard. Ellisville, Mo.: A.J. Ostergaard, 2001. 116pp., illustrated.

Meisinger served in the United States as a sergeant and second lieutenant, first in the 134th Regimental Band and the statistical section of the 34th Division, and then in various Signal Corps posts. A desktop publication, of family interest only.

1210. Mellon, Thomas, Jr. *Army "Y" Diary*. Pittsburgh: The Crescent Press, 1920. 37pp., illustrated.

Diary, September–December 1918. Mellon served as a Y.M.C.A. secretary in Washington, D.C. Unremarkable.

1211. Menne, Edward P. *Diary of a Doughboy*. Edited by Jeanne Kosmoski. Privately printed, n.d. 26pp., illustrated.

Diary, April 1917–January 1919. Menne was an enlisted man in the 121st Field Artillery Regiment, 32nd Division. Good entries on August–September 1918.

1212. Merkle, Henry B. *Memoirs of an Infantryman*. Edited by Edward B. Merkle. Orrville, Ohio: Bunker Hill Publications, 1989. 40pp., illustrated.

Transcript of taped memoirs recorded in 1968, covering April 1917–1919. Merkle was drafted in April 1918 and eventually joined the 104th Infantry Regiment, 26th Division, as a scout and sniper. He fought at Château-Thierry, St. Mihiel, and the Meuse-Argonne, and retained surprisingly complete memories of his combat experiences.

1213. Merrick, Robert G. *World War I: A Diary*. Baltimore: Privately printed, 1982. 125pp., illustrated.

Memoir, originally written in 1919, covering April 1917–January 1919. Merrick was a captain in the 10th Field Artillery Regiment, 3rd Division, and participated in most of the major American engagements in the autumn of 1918. Plainly written but absorbing.

1214. Metcalf, Stanley W. *Personal Memoirs: A Narrative of the Experiences of an American in France and Germany in 1917–1919*. Fulton, N.Y.: The Morrill Press, 1927. 254pp., illustrated.

Memoir, April 1917–August 1919. Metcalf served in the Norton-Harjes ambulance unit, S.S.U. 5 until January 1918, when he was commissioned a second lieutenant in the 17th Field Artillery, 2nd Division. He saw action in the Soissons and Champagne sectors, and participated in the occupation of Germany. Rare but exciting account, deserves reprinting.

1215. Miles, Perry Lester. *Fallen Leaves: Memories of an Old Soldier.* Berkeley, Calif.: Wuerth Pub. Co., 1961. 311pp.

Autobiography, describing the author's experiences as a brigadier general in the Spanish-American War and World War I.

1216. Millard, Shirley. *I Saw Them Die: Diary and Recollections of Shirley Millard.* Edited by Adele Comandini. New York: Harcourt Brace, 1936. 115pp.

Memoir with diary excerpts, March–November 1918. Millard volunteered for service with a French evacuation hospital near Soissons. She describes her experiences in a graphic, self-consciously wrenching manner, meant to drive home the folly of war.

1217. Millen, DeWitt Clinton. *Memoirs of 591 in the World War.* Ann Arbor, Mich.: D.C. Millen, 1932. 99pp., illustrated.

Memoir, September 1917–April 1919. Millen served in U.S.A.A.S. ambulance unit 591, which was attached to the French 4th and 27th Divisions. Episodic and uneven, but with good illustrations. Millen was antiwar from the beginning.

1218. Miller, Walter H. *Diary of a Yankee Doughboy in World War I: A Story of Bombs, Shells, Mud, Rats and God.* Portland, Maine: Seavey Printers, 1975. 61pp., illustrated.

Diary, May 1917–March 1919. Lively, charming diary of an enlisted man in the 54th and 51st Artillery, C.A.C., best on the summer and late autumn of 1918 but interesting even when Miller was not at the front.

1219. Millholland, Ray. *The Splinter Fleet of the Otranto Barrage.* New York: Bobbs-Merrill, 1936. 307pp., illustrated.

Memoir, August 1917–1919. The author was chief engineer on board a submarine chaser (or "splinter boat"), serving in the Mediterranean and Adriatic and participating in the October 1918 raid on Durazzo. A readable, fast-paced memoir.

1220. Mills, Quincy Sharpe. *One Who Gave His Life: War Letters of Quincy Sharpe Mills; with a Sketch of His Life and Ideals; A Study in Americanism and Heredity.* New York: G.P. Putnam's Sons, 1922. 490pp.

1221. Minder, Charles Frank. *This Man's War: The Day-by-Day Record of an American Private on the Western Front*. New York: Pevensey Press, 1931. 368pp.

Letters, April–October 1918, with portions that were originally censored rewritten from Minder's diaries. Minder served with the 306th Machine Gun Battalion, 77th Division, and saw a great deal of the front before being gassed in the Meuse-Argonne in October 1918. His letters to his mother become progressively antiwar.

1222. Minturn, Joseph Allen. *The American Spirit*. Indianapolis: Globe Publishing, 1921. 364pp., illustrated.

Memoir, April 1917–June 1919. Initially rejected for being overage—he was 56—Minturn eventually gained a commission in the 309th Engineers but saw nothing of the front. Personal story, little of interest.

1223. Mitchell, Clarence van Schaick. *Letters from a Liaison Officer* 1918–1919. Princeton: Princeton University Press, 1920. 105pp., illustrated.

Diary, January 1918–January 1919. Mitchell, a captain, served as a liaison officer on the staff of French General de Castlenau. Though a staff officer, he spent a fair amount of time at the front, and his diary makes interesting reading.

1224. Mitchell, Mildred. *Letters from an American Girl in the War Zone, 1917–1919*. Princeton University Press, 1920. 69pp.

Letters, dating from December 1917 to January 1919. The author served in a Red Cross canteen at Chalons-sur-Marne, then as a volunteer nurse in a French hospital at Écury. Notable chiefly for an intimate and sympathetic view of *poilus* and French civilians.

1225. Mitchell, William. *Memoirs of World War I: "from Start to Finish of our Greatest War."* New York: Random House, 1960. 312pp., illustrated.

"Billy" Mitchell describes his experiences as head of the U.S. Army's aviation section and as an observer at the Marne and Argonne. Particularly valuable for Mitchell's discussion of his controversial ideas on the uses of air power.

1226. Moffat, Alexander White. *Maverick Navy*. Middletown, Conn.:

Wesleyan University Press, 1976. 157pp., illustrated.

Memoir, June 1917–January 1918. Moffat was an ensign commanding subchasers No. 77 and No. 143 in the Atlantic. He warns that "This is definitely not a war book," but provides an interesting view of anti-submarine warfare.

1227. Montague, Edgar Sclater. *Lead, Swing and Wheel.* Hampton, Va.: Privately printed, 1959. 76pp.

Memoir in diary form, December 1917–November 1918. Montague served in the St. Mihiel and Meuse-Argonne offensives as a second lieutenant with the 123rd Field Artillery Regiment until late October, when he became a first lieutenant in the 124th Field Artillery Regiment; both units were attached to the 33rd Division. He was horse officer in both units, and although the narrative is disjointed it provides some useful information on artillery transport.

1228. Montgomery-Moore, Cecil. *"That's My Bloody Plane": The World War I Experiences of Major Cecil Montgomery-Moore, as Told to Peter Kilduff.* Chester, Conn.: Pequot Press, 1975. 157pp., illustrated.

Memoir transcribed from tape recordings, August 1917–January 1919. American-born, Montgomery-Moore was living in Bermuda when the war began. He joined the R.F.C. in the summer of 1917 and flew Sopwith 5F.1 Dolphins for No. 19 and 90 Squadrons in 1918. After the war's end he test-flew various German aircraft. Beautifully illustrated memoir; the exciting text has much of interest to aviation enthusiasts.

1229. Moore, Howard W. *Plowing My Own Furrow.* New York: W.W. Norton, 1985. 225pp., illustrated.

Autobiography of a conscientious objector from rural New York state who endured the "varied horrors" of imprisonment for two years at Fort Douglas, Utah, and elsewhere because of his refusal to serve in either combatant or non-combatant status.

1230. Moore, Waldo Wightman. *World War I: Anabasis and Katabasis of Waldo W. Moore.* Privately printed, 1981.

1231. Morgan, Daniel E. *When the World Went Mad: A Thrilling Story of the Late War, Told in the Language of the Trenches.* Boston: The Christopher Publishing House, 1931. 163pp.

Memoir, August 1914–1922. The author enlisted in the marines before the United States entered the war, and served in the 6th Machine Gun Battalion at Château-Thierry, Belleau Wood, and Soissons. Extremely bitter antiwar memoir—atypical of American and marine accounts—emphasizing the incompetence of officers, despair of the men, and the difficulty of returning to civilian life.

1232. Morrison, Elton J. *My Experiences Overseas in World War I.* New York: Vantage Press, 1983. 114pp., illustrated.

Memoir, July 1917–May 1919. Morrison, a second lieutenant, trained with the British. He served briefly with the 82nd and 78th Divisions before joining the 167th Infantry Regiment of the 42nd Division in August 1918. After participating in the St. Mihiel battles for a few days, he came down with the flu and spent the rest of the war in a hospital.

1233. Morse, Katherine Duncan. *The Uncensored Letters of a Canteen Girl.* New York: Henry Holt and Company, 1920. 265pp.

Letters, November 1917–April 1919. Really a diary written in letter form, since the author never mailed the letters but brought them home to avoid censorship. Morse served at Y.M.C.A. canteens throughout France; her relentlessly cheerful letters include the usual rumors and anecdotes but also a lot of useful detail.

1234. Moseley, George Clark. *Extracts from the Letters of George Clark Moseley During the Period of the Great War.* Chicago: Privately printed, 1923. 239pp., illustrated.

Letters, April 1917–November 1918. Moseley flew a Nieuport in French Escadrille Spad 150 from December 1917 to February 1918. From March to June 1918 he was a member of the U.S. Naval Seaplane Station at Dunkirk, from July to September 1918 he flew a D.H. 9 day bomber with R.F.C. Squadron No. 218, and from September to the end of the war Moseley was attached to French Escadrille de Saint-Pol. Excellent, extensive letters.

1235. Murnane, Mark Raymond. *Ground Swells; of Sailors, Ships, and Shellac.* New York: Exposition Press, 1949. 482pp.

Memoir, January 1917–1919. Overlong, tedious memoir of the author's training at the Great Lakes Naval Station and his daily life as a sailor on the battleship *Texas.*

1236. Muse, Benjamin. *Tarheel Tommy Atkins*. New York: Vantage Press, 1963. 140pp., illustrated.

Memoir, January 1917–April 1919. Muse enlisted as a rifleman in the 11th King's Royal Rifles of the British army in January 1917, serving at Passchendaele before being captured at the end of November 1917. In prison he developed sympathy for the German people and contempt for war propaganda. Thoughtful and candid view of the effect of propaganda, and of British soldiers from an outsider's perspective. Incorporates his rare early book *The Memoirs of a Swine in the Land of Kultur* (1919).

1237. Muston, W. H. *Over There: The Story of a Sky Pilot*. Yoakum, Tex.: W.H. Muston, 1923. 207pp., illustrated.

The author was a chaplain with the 25th Engineers and the 309th Infantry Regiment, 78th Division. A series of anecdotal stories based on his experiences.

1238. Myrland, E. H. *War, Women & Wine*. Winona, Minn.: Apollo Books, 1985. 218pp., illustrated.

Autobiography, with text and numerous letters relating to Myrland's service as a lieutenant attached to the Army Intelligence School at Langres, France, and as an escort for German prisoners.

1239. Nell, John W. *The Lost Battalion: A Private's Story*. San Antonio, Tex.: The Historical Publishing Network, 2001. Edited by Ron Lammert. 124pp., illustrated.

Memoir, heavily rewritten by Lammert, September 1917–January 1919. Nell was an enlisted man in the 308th Infantry Regiment, 77th Division, and became one of the few survivors of the famed Lost Battalion. A gripping account, originally written in the 1930s and strongly antiwar.

1240. Nelson, David Theodore. *Letters and Diaries of David T. Nelson, 1914–1919*. Waukon, Iowa: J.P. Nelson, 1996. 189pp., illustrated.

Letters, September 1914–July 1919. Best on Nelson's service with the Belgian Relief Commission in 1914–1915 and his service with A.F.S. ambulance section No. 1 from December 1915 to May 1916. Nelson entered the U.S. Army in April 1917 and worked in military intelligence. Though skeptical at first of anti-German propaganda, Nelson became pro-Allied.

1241. Nichols, Alan H. *Letters Home from the Lafayette Flying Corps.* Edited by Nancy Nichols. San Francisco: J.D. Huff, 1993. 296pp., illustrated.

Letters, February 1917–May 1918. Nichols was an ambulance driver with S.S.U. 14 of the A.F.S. until July 1917, when he left for aviation training and eventual service as a lieutenant flying Nieuports with French Escadrilles Spad 98 and 85. He was shot down and killed in June 1918.

1242. Noble, Carl. *Jugheads Behind the Lines.* Edited by Grace Stone Coates. Caldwell, Idaho: The Caxton Printers, 1938. 208pp., illustrated.

Memoir, September 1917–August 1919. Uneventful memoir of a wagoner in a supply company of the 60th Infantry Regiment, 5th Division.

1243. O'Brian, Alice Lord. *No Glory; Letters from France, 1917–1919.* Buffalo, N.Y.: Airport Publishers, 1936. 184pp., illustrated.

Letters, September 1917–March 1919. Letters of a Red Cross nurse at St. Germain-des-Fossés, presented "to convince a careless generation of the futility of war" despite being unrelentingly peppy and cheerful.

1244. O'Brien, Howard Vincent. *Wine, Women and War: A Diary of Disillusionment.* New York: J.H. Sears & Company, 1926. 321pp.

The author, an American gunner, was kept against his will in various jobs behind the lines, including censorship and counterespionage. Very critical of Americans, especially officers.

1245. Oechsner, John G. *Kaiser Bill: An Autobiography of El Pasoan John Oechsner, Machinist, Soldier, Aviation Pioneer.* Edited by Erwin H. Koehler. Fort Bliss, Tex.: U.S. Army Noncommissioned Officer Museum Association, 1984. 162pp., illustrated.

Autobiography retold by Koehler. Uneventful story of a machinist sergeant in the 351st Aero Service Squadron.

1246. Ogburn, Milton. *Wings of World War I; My First 26 Years.* New York: Exposition Press, 1970. 117pp.

Autobiography, most on World War I. The author enlisted in the air service in February 1918 and spent most of his time in support units in the United States. Not very interesting.

1247. Olsmith, Vernon G. *Recollections of an Old Soldier.* San Antonio,

Tex.: Privately printed, 1963. 313pp.

Autobiography, with about 45pp. on World War I, when he served as a captain in the 6th Infantry Regiment, 5th Division, and, from the end of August 1918, as a major in the 128th Infantry Regiment, 32nd Division. Olsmith saw fighting at Juvigny and the Argonne.

1248. Page, L. Rodman. *War Without Fighting: Being the Experiences of L. Rodman Page, Jr. on the Mexican Border and in the World War Against Germany*. New York: Derrydale Press, 1928. 59pp.

Rare book, mostly about campaigns against Pancho Villa.

1249. Paikowski, Edward F. *Les Terribles*. Edited by Sylvia Scharmach. New York: Pageant Press, 1967. 86pp., illustrated.

Memoir, May 1917–November 1918. The author was a private in Ambulance Company 125, 32nd Division, and saw fighting at Château-Thierry and the Meuse-Argonne. Short but with good accounts of combat.

1250. Palmer, Frederick. *With My Own Eyes: A Personal Story of Battle Years*. Indianapolis: Bobbs-Merrill, 1933. 396pp.

Autobiography, about 80pp. on World War I, when Palmer was a war correspondent with the British army and saw very little of the front. In 1917–1918 he worked in censorship and propaganda.

1251. Parrish, Fred Louis. *A Yank in the British YMCA in 1917*. Manhattan, Kans.: Aerospace Historian, 1974. 177pp.

Memoir/Diary, April 1917–February 1918. Rough, unremarkable typescript memoir of the author's brief Y.M.C.A. service in Britain.

1252. Parsons, Edwin C. *The Great Adventure: The Story of the Lafayette Escadrille*. Garden City, N.Y.: Doubleday, Doran, 1937. 335pp., illustrated.

A combination memoir and history of the Lafayette Escadrille, roughly 1916–1918. Some good descriptions of combat.

1253. Patch, Joseph Dorst. *A Soldier's War; The First Infantry Division, A.E.F.* Corpus Christi, Tex.: Mission Press, 1966. 171pp., illustrated.

Memoir/unit history, April 1917–November 1918. Professional, detached account of the 26th Infantry Regiment, 1st Division, at Soissons. Patch was a junior officer in his unit.

1254. Peixotto, Ernest. *The American Front.* New York: Charles Scribner's Sons, 1919. 230pp., illustrated by the author.

Memoir, March–December 1918. Peixotto, who was too old to enter active service in the army, was granted a commission as a captain in the engineers in February 1918 and made one of eight official War Department artists. He followed American troops throughout their 1918 battles and the occupation of Germany, and many of his war paintings are reproduced in this unique and interesting book.

1255. Perrin, Edna. *Letters to Her Family, Supplemented by Selections from Her Diary. Her Year of Service with the YMCA, 1918–1919.* Privately printed, 1994. 84pp., illustrated.

Letters/diaries, December 1918–December 1919. Perrin served with the Y.M.C.A. in London until April 1919, then worked in France. Some interesting accounts of wounded soldiers and the travails of England and France in the aftermath of war.

1256. Pershing, John J. *My Experiences in the World War.* New York: Frederick A. Stokes Company, 1931. 2 vols., 400 and 436pp., illustrated.

Memoir, May 1917–November 1918. Standard work on the American army and Pershing's efforts to maintain it as an independent and effective force.

1257. Peterson, Harold H. *With the Indian Army in the Great War 1916–1919; A Personal Narrative.* Privately printed, 1970. 152pp., illustrated.

Memoir, June 1916–1919, of the author's service as a Y.M.C.A. secretary in India, China, Mesopotamia, and Persia. Little on the war itself.

1258. Peterson, Wilbur. *I Went to War.* Marshall, Minn.: The Messenger Press, 1938. 76pp.

Memoir, "a series of word pictures," 1917–1918. Peterson was an enlisted soldier in the 151st Field Artillery, 42nd Division. His later book, *Soldier WWI* (1988), includes *I Went to War* plus a more conventional narrative of his experiences.

1259. Pfennig, Clair M. *All for Heaven, Hell, or Hoboken: The World War I Diary and Letters of Clair M. Pfennig, Flash Ranger, Company D,*

29th Engineers, A.E.F. Edited by Anthony G. Finan. St. Louis: Crimson Shamrock Press, 1998. 243pp., illustrated.

Diary/letters, May 1918–March 1919. Pfennig, a draftee, worked with flash and sound ranging equipment in a unit attached to the 2nd Army. Sketchy diaries, heavily padded by the editor.

1260. Phillips, Claude. *"Dear Mother and Folks at Home": Iowa Farm to Clermont-Ferrand, 1917–1918.* Austin, Tex.: Eclectic Owl Publications, 1987. 265pp., illustrated.

1261. Pickell, James Ralph. *Twenty-Four Days on a Troopship.* Chicago: Rosenbaum Review, 1919. 145pp., illustrated.

Strange story of the events on board a homeward bound troopship in June–July 1919, based on the author's own experiences.

1262. Pickens, J. D. *Two Brothers, One Shell: A Story of World War I.* Morrison Print Co., 1954. 61pp., illustrated.

Memoir, July–October 1918. Author served with 38th Infantry Regiment, 3rd Division, on the Vesle and Meuse-Argonne.

1263. Piper, Edgar Bramwell. *Somewhere Near the War; Being an Authentic and More or Less Diverting Chronicle of the Pilgrimage of Twelve American Journalists to the War Zone, with Some Account of Their Adventures There and Thereabouts.* Portland, Or.: Morning Oregonian, 1919. 141pp.

1264. Pottle, Frederick Albert. *Stretchers; The Story of a Hospital Unit on the Western Front.* New Haven: Yale University Press, 1929. 366pp.

Memoir, November 1917–November 1918. Pottle served as an orderly with Evacuation Hospital No. 8, based at the Collège de Juilly, Seine-et-Marne. Based on Pottle's own letters and diaries as well as those of his comrades, with realistic descriptions of surgery and other hospital work.

1265. Powell, Edward Alexander. *Slanting Lines of Steel.* New York: Macmillan, 1933. 307pp.

Memoir, August 1914–November 1918. Powell was a war correspondent in Belgium during the first months of the war, accompanying the German armies and witnessing the fall of Antwerp. He also witnessed the

Champagne offensive, reported on the Italian front, and served in U.S. military intelligence after 1917. Colorful, readable account.

1266. Putnam, Elizabeth Cabot. *On Duty and Off: Letters of Elizabeth Cabot Putnam: Written in France, May, 1917—September, 1918.* Cambridge, Mass.: Riverside Press, 1919. 222pp.

Letters, May 1917–September 1918. Putnam worked in Red Cross Hospital No. 1 at Neuilly-sur-Seine until September 1917, when she took up secretarial work at U.S. Air Service headquarters in Paris. She joined Base Hospital No. 24 at Limoges in June 1918. Cheerful but interesting and fairly objective.

1267. Pratt, Joseph Hyde. *Diary of Colonel Joseph Hyde Pratt: Commanding 105th Engineers, A.E.F.* Raleigh, N.C.: Edwards & Broughton, 1926. 318pp., foldout maps.

Diary, May 1918–May 1919. Pratt served as major, lieutenant colonel, and colonel of the 105th Engineer Regiment, 30th Division, participating in the St. Miheil and Meuse-Argonne battles. Very detailed but readable diary.

1268. Quermbach, Harry V. *Doughboy!: Experiences in the Great War.* Edited by Q. LaBurn and Nancy Q. Werstein. Quality Books, 1997. 194pp., illustrated.

Memoir, June 1917–February 1919. Mildly interesting of a private on an observation team in the 32nd Division, who saw most of the division's battles in the autumn of 1918 from behind the lines.

1269. Quinn, James E. *Letters to Mam: The Wartime letters of Cpl. James E. Quinn, (1918–1919): with a Newspaper Survey of Events in Canton, Ohio, the United States, and the World.* Edited by Robert D. Quinn. Westlake, Ohio: Hedgewood Press, 1993. 150pp., illustrated.

Letters, January 1918–May 1919. Quinn was drafted into the 329th Infantry Regiment, then served in the headquarters company of the 9th Infantry Regiment, 2nd Division, in France. Heavily censored letters; most of the book is made up of newspaper clippings.

1270. Ranlett, Louis Felix. *Let's Go! The Story of A.S. no. 2448602.* Boston: Houghton Mifflin, 1927. 291pp., illustrated.

Memoir, December 1917–October 1918. Ranlett was a corporal in the

308th Infantry Regiment, 77th Division, until July 1918, when he was commissioned a second lieutenant in the 23rd Infantry Regiment, 2nd Division. Exciting, readable memoir describing fighting from the Aisne-Marne to the Meuse-Argonne, where Ranlett was badly wounded.

1271. Raymond, Anan. *Letters, April, 1917, June, 1919*. Omaha, Nebr.: Privately printed, 1926. 243pp., illustrated.

Letters, April 1917–June 1919. Raymond was a captain in the 349th Infantry Regiment, 88th Division, until May 1918, when he was promoted to major and placed in command of the 3rd Battalion of the regiment. Dense and largely uneventful letters. See also his autobiography, *Not So Long Ago* (1965).

1272. Reece, Robert H. *Night Bombing with the Bedouins*. Boston: Houghton Mifflin, 1919. 99pp., illustrated.

Memoir, 1917–1918. Reece, an American, was a lieutenant in the British "Bedouin" Squadron of Handley-Page bombers. Full of hilarity and colorful characters, but disappointingly short of detail on the bombers or Reece's own experiences.

1273. Reed, David Aiken. *Letters, 1918–1919*. New York: The Knickerbocker Press, 1919. 99pp.

Letters, July 1918–January 1919. Reed was a major with the 311th Field Artillery Regiment, 79th Division. His unit reached the front only in early November 1918 and these letters contain little more than anecdotes of training and life in the rear areas.

1274. Reifsnyder, Henry J. *A Second Class Private in the Great World War*. Philadelphia, 1923. 198pp.

Diary, May 1917–May 1919, of a soldier in the 103rd Engineers.

1275. Rendigs, August A., Jr. *332nd Infantry USA, World War I*. Privately printed, n.d.

A firsthand memoir of service in Italy.

1276. Rendinell, Joseph Edward, and George Pattullo. *One Man's War: The Diary of a Leatherneck*. New York: J.H. Sears, 1928. 177pp.

Memoir, April 1917–February 1919. Rendinell's diaries of service as a corporal in the 6th Marines are put in narrative form by Pattullo.

Rendinell served in Belleau Wood, the Aisne-Marne, and at Mont Blanc, being wounded twice and badly gassed. Quick read; good depiction of a marine's outlook.

1277. Richards, Elmer Eugene. *Chronicles of a Soldier: The 1918 Diary and Letters of Pvt. Elmer Eugene Richards, Company E, 107th Ammunition Train, 32nd Division, American Expeditionary Force.* Edited by Robert Eugene Richards. Privately printed, 1994. 80pp., illustrated.

Diary/letters, August 1917–April 1919. Carefully annotated but scant.

1278. Richards, John Francisco. *War Diary and Letters of John Francisco Richards II, 1917–1918.* Kansas City, Mo.: Lechtman Printing Co., 1925. 184pp., illustrated.

Diary/letters, March 1917–September 1918. Richards joined the 1st Aero Squadron as a lieutenant in January 1918, and was killed in action while flying a Salmson 2A2 observer plane over the Argonne in September 1918. Very good diaries, more detailed than most.

1279. Richardson, Roland W. *An American Pursuit Pilot in France: Roland W. Richardson's Diaries and Letters, 1917–1919.* Edited by Ritchie Thomas and Carl M. Becker. Shippensburg, Pa.: White Mane Publishing, 1994. 198pp., illustrated.

Diary/letters, July 1917–February 1919. Richardson was a first lieutenant in the 213th Aero Squadron, 3rd Pursuit Group. He flew a Nieuport 27 and Sopwith Camel in training, among other planes, and a Spad XIII over the lines from August 1918. Richardson saw little combat, but the book is a useful guide to the daily routine of life in the air service.

1280. Rickenbacker, Eddie. *Fighting the Flying Circus.* New York: Frederick A. Stokes, 1919. 371pp., illustrated.

Classic memoir of Rickenbacker's service with the 94th Aero Squadron, with which he scored 26 victories.

1281. Rideout, Percy A. *Dear Heart: A Diary Letter, 1917–1918.* Concord, Mass.: Privately printed, 1965. 74pp.

Letters written in diary form, September 1917–October 1918. Rideout enlisted in the 101st Engineers, 26th Division in August 1917, and became a lieutenant early the following year. He transferred to the 1st Gas Regiment in May 1918 and was killed in action that October. More revealing in many respects than William L. Langer's book on the same unit; deserves republication.

1282. Ridout, George W. *The Cross and Flag: Experiences in the Great World War*. Louisville, Ky.: Pentecostal Pub. Co., 1919. 178pp.

Memoir, April 1917–May 1919. Ridout, a Methodist minister, joined the Y.M.C.A. at the declaration of war and then continued as a chaplain in the 38th Infantry Regiment, 3rd Division. Patriotic and religious, but with realistic depictions of war, especially at the Aisne-Marne in the summer of 1918.

1283. Riegelman, Harold. *War Notes of a Casual*. New York: Privately printed, 1931. 191pp.

Diary, January–November 1918. In February 1918 the author was detailed to the staff as Assistant War Risk Officer in charge of insurance, and in July he transferred to the Chemical Warfare Service with the headquarters of the 28th Division. He eventually became gas officer of the 3rd Battalion, 109th Infantry Regiment, and in September was made Assistant Corps Gas Officer of the 5th Corps. Some interesting details on gas warfare research.

1284. Riordan, John J. *Horses, Mules, and Remounts: The Memoirs of a World War I Veterinary Officer*. Edited by John F. Riordan. Glendale, Calif.: J.F. Riordan, 1983. 115pp., illustrated.

Memoir, April 1917–September 1919. Riordan, a lieutenant in the Veterinary Reserve Corps, served until the end of the war with Veterinary Hospital No. 5 at St. Nazaire, and with the 4th Corps Mobile Veterinary Hospital at Toul, despite his efforts to gain a transfer to aviation. He gives almost no information on his actual work at the hospital.

1285. Rizzi, Joseph N. *Joe's War: Memoirs of a Doughboy*. Huntington, W. Va.: Der Angriff Publications, 1983. 144pp., illustrated.

The author served in the 110th Engineers, 35th Division.

1286. Rockwell, Kiffin Yates, ed. Paul Rockwell. *War Letters of Kiffin Yates Rockwell, Foreign Legionnaire and Aviator, France, 1914–1916*. Garden City, N.Y.: The Country Life Press, 1925. 202pp.

Rockwell joined the Lafayette Escadrille in April 1916 and was killed that September.

1287. Roderick, Mary Louise Rochester. *A Nightingale in the Trenches*. New York: Vantage Press, 1966. 289pp., illustrated.

Diary, February 1918–October 1920. Roderick joined the Y.M.C.A. to sing for American troops throughout France.

1288. Rodman, Hugh. *Yarns of a Kentucky Admiral*. Indianapolis: Bobbs-Merrill, 1928. 320pp.

Autobiography, with 2 chapters on World War I, when Rodman was admiral of a division of battleships that worked with the British Grand Fleet in the North Sea, 1917–1918. Anecdotal, but useful administrative account.

1289. Rogers, Alden. *The Hard White Road: A Chronicle of the Reserve Mallet*. Buffalo: Privately printed, 1923. 113pp., illustrated.

Memoir, June 1917–June 1919. Good illustrations, but otherwise unremarkable memoir of the exploits of a motorized ammunition train.

1290. Rogers, Bogart. *A Yankee Ace in the RAF: The World War I Letters of Captain Bogart Rogers*. Lawrence: University Press of Kansas, 1996. Edited by John H. Morrow, Jr., and Earl Rogers. 264pp., illustrated.

Letters, August 1917–April 1919. Rogers trained for the R.F.C. in Canada, Texas, and England on the Curtiss JN-4 Jenny and Avro 504, entering the war in May 1918 as a first lieutenant in the 32nd Squadron of the R.A.F. and flying an SE-5. Rogers's letters, all to his girlfriend, were naturally censored but contain a surprising amount of information and good accounts of air combat. He was promoted to captain and awarded the Distinguished Flying Cross after the end of the war.

1291. Rogers, Horatio. *The Diary of an Artillery Scout*. North Andover, Mass.: Horatio Rogers, 1975. 268pp., illustrated. Also published as *World War I Through My Sights*.

Memoir, July 1917–April 1919. Rogers was a corporal in the 101st Field Artillery, 26th Division. Very well written, one of the best American accounts, documenting how men became increasingly "fed up" with the war after service at the Aisne-Marne and St. Mihiel.

1292. Rogers, Randolph. *Pour le Droit*. Ann Arbor, Mich.: G. Wahr, 1919. 103pp., illustrated.

1293. Rohrbough, Fred W. *A Soldier Remembers That War Was Declared.* New Orleans: Harvey Press, 1978. 67pp., illustrated.

Memoir, April 1917–August 1919. Ostensibly a private in the 497th Aero Squadron, the author actually spent the war driving trucks to and from the front lines. In 1919 he served as a liaison officer in the American Red Cross.

1294. Romedahl, Joe. *An Iowa Soldier in World War I.* Edited by Mildred Romedahl Steele. Boone, Iowa: JRS/MRS Enterprises, 1993. 136pp., illustrated.

Memoir, April 1917–June 1919. Romedahl was drafted a private in the 129th Infantry Regiment, 33rd Division, and was wounded during the Meuse-Argonne offensive. Clumsily printed but with some interesting reminiscences and useful appendixes.

1295. Romeo, Giuseppe. *Diary of Pvt. Giuseppe Romeo.* Tacoma: T.V. Copeland & Son, 1919. 70pp., illustrated. Also printed in shorter, unedited version at 38pp.

Diary, October 1917–May 1919. Basic diary of an Italian immigrant who was drafted in October 1917 and promptly became a discipline problem. Little on the front lines except the first days of the Meuse-Argonne.

1296. Roosevelt, Kermit. *War in the Garden of Eden.* New York: Charles Scribner's Sons, 1919. 253pp., illustrated.

Memoir, approximately spring 1917–January 1919. Roosevelt served with the British on the Mesopotamian front, commanding Ford tender vans attached to the 14th Battery of Rolls-Royce armored cars, Motor Machine Gun Corps. In the summer of 1918 he joined the U.S. Army as captain of C Battery, 7th Field Artillery attached to the 1st Division. Interesting on Mesopotamia; no account of fighting in France, but recounts occupation of Germany.

1297. Roosevelt, Quentin. *Quentin Roosevelt; A Sketch with Letters.* Edited by Kermit Roosevelt. New York: Charles Scribner's Sons, 1921. 282pp., illustrated.

Letters, February 1917–July 1918. The author, son of former president Theodore Roosevelt, joined the 95th Aero Squadron and was shot down and killed in July 1918. This book contains mostly tributes by others, though some of Quentin's own letters are interesting.

1298. Rose, Harold W. *Brittany Patrol: The Story of the Suicide Fleet.* New York: W.W. Norton, 1937. 367pp., illustrated.

Memoir, July 1917–December 1918. The author served as a wireless operator on the yacht *Emeline*, part of an anti-submarine patrol operating from Brittany. He was promoted ensign and transferred to the destroyer *Wadsworth* in September 1918. Well written, more exciting than most World War I naval memoirs.

1299. Ross, Warner Anthony. *My Colored Battalion.* Chicago: Warner A. Ross, 1920. 119pp.

Memoir, originally a speech given to veterans, August 1917–March 1919. Ross was a white officer, serving as captain and major of the 365th Infantry Regiment, 92nd Division. Ross describes his own experiences while praising the bravery of his troops in their engagements in 1918. Slightly overdramatized but worthwhile.

1300. Ross, William O., and Duke L. Slaughter. *With the 351st in France.* Baltimore: Afro-American Company, 1923. 49pp., illustrated.

Diary, June 1918–February 1919. Apparently combined from the diaries of both officers; rare account of an African American unit.

1301. Rounds, Ona Mahitta. *Buck Privates on Parnassus.* Boston: Meador, 1933. 217pp., illustrated.

Memoir, 1917–June 1919. Bubbly tale of a woman working in a Y.M.C.A. camp library at Châtillon-sur-Seine.

1302. Rowe, Josiah P., Jr. *Letters from a World War I Aviator.* Edited by Genevieve Bailey Rowe and Diana Rowe Doran. Boston: Sinclaire Press, 1986. 151pp., illustrated.

Letters, October 1917–December 1918. Rowe trained in Foggia, Italy, and was commissioned a second lieutenant in May 1918, joining the 147th Aero Squadron, First Pursuit Group, in Rembercourt, France. Flying a Spad XIII, Rowe saw little action and the letters are unexceptional; but excellent photographs.

1303. Russel, William Muir. *A Happy Warrior: Letters of William Muir Russel, an American Aviator in the Great War, 1917–1918.* Detroit,

Mich.: Saturday Night Press, 1919. 212pp., illustrated.

Letters, April 1917–August 1918. Lieutenant Russel flew a Spad XIII with the 95th Aero Squadron and was killed in action in August 1918, a month after reaching the front. Almost all of his letters describe training.

1304. Saxe, Marvin Stowe. *An Old Veteran Reminisces*. Somerville, N.J.: Somerset Press, 1978. 142pp., illustrated.

Memoir, April 1917–1919. Saxe served in U.S.A.A.S. section 592, driving Fords and Fiats in the Vosges, until February 1918, when he became a private in the 304th Brigade, Tank Corps, or 1st Tank Brigade. Saxe stayed at headquarters and did not actually serve in the tanks, but he has some interesting memories of Patton and how tanks fought at St. Mihiel and the Meuse-Argonne.

1305. Schellberg, William. *Your Brother Will: The Great War Letters and Diary of William Schellberg, Machine Gun Company, 313th Infantry, "Baltimore's Own," 157th Brigade, 79th Division*. Edited by Jerry Harlowe. Ellicott City, Md.: Patapsco Falls Press, 1992. 193pp., illustrated.

Letters/diary, October 1917–June 1919. Heavily padded by the editor. Some diary entries are worth perusing; most are fairly routine.

1306. Schiani, Alfred. *A Former Marine Tells it Like it Was, and Is*. New York: Carlton Press, 1988. 64pp.

Autobiography, mostly on 1917–1918. Schiani, a Brooklyn Italian, rushes at breakneck speed through his experiences as an enlisted man in the 5th Marines, 2nd Division. He was wounded and won both the Distinguished Service Cross and the Navy Cross.

1307. Schierholt, William J. *Diary of William J. Schierholt in World War I*. Manhattan, Kans.: Military Affairs/Aerospace Historian Pub., 1978. 17pp.

Diary/memoir, March 1918–August 1919. Rough transcript of the memories of a soldier in an unnamed unit; not annotated and therefore confusing.

1308. Schultze, Walter H. *Captain Walter H. Schultze: The Peace Messenger*. Chicago: Rodgers & Co., 1925. 102pp., illustrated.

Memorial book with a few letters. Schultze, a captain in the 138th

Aero Squadron, was killed when his Spad crashed in June 1919.

1309. Scudder, Robert Author. *My Experience in the World War*. Dover, N.J.: R.A. Scudder, 1921. 143pp., illustrated.

1310. Scully, Charles Alison. *The Course of the Silver Greyhound*. New York: G.P. Putnam's Sons, 1936. 93pp.

Memoir, March–June 1919. Describes the author's experiences in the Courier Service, or the Postal Express Service of the A.E.F., in eastern Europe.

1311. Searcy, Earl B. *Looking Back*. Springfield, Ill.: The Journal Press, 1921. 161pp.

Memoir, April 1918–March 1919. Searcy was a private in the 311th Infantry Regiment, 78th Division. Very good memoir, with extended reminiscences of St. Mihiel and the Argonne.

1312. Sears, Herbert Mason. *Journal of a Canteen Worker: A Record of Service with the American Red Cross in Flanders*. Boston: Marymount Press, 1919. 213pp., illustrated.

Diary, August 1917–April 1918. Careful observations on the war, as much as Sears could see of it from well behind the lines.

Secor, Lella. *See* Florence, Lella Secor.

1313. Seibert, Raymond Smith. *Raymond Smith Seibert, M.D., F.A.C.S.: His Autobiography and Some Poems, Plus His Seibert Ancestry: Born August 31, 1883, Harrisburg, Pa., Physician and Surgeon, Died February 23, 1931, Trenton, N.J.: Captain, Medical Corps, France, June 27 to December 18, 1918*. Coralville, Iowa: R.M. Bell, 1996. 40pp.

Autobiography, very roughly printed, with a short section on the author's experiences as a surgeon attached to the 113th Infantry Regiment, 29th Division.

1314. Sergeant, Elizabeth Shepley. *Shadow-Shapes: The Journal of a Wounded Woman, October 1918–May 1919*. Boston: Houghton Mifflin, 1920. 237pp.

Memoir in diary form. The author, war correspondent for the *New Republic*, was badly wounded by the explosion of a piece of ordnance while visiting old battlefields near Rheims shortly before the end of the war. She describes her extended convalescence in a Paris hospital, witnessing the suffering of wounded soldiers and the lives of civilians with thoughtfulness and sensitivity.

1315. Shaffer, Walter. *Exploding Flying Myths.* Atlanta: Williams Printing Co., 1968. 89pp., illustrated.

Autobiography, part on World War I, when Shaffer flew in French Escadrilles 94 and 156, and Spad 38, shooting down one plane and one balloon before being downed and captured by the Germans.

1316. Shainwald, Richard H. *Letters and Notes From France, June 30, 1917–November 6, 1918.* San Francisco: Abbott Press, 1919. 69pp.

1317. Shanks, David C. *As They Passed Through the Port.* Washington, D.C.: Cary Publishing Company, 1927. 351pp., illustrated.

Memoir, July 1917–July 1920. Major General Shanks was commander of the Port of Embarkation at Hoboken, New Jersey, and briefly led the 16th Division at the end of the war. This heavily anecdotal memoir describes the departure and return of the Doughboys along with Shanks's own administrative duties.

1318. Sheely, Irving Edward. *Sailor of the Air: The 1917–1919 Letters & Diary of USN CMM/A Irving Edward Sheely.* Edited by Lawrence D. Sheely. Tuscaloosa: University of Alabama Press, 1993. 221pp., illustrated.

Letters/diary, March 1917–January 1919. Sheely served with the Navy's First Aeronautical Detachment as a petty officer, flying a variety of aircraft on patrol missions including Farman, Nieuport, B.E. 2, and a Curtiss flying boat. He also served combat missions with R.A.F. No. 202 and No. 218 Reconnaissance Squadrons, flying as an observer in D.H. 4 and D.H. 9 aircraft. Cryptic diary but good letters and annotation as well as an interesting reproduction of Sheely's training notebook.

1319. Sherwood, Elmer W. *Diary of a Rainbow Veteran.* Terre Haute, Ind.: Moore-Langen, 1929. 217pp. Also printed as *Rainbow Hoosier.*

Diary, July–November 1918 of 122 days in the 150th Field Artillery at Château-Thierry, St. Mihiel, and the Argonne.

1320. Shillinglaw, David Lee. *An American in the Army and YMCA, 1917–1920: The Diary of David Lee Shillinglaw*. Privately published, 1971. 219pp., illustrated.

Diary with letters and author's commentary, July 1917–January 1920. Shillinglaw served as head of the Y.M.C.A. Construction Department until August 1918, when he joined the Corps of Engineers, being commissioned a second lieutenant and working in a succession of administrative positions. In January 1919 he returned to the Y.M.C.A. in the Salvage Department. Of administrative interest only.

1321. Shortall, Katherine. *A "Y" Girl in France*. Boston: Richard G. Badger, 1919. 80pp.

The amusing if somewhat cloying letters of a young woman from Chicago who volunteered to serve in one of the Y.W.C.A. organizations tending to American soldiers in France. Ms. Shortall arrived in France in early 1919, after the war had ended; but as a witness of the impatient American troops waiting to be demobilized and a visitor to the battlefields in the Argonne and Verdun immediately after the close of the war, her letters belong in this bibliography. There is an interesting vignette on race relations between white and black soldiers in the U.S. Army.

1322. Sims, William Sowden. *The Victory at Sea*. Garden City, N.Y.: Doubleday, Page, 1920. 410pp., illustrated.

Memoir, March 1917–November 1918. Rear Admiral Sims commanded U.S. naval forces in European waters during the war; his memoir includes useful information on submarine fighting and transporting the American troops overseas.

1323. Sirmon, W. A. *That's War: An Authentic Diary*. Atlanta: The Linmon Company, 1929. 277pp., illustrated.

Diary, January–November 1918. Sirmon, a first lieutenant who was promoted to captain near the end of the war, served for several months as an aide to Brigadier General Marcus D. Cronin of the 163rd Infantry Brigade, 82nd Division. In August 1918 Sirmon left Cronin in disgust and joined the 325th Regiment of the same brigade. Sirmon won a D.S.C. on patrol, fought and was gassed in the Argonne Forest. Very patriotic in tone.

1324. Smart, Lawrence. *The Hawks that Guided the Guns*. Privately printed, 1968. 70pp., illustrated.

Memoir, April 1917–November 1918. Smart went into action in August 1918 as a lieutenant and eventually flight commander in the 135th Aero Squadron, flying D.H.4 aircraft. Good account, well illustrated.

1325. Smith, Dean C. *By the Seat of My Pants*. Boston: Little, Brown, 1961. 245pp.

Autobiography, part on World War I, when Smith enlisted at age sixteen and served in the 125th Aero Squadron. He trained in a Jenny but never left the United States.

1326. Smith, Harry L., and James R. Eckman. *Memoirs of an Ambulance Company Officer*. Rochester, Minn.: Doomsday Press, 1940. 226pp., illustrated.

Memoir, April 1917–August 1919. Smith, a doctor, served in ambulance company No. 21 of the 4th Division at the Aisne-Marne, St. Mihiel, and Meuse-Argonne. Written to discourage entry into World War II.

1327. Snively, Harry Hamilton. *The Battle of the Non-Combatants; The Letters of Dr. Harry Hamilton Snively to His Family from Russia, Poland, France, Belgium, Persia, etc., Assembled by His Daughter, Marjorie Knowton Snively*. New York: The Business Bourse, 1933. 252pp.

1328. Snow, William J. *Signposts of Experience: World War Memoirs*. Washington, D.C.: U.S. Field Artillery Association, 1941. 317pp., illustrated.

Memoir, February–November 1918. Brigadier General Snow was appointed Chief of Field Artillery in February 1918. Highly technical but invaluable look at the organization of the U.S. Artillery.

1329. Speakman, Harold. *From a Soldier's Heart*. New York: The Abington Press, 1919. 163pp., illustrated.

Memoir, approximately spring 1918–spring 1919. Author was a first lieutenant in the 332nd Infantry Regiment, 83rd Division. Impressionistic, uneventful memoir of American troops in Italy in 1918 who found themselves in the middle of a revolution in Montenegro after the end of the war.

1330. Speakman, Marie Anna Vuilleumier. *Memories*. Wilmington, Del.: Greenwood Bookshop, 1937. 191pp., illustrated.

Memoir, June 1915–November 1918. The experiences of Mrs. Speakman, who served on the War Relief Committee, combined with letters and diary entries of her husband, Dr. William Cyrus Speakman, a dentist with the American Ambulance at Neuilly and other hospitals.

1331. Speranza, Gino Charles. *The Diary of Gino Speranza, Italy, 1915–1919*. New York: AMS Press, 1941. 2 volumes, 406 and 336pp., illustrated.

The author was a war correspondent in Italy from 1915 until April 1917, when he took up work with the U.S. Embassy in Rome. Useful for research in Italian wartime politics and society.

1332. Spitz, Leon. *The Memoirs of a Camp Rabbi*. New York: Bloch Pub. Co., 1927. 44pp., illustrated.

1333. Spring, Harry. *An Engineer's Diary of the War*. Edited by Terry M. Bareither. West Lafayette, Ind.: Purdue University Press, 2002. 259pp., illustrated.

Diary, September 1917–April 1919. Spring was a second lieutenant in F Company of the 37th Engineer Regiment, which served in support of various divisions during the Meuse-Argonne offensive. Most of the diary deals with activities behind the lines, but it is an interesting and useful record of work done by the engineers. Well annotated.

Springs, Elliott White. *See*: Grider, John MacGavock.

1334. Stamas, Christ K. *The Road to St. Mihiel*. New York: Comet Press Books, 1957. 95pp.

1335. Stansbury, Henry D. *Maryland's 117th Trench Mortar Battery in the World War, 1917–1919*. Baltimore: Maryland Chapter Rainbow Division Veterans, 1942. 142pp., illustrated.

This unit history, covering April 1917–April 1919, has enough of a personal touch to merit inclusion here. The 117th was attached to the 42nd Division, participating in all of that unit's engagements from the Champagne to the Argonne. Stansbury records the uglier side of war and bombardments with gritty realism; good illustrations too.

1336. Stearns, Gustav. *From Army Camps and Battle-Fields.* Minneapolis, Minn.: Augsburg Publishing House, 1919. 281pp., illustrated.

Letters, December 1917–March 1919. Stearns was chaplain of the 127th Infantry Regiment, 32nd Division. Good illustrations, and some interesting letters on the Aisne-Marne and subsequent engagements.

1337. Stephens, D. Owen. *With Quakers in France.* London: C.W. Daniel, 1921. 336pp., illustrated.

Diary, September 1917–March 1919. Thoughtful, inspiring, but non-polemical account of a pacifist serving with the American Friends' Reconstruction Unit, rebuilding destroyed homes in France.

1338. Stevenson, Sarah Sand. *Lamp for a Soldier: The Caring Story of a Nurse in World War I.* Bismarck, N.D.: North Dakota State Nurses' Association, 1976. 112pp., illustrated.

1339. Stewart, Lawrence O. *Rainbow Bright.* Philadelphia: Dorrance, 1923. 145pp., illustrated.

Memoir, autumn 1917–November 1918. Stewart was a member of the sanitary corps of the 168th Infantry Regiment, 42nd Division. Mostly humorous and anecdotal, but with some serious depictions of Château-Thierry, St. Mihiel and the Argonne.

1340. Stewart, Jr., William Galbraith, ed. Robert Cady Gates. *The Ancestry and World War I Letters of William Galbraith Stewart, Jr. (1896–1935) of Wilkinsburg, Allegheny County, Pennsylvania.* Edited by Robert Cody Gates. Springfield, Mo.: R.C. Gates, 1995. 158pp., illustrated.

Biography/letters, November 1917–August 1920. Stewart served aboard Subchaser No. 92, based at Corfu. Mundane, little of interest.

1341. Stone, Ernest. *Battery B Thru the Fires of France.* Los Angeles: Wayside Press, 1919. 242pp.

Memoir, May 1918–January 1919. Stone served in the 2nd Battalion of Anti-Aircraft Artillery, C.A.C., and participated in most major American engagements of the war. Fascinating, detailed, and rare study of an obscure but important service.

1342. Storer, Herbert Stone. *World War I Letters of Lieutenant Herbert*

Stone Storer Thirteenth Field Artillery, Fourth Division American Expeditionary Forces. Edited by Robert L. and Marguerite Storer Redmond. Savannah, Ga.: R.L. and M.S. Redmond, 1993. Unpaginated.

Letters, April 1918–August 1919. Mundane, but with some good letters on St. Mihiel and the Meuse-Argonne.

1343. Straub, Elmer Frank. *A Sergeant's Diary in the World War; The Diary of an Enlisted Member of the 150th Field Artillery (Forty-second <Rainbow> Division) October 27, 1917, to August 7, 1919.* Indianapolis: Indiana Historical Commission, 1923. 356pp., illustrated.

1344. Strickland, Riley. *Adventures of the A.E.F. Soldier.* Austin, Tex.: Von Boeckmann-Jones, 1920. 338pp., illustrated.

Memoir, April 1918–June 1919. Detached account of the author's experiences as an enlisted man in the 315th Engineers, 90th Division, at St. Mihiel and the Meuse-Argonne. Good illustrations.

1345. Stringfellow, John S. *Hell! No! This and That: A Narrative of the Great War.* Boston: Meador Publishing Company, 1936. 362pp., illustrated.

Memoir, April 1917–May 1919. Stringfellow was a captain in the 320th Regiment, 80th Division. His unit was attached to the British army for a few months before joining the U.S. Army in St. Mihiel and Meuse-Argonne. Often anecdotal but honest, with good accounts of training and combat, excellent illustrations.

1346. Sullivan, Vincent F. *With the Yanks in France: A Story of America in France.* New York: V.F. Sullivan, 1921. 137pp.

Memoir, January 1918–May 1919. Sullivan was a wagoner in the 58th Artillery, C.A.C., and participated in the latter stages of the Meuse-Argonne offensive.

1347. Taber, Sydney Richmond. *Arthur Richmond Taber: A Memorial Record Compiled by His Father.* Princeton: Privately printed, 1920. 203pp., illustrated.

Includes war letters dating November 1915–February 1919. The best letters relate to Taber's service as an ambulance driver in S.S.U. 4 from November 1915 to February 1916, after which he returned to the United States. Taber went back to Europe after his country entered the war, trained at Oxford and Issoudun, and then served as a transfer pilot until his accidental death in February 1919.

1348. Tarbot, Jerry. *Jerry Tarbot, the Living Unknown Soldier*. New York: Tyler Publishing Co., 1928. 182pp., illustrated.

Memoir, covering mainly the postwar period. The author claims to have served in the 6th Marine Regiment, 2nd Division, but to have lost his identity through shell shock-induced amnesia before "awaking" in a California hospital in 1923. This book chronicles his attempts to reclaim his identity, and get recognition from the government. Tarbot's story is probably fraudulent.

1349. Taussig, Joseph K. *The Queenstown Patrol, 1917: The Diary of Commander Joseph Knefler Taussig, U.S. Navy*. Edited by William N. Still, Jr. Newport, R.I.: Naval War College Press, 1996. 208pp., illustrated.

Diary, April–November 1917. Commander Taussig was in charge of a division of U.S. destroyers stationed at Queenstown, now Cobh, Ireland. His own ship was the USS *Wadsworth*. This well-annotated diary contains useful information on American anti-submarine tactics and Ireland in wartime.

1350. Taylor, Edgar. *It's a Long Way to Camas Meadows: The Flying Log, Letters, and Diary of Lieutenant Edgar Taylor*. Pocatello: Idaho State University Press, 1976. 155pp., illustrated.

1351. Terriberry, Gladys. *Diary of Gladys Terriberry: American Army Nurse, France, 1918*. New Brunswick, N.J.: David Joseph Riley, 1998. 16pp.

1352. Thompson, Terry Brewster. *Take Her Down, a Submarine Portrait*. New York: Sheridan House, 1937. 317pp.

Memoir, April 1917–1919, of the first executive officer and later commander of the submarine *L-9*. Well-written, readable account of the first halting steps of the U.S. Submarine Service.

1353. Thornton, Floyd. *Letters from Camp, Written in 1917 and 1918*. Pittsburgh, Pa.: Dorrance Publishing, 2001. 152pp.

Letters, May 1917–June 1919. Mundane letters on family affairs and camp life at Camp Perry, Ohio, and the author's service in the 112th Field Signal Battalion. Nothing on front lines.

1354. *Those War Women: By One of Them.* New York: Coward McCann, 1929. 283pp.

Rewritten diary, February–August 1919. Author traveled throughout France as an entertainer for the demobilizing A.E.F. Her diary is rewritten as a social document and is probably semi-fictional.

1355. Tippett, Edwin James, Jr. *Who Won the War?: Letters and Notes of an M.P. in Dixie, England, France and Flanders.* Toledo, Ohio: Toledo Type-Setting & Printing Co., 1920. 237pp., illustrated.

Memoir/diary, July 1917–April 1919. Tippett was a corporal in the 112th Military Police, 37th Division. Uncommon look at the war from a member of the much-despised military police; very good at describing a typical M.P.'s daily duties and attitude toward his critics.

1356. Todd, Robert M. *Sopwith Camel Fighter Ace.* Falls Church, Va.: AJAY Enterprises, 1978. 112pp., illustrated.

Memoir, April 1917–November 1918. Todd enlisted in August 1917 and became a second lieutenant in the 17th Aero Squadron, flying Sopwith Camels. He was shot down and captured in August 1918 after becoming an ace. Includes Todd's letters.

1357. Townsend, Harry Everett. *War Diary of a Combat Artist.* Edited by Alfred E. Cornebise. Boulder: University of Colorado Press, 1991. 284pp., illustrated.

Diary, 1918, of one of the United States' eight official combat artists. Includes excellent illustrations.

1358. Triplet, William S. *A Youth in the Meuse-Argonne: A Memoir, 1917–1918.* Edited by Robert H. Ferrell. Columbia: University of Missouri Press, 2000. 326pp., illustrated.

Memoir, 1917–1919, of a sergeant in the 140th Infantry Regiment, 35th Division, describing his experiences in most of the major battles of 1918, especially the Meuse-Argonne. Extraordinarily vivid and readable accounts of combat and how the soldiers dealt with it physically and psychologically. Highly recommended.

1359. Trowbridge, Augustus. *War Letters of Augustus Trowbridge, August 28, 1917, to January 19, 1919*. New York: The New York Public Library, 1940. 152pp.

Trowbridge, a major and lieutenant colonel of engineers, served on the general staff and organized the Sound and Flash Ranging services of the A.E.F. His letters to his wife are extensive but, unsurprisingly, lack technical detail.

1360. Trueblood, Edward Alva. *Observations of an American Soldier During His Service with the A.E.F. in France, in the Flash Ranging Service*. Sacramento, Calif.: The News Publishing Co., 1919. 78pp., illustrated.

Memoir, June 1918–February 1919. Trueblood, a private in the 29th Engineers, participated in the St. Mihiel offensive before being gassed, wounded, and evacuated. Good description of his brief front-line service.

1361. Tunney, Thomas J., and Paul Merrick Hollister. *Throttled! The Detection of the German and Anarchist Bomb Plotters*. Boston: Small, Maynard and Company, 1919. 277pp., illustrated.

Memoir, 1914–1918. Inspector Tunney, head of the bomb squad of the New York Police Department, tells how he thwarted German, "Hindu-Boche," anarchist, and other plots in the United States during the war.

1362. Turnure, George Evans. *Flight Log and War Letters*. New York: Whitney Press, 1936. Unpaginated, illustrated.

Letters, February 1917–December 1918. Most of these letters concern Turnure's experiences with French Escadrille Spad 103, the Lafayette Escadrille, and the 103rd Aero Squadron from July 1917 to August 1918. He then became flight commander of the 28th Aero Squadron. Good illustrations and long, interesting letters.

1363. Tuthill, Cuyler Beebe. *The YMCA/World War I Memoirs of Colonel Cuyler Beebe Tuthill*. New York: Y.M.C.A. Historical Library, 1964. 10pp.

Memoir, roughly 1917–1920. Tuthill served with the Y.M.C.A. in Virginia throughout the war; this pamphlet includes just a few of his memories.

1364. Tyler, Elizabeth Stearns. *Letters of Elizabeth Stearns Tyler*.

Norwood, Mass.: The Plimpton Press, 1920. 87pp.

1365. Tyler, John C. *Selections from the Letters and Diary of John Cowperthworth Tyler; from August 1917 to September 1918.* Camden, N.J.: Haddon Craftsmen, 1938. 152pp.

The author served in the 11th Aero Squadron before being killed in September 1918.

1366. Upson, William Hazlett. *Me and Henry and the Artillery.* Garden City, N.Y.: Doubleday, Doran & Co., 1928. 271pp.

Memoir, September 1918–1919. Upson served in an unnamed unit of 155mm guns in the 4th Division at St. Mihiel and the Meuse-Argonne. He swears that "it was a lousy life," but writes a funny and engaging memoir about it.

1367. Van Schaick, John, Jr. *Love That Never Failed: Memories of the World War.* Boston: The Universalist Publishing House, 1933. 279pp.

Memoir, June 1914–April 1919. Dense, anecdotal account of the author's service doing relief work on both sides of the Western Front through the Belgian Relief Commission and the Red Cross Commission. Partly reprinted from articles in the *Christian Leader.*

1368. Vaughn, George A., Jr. *War Flying in France.* Edited by Marvin L. Skelton. Manhattan, Kans.: Military Affairs/Aerospace Historian, 1980. 171pp., illustrated.

Memoir/letters, February 1917–February 1919. Vaughn was the first American to receive the Distinguished Flying Cross as a lieutenant flying an S.E.5A in R.F.C. Squadron No. 84. He went on to become a flight leader in the U.S. 17th Aero Squadron. Clumsily printed, but an invaluable record of one of America's best pilots.

1369. Veil, Charles. *Adventure's a Wench: The Autobiography of Charles Veil as Told to Howard Marsh.* New York: William Morrow, 1934. 340pp., illustrated.

Autobiography, with several chapters on World War I, 1917–1918. Veil flew a Spad XIII with French Escadrille Spad 150 from December 1917 to the end of the war. "I like war," he writes, and describes it and his womanizing at a frenetic pace.

1370. Voska, Emanuel Victor, and Will Irwin. *Spy and Counterspy*. New York: Doubleday, Doran, 1940. 322pp.

Memoir, May 1914–March 1939. Account of the work of Voska and other Czech Americans who countered German espionage in America and worked to undermine the Austro-Hungarian army.

1371. Wallach, Mike. *"Farmer, Have You a Daughter Fair?" A Traveling Salesman Meets the Mamselles from Armentières*. New York: The Vanguard Press, 1929. 231pp.

Memoir, roughly January–November 1918. Wallach was an enlisted man in a unit whose identity is disguised. Despite the title, lighthearted moments of revery and womanizing alternate with gripping depictions of battle in the Aisne-Marne offensive of summer 1918.

1372. Washburn, Slater. *One of the Yankee Division*. Boston: Houghton Mifflin, 1919. 163pp., illustrated.

Memoir, April 1917–August 1918. Washburn was a corporal in the 101st Field Artillery, 26th Division. Readable but largely uneventful except for a brief account of Château-Thierry.

1373. Washburn, Stanley. *On the Russian front in World War I: Memoirs of an American War Correspondent*. New York: R. Speller and Sons, 1982. 332pp., illustrated.

Memoir, August 1914–November 1918. Washburn, an American who worked for the London *Times* as the most prominent war correspondent in Russia, witnessed most of the major battles on the Eastern Front from late 1914 to the end of 1916. He also visited the Verdun battlefields in the spring of 1916. His sometimes astonishing conceit as an armchair strategist detracts from the value of his observations, however.

1374. Watson, Samuel Newell. *Those Paris Years: With the World at the Cross-roads*. New York: Fleming H. Revell Company, 1936. 347pp.

Autobiography, half on World War I, when the author supervised various forms of relief work in France. Tedious.

1375. Wayne, Wallace Alexander. *The Memoirs of Wallace Alexander Wayne*. Lafayette, Calif.: K&K Publications, 1987. 101pp., illustrated.

Autobiography, with a chapter on World War I, when Wayne served as a horseman with the 147th Field Artillery, part of the Army Artillery and the 32nd Division. A few mildly interesting anecdotes.

1376. Werner, Morris Robert. *"Orderly!"* New York: Jonathan Cape & Harrison Smith, 1930. 214pp.

Memoir, spring 1917–January 1919. Author was a private and orderly in a base hospital for British soldiers at Etretat in Normandy. Excellent details on work in a base hospital from an orderly's point of view; gently ironic and antiwar.

1377. West, William Benjamin. *The Fight for the Argonne, Personal Experiences of a "Y" Man*. New York: Abingdon Press, 1919. 124pp., illustrated.

Memoir, 1917–1918. Patriotic and pious account by a preacher with the Y.M.C.A. attached to the 37th Division.

1378. Westbrook, Stillman Foote. *Those Eighteen Months. October 9, 1917—April 8, 1919: from the War Letters of Stillman F. Westbrook*. Hartford, Conn.: Case, Lockwood & Brainard, 1934. 229pp., illustrated.

Letters, with explanatory passages by the author. Westbrook was an officer in the machine gun company of the 104th Infantry Regiment, 26th Division; his letters on the Aisne-Marne and Meuse-Argonne are of interest.

1379. Whitehouse, Arthur George Joseph. *The Fledgling: An Autobiography*. London: Nicholas Vane, 1964. 307pp., illustrated.

Memoir, August 1914–November 1918. Whitehouse, an American born in Britain, enlisted in the 3/1st Northamptonshire Yeomanry in late 1914. Disgusted with ground service, he transferred to the R.F.C., and was eventually commissioned a lieutenant in No. 22 Squadron. He flew various planes, lastly the Sopwith Camel, and scored 16 victories. One of the best American aviation memoirs, readable and always interesting.

1380. Whitehouse, Vira B. *A Year as a Government Agent*. New York: Harper & Brothers, 1920. 316pp., illustrated.

Memoir, November 1917–November 1918. Whitehouse served as director of the Committee on Public Information in Switzerland. Useful perspective on the war of propaganda and secret services in that country.

1381. Wilder, Amos Niven. *Armageddon Revisited: A World War I*

Journal. New Haven: Yale University Press, 1994. 168pp., illustrated.

Memoir, September 1916–November 1918. Amos Wilder, brother of author Thornton Wilder, enlisted in the A.F.S. while a Yale student in September 1916, serving subsequently in S.S.U. 2 in the Argonne, February to May 1917, and S.S.U. 3 on the Salonika front, June to October 1917. In November 1917 he became a private, later corporal in the 17th Field Artillery, 2nd Division. His battery was equipped with 155mm guns and participated in battles at Château-Thierry and Soissons before Wilder was hospitalized due to illness; he worked in headquarters for last two weeks of war. A detached, stiff, and somewhat priggish narrative.

1382. Wilder, Fred Calvin. *War Experiences of F.C. Wilder.* Belchertown, Mass.: Lewis H. Blackmer, 1926. 119pp.

Memoir, May 1917–November 1918. Simply written but good memoir of the author's experiences with the 101st Infantry Regiment, 26th Division, at Soissons, Château-Thierry, and St. Mihiel.

1383. Wilgus, William. *Transporting the A.E.F. in Western Europe, 1917–1919.* New York: Columbia University Press, 1931. 612pp.

An important work on one of the weakest links of the A.E.F.

1384. Williams, Ashby. *Experiences of the Great War; Artois, St. Mihiel, Meuse-Argonne.* Roanoke, Va.: Stone Printing and Manufacturing, 1919. 197pp.

Memoir, May 1918–June 1919. Williams was a lieutenant colonel in the 320th Infantry Regiment, 80th Division, and served in British sectors as well as in those given in the title. Meticulously detailed, readable as both unit history and memoir.

1385. Williams, John Francis II. *Experiences in the Great War.* Pacific Beach, Calif.: Privately printed, 1975. 69pp.

Memoir, May 1918–January 1919. Williams was a lieutenant in the 120th Infantry Regiment, 30th Division, which fought alongside the British in Flanders. Williams saw a great deal of fighting, and he describes it colorfully in this account originally written in 1919.

1386. Williams, Ralph L. *The Luck of a Buck.* Madison, Wis.: Fitchburg Press, 1985. 184pp.

Memoir, April 1917–1919. Williams was a private in the 2nd Engineers, 2nd Division, and experienced heavy fighting at Château-Thierry, the Aisne-Marne, St. Mihiel, and the Argonne. Gassed and badly wounded, he suffered the aftereffects, including nightmares, for years after the war. A disturbing memoir that richly deserves a wider printing.

1387. Winant, Cornelius. *A Soldier's Manuscript*. Boston: D.B. Updike, The Merrymount Press, 1929. 141pp.

Memoir, June 1916–November 1918. Despite having a heart defect, Winant drove an ambulance for S.S.U. 3 of the A.F.S. in France and Salonika in 1916–17, joined the French 236th Field Artillery in January 1918, helped to stem the March offensive, was captured by the Germans in June, and escaped to Holland in September. Very interesting account of the war from an unconventional perspective.

1388. Winn, Hiram W. *Fighting the Hun on the U.S.S. Huntington*. Privately printed, 1919. 126pp., illustrated.

Memoir, April 1917–January 1919. Winn served as a blacksmith first class on his ship, a cruiser, as it escorted convoys and hunted submarines in the Atlantic. Upbeat, well illustrated, and uneventful.

1389. Winter, James E. *Memoirs of James E. Winter, M.D.* Masonic Home Journal, 1970. 84pp.

Autobiography, with one chapter on World War I. Vague memories of the author's service as a private in Base Hospital No. 25.

1390. Winton, David J. *Recollections of the Great War*. Privately printed, 1976. 162pp., illustrated.

1391. Wise, Frederick M., and Meigs O. Frost. *A Marine Tells it to You*. New York: J.H. Sears, 1929. 366pp.

Autobiography, about 150pp. on World War I, when Wise was a lieutenant colonel commanding a battalion of the 5th Marines. He was decorated for his service in Belleau Wood and the Meuse-Argonne. Exciting and readable.

1392. Withington, Alfreda Bosworth. *Mine Eyes Have Seen; A Woman Doctor's Saga*. New York: E.P. Dutton, 1941. 311pp., illustrated.

Autobiography, about 50pp. on World War I, when the author, a pioneering woman physician, served with the Red Cross in France and fought tuberculosis and cared for refugees.

1393. Witt, William Henry. *Here, There, Yonder*. Nashville, Tenn.: W.H. Witt, n.d., apparently 1954. 177pp., illustrated.

Autobiography, with World War I diary and letters dating December 1917–March 1919. Witt was a major in the Vanderbilt University Hospital Unit, which functioned alternately as Base Hospital No. 17 at Dijon and Camp Hospital No. 28 at Nevers. Unexceptional.

1394. Wolfe, S. Herbert. *In Service*. Privately printed, 1922. 107pp.

Memoir, January 1916–April 1919. Wolfe was a captain and major in the Quartermaster Reserve Corps, and also worked with the Treasury Department. Dull administrative account.

1395. Wood, Lambert Alexander. *His Job: Letters Written by a 22-Year-Old Lieutenant in the World War to His Parents and Others in Oregon*. Portland, Oreg.: Metropolitan Press, 1932. 88pp., illustrated.

Letters, October 1917–July 1918. Wood served in the 9th Infantry Regiment, 2nd Division, and was killed in action near Soissons in July 1918. A few of his letters deal with Château-Thierry and the Aisne-Marne.

1396. Woodcock, A. W. W. *Golden Days*. Salisbury, Md.: Privately printed, 1951. 244pp.

Autobiography, about two-thirds on World War I, when Woodcock was a captain of the 115th Infantry Regiment, 29th Division, at the Meuse-Argonne. Mostly anecdotal, with little on combat.

1397. Woodward, Houston. *A Year for France: War Letters of Houston Woodward*. New Haven: Yale Publishing Association, 1919. 196pp., illustrated.

Letters, March 1914–March 1918. Woodward went to France in March 1917 as an ambulance driver in S.S.U. 13. Horrified by what he saw of the land war near Verdun, Woodward began to see the war as "terribly hopeless" and unwinnable; but he transferred to the air service as a corporal in French Escadrille Spad 94. He was shot down and killed in April 1918. Woodward's surprisingly frank letters present an intriguing picture of his changing attitude and tragic end.

1398. Woolley, Knight. *In Retrospect, a Very Personal Memoir*. Privately printed, 1975. 96pp., illustrated.

The author served with the 308th Field Artillery Regiment of the 78th Division.

1399. Wrentmore, Ernest L. *In Spite of Hell: A Factual Story of Incidents that Occurred During World War I, as Experienced by the Youngest Soldier to Have Seen Combat Duty with the American Expeditionary Forces in France, as a Member of the Famous Company I, 60th Infantry, Fifth (Red Diamond) Division*. New York: Greenwich Book Publishers, 1958. 193pp.

1400. Wright, William M. Meuse-Argonne Diary: A Division Commander in World War I. Columbia: University of Missouri Press, 2004.

The author commanded the 89th Division, and eventually the 3rd Army Corps.

1401. Wunderlich, Raymond. *From Trench and Dugout*. Stockton, Calif.: Wunderlich, 1919. 82pp.

1402. Yardley, Herbert O. *The American Black Chamber*. Indianapolis: Bobbs-Merrill, 1931. 375pp., illustrated.

Memoir, 1913–1929. Yardley recounts his founding during the war of the top secret MI-8, or the American Black Chamber, and its subsequent work in code-breaking, cryptography, and espionage until the government closed it down in 1929. The details provided in this book apparently enraged the U.S. Army and alarmed foreign governments.

1403. York, Alvin. *Sergeant York: His Own Life Story and War Diary*. Garden City, N.Y.: Doubleday, Doran and Company, Inc., 1928. 309pp., illustrated.

Classic tale of York's service with the 328th Infantry Regiment, 82nd Division, and his famous exploit on October 8, 1918, that made him the biggest American hero of the war. His excellent diary covers June 1917–May 1919.

1404. Young, Rush Stephenson. *Over the Top with the 80th*. Washington, D.C.: Privately printed, 1933. Unpaginated, illustrated.

Memoir, September 1917–May 1919. Young was a private in the

318th Infantry Regiment, 80th Division. His personal narrative is especially good on the Meuse-Argonne battles. Well illustrated.

1405. Zander, Harry William. *Thirteen Years in Hell.* Boston: Meador Publishing Company, 1933. 307pp., illustrated.

Novelized memoir, 1917–1930, as told by Zander to "Tinkle Bell," who wrote the foreword. Zander was a private in the 4th Engineers, 4th Division, fighting in the Aisne-Marne, St. Mihiel, and Argonne battles before joining in the occupation of Germany. He writes with extreme bitterness about his treatment by employers and the government after returning home to Atlanta, where he had trouble finding a job and was hospitalized from the aftereffects of gas.

Chapter 12

Other

1406. Coppens de Houthulst, Willy. *Days on the Wing, Being the War Memoirs of Major the Chevalier Willy Coppens de Houthulst.* Translated by A.J. Insall. London: John Hamilton, 1934. 291pp., illustrated.

Memoir, August 1914–November 1918. Dry, technical, and finally disappointing memoir, but it provides some useful information on the author's service with the Belgian Flying Corps from 1917 to 1918.

1407. Dyboski, Roman. *Seven Years in Russia and Siberia, 1914–1921.* Translated by Marion Moore Coleman. Cheshire, Conn.: Cherry Hill Books, 1971. 177pp. Polish edition: *Siedem lat w Rosji I na Syberji* (1922).

1408. Fokker, Anthony H. G., and Bruce Gould. *Flying Dutchman: The Life of Anthony Fokker.* London: G. Routledge, 1931. 302pp., illustrated.

Memoir of the Dutch aircraft designer who built some of the best German airplanes of the war.

1409. Górecki, Roman. *Under the Shadow of Death: Reminiscences of Experiences in 1918.* Warsaw: 1933. 70pp.

Memoir, February–November 1918. Brief memoir of a brigadier general in the budding Polish army of 1918.

1410. McKenna, Marthe Cnockaert. *I Was a Spy*! London: Jarrolds, 1932. 288pp., illustrated.

Memoir, August 1914–November 1918. Romantic account of a Belgian woman who became a spy for the Allies. Lurid tales of German atrocities, complete with babies on bayonets.

1411. Mimovic, Ilija Miletin. *Blackbirds' Field.* New York: R.D. Henkle,

1934. 319pp.

Practically the only Serbian account of the war published in English.

1412. Pirenne, Henri. *The Journal de Guerre of Henri Pirenne*. Amsterdam: North-Holland, 1976. 202pp., illustrated.

Account of a Belgian prisoner of war in Germany.

Appendix:

List of Notable and Recommended Books

(References are to entry numbers)

Adamson, Agar. *Letters of Agar Adamson, 1914 to 1919, Lieutenant Colonel, Princess Patricia's Canadian Light Infantry*: 199.

Aitken, Alexander. *Gallipoli to the Somme: Recollections of a New Zealand Infantryman*: 3.

Allen, Hervey. *Toward the Flame: A War Diary*: 986.

Archibald, Norman. *Heaven High, Hell Deep, 1917–1918*: 990.

Ashurst, George. *My Bit: A Lancashire Fusilier at War, 1914–1918*: 364

Baker, C. Earl. *Doughboy's Diary*: 993.

Barber, Thomas H. *Along the Road*: 997.

Barkley, John Lewis. *No Hard Feelings!*: 999.

Bartley, Albert Lea. *Tales of the World War*: 1001.

Bean, C. E. W. *Gallipoli Correspondent: The Frontline Diary of C. E. W. Bean*: 8.

Biddle, Charles John. *The Way of the Eagle*: 1004.

Bird, Will R. *Ghosts Have Warm Hands: A Memoir of the Great War, 1916–1919*: 206.

Blunden, Edmund. *Undertones of War*: 403.

Boyd, Donald. *Salute of Guns*: 410.

Brereton, Cyprian Bridge. *Tales of Three Campaigns*: 13.

Brittain, Vera. *Testament of Youth: An Autobiographical Study of the Years 1900–1925*: 414.

Brooks, Alden. *As I Saw It*: 1017.

Campbell, Patrick James. *The Ebb and Flow of Battle*: 439.

Carrington, Charles [pseud. Charles Edmonds]. *A Subaltern's War: Being a Memoir of the Great War from the Point of View of a Romantic Young Man, with Candid Accounts of Two Particular Battles, Written Shortly After They Occurred, and an Essay on Militarism*: 444.

Chandler, Les G. *Dear Homefolks: Letters Written by L. G. Chandler During the First World War*: 20.

Chapman, Guy. *A Passionate Prodigality: Fragments of Autobiography*: 452.

Clapham, H. S. *Mud and Khaki: The Memories of an Incomplete Soldier*: 454.

Congreve, Billy. *Armageddon Road: A VC's Diary, 1914–16*: 467.

Corbett, Elsie. *Red Cross in Serbia, 1915–1919; A Personal Diary of Experiences*: 473.

Cushing, Harvey. *From a Surgeon's Journal, 1915–1918*: 1065.

Desagneaux, Henri. *A French Soldier's War Diary, 1914–1918*: 281.

Dunham, Frank. *The Long Carry: The Journal of Stretcher Bearer Frank Dunham, 1916–18*: 520.

Emmett, Chris. *Give 'Way to the Right: Serving with the A.E.F. in France During the World War*: 1083.

Farmborough, Florence. *Nurse at the Russian Front: A Diary, 1914–18*: 534.

Feilding, Rowland Charles. *War Letters to a Wife, France and Flanders, 1915–1919*: 537.

Fraser, Donald. *The Journal of Private Fraser, Canadian Expeditionary Force*: 226.

Gibbs, A. Hamilton. *Gun Fodder: The Diary of Four Years of War*: 563.

Glubb, John. *Into Battle: A Soldier's Diary of the Great War*: 571.

Graves, Robert. *Good-bye to All That*: 583.

Gray, John Lyons [pseud. Donald Black]. *Red Dust: An Australian Trooper in Palestine*: 57.

Griffith, Wyn. *Up to Mametz*: 589.

Heinrichs, Waldo Huntley. *First to the Front: The Aerial Adventures of 1st Lt. Waldo Heinrichs and the 95th Aero Squadron, 1917–1918*: 1125.

Heinz, Max. *Loretto, Sketches of a German Volunteer*: 309.

Hickey, Daniel Edgar. *Rolling into Action: Memoirs of a Tank Corps Section Commander*: 629.

Hitchcock, F. C. *Stand To! A Diary of the Trenches, 1915–18*: 634.

Idriess, Ion Llewellyn. *The Desert Column: Leaves from the Diary of an Australian Trooper in Gallipoli, Sinai, and Palestine*: 81.

Jünger, Ernst. *The Storm of Steel: From the Diary of a German Storm-Troop Officer on the Western Front*: 315.

Kelly, R. B. Talbot. *A Subaltern's Odyssey: Memoirs of the Great War, 1915–1917*: 667.

King, Olive. *One Woman at War: Letters of Olive King, 1915–1920*: 94.

Laidlaw, James Maxwell. *For King and Country*: 99.

Lawrence, Cyril. *The Gallipoli Diary of Sergeant Lawrence of the Australian Engineers, 1st A.I.F., 1915*; sequel, *Sergeant Lawrence Goes to France*: 101.

Leland, Claude Granger. *From Shell Hole to Château with Company I; Personal Recollections of a Line Officer of the 107th U.S. Infantry, 27th Division, in France, 1918*: 1178.

Lucy, John. *There's a Devil in the Drum*: 707.

Lynch, John William. *Princess Patricia's Canadian Light Infantry, 1917–1919*: 1189.

Mackin, Elton. *Suddenly We Didn't Want to Die: Memoirs of a World War I Marine*: 1198.

Marks, Thomas Penrose. *The Laughter Goes from Life: in the Trenches of the First World War*: 722.

Millard, Shirley. *I Saw Them Die: Diary and Recollections of Shirley Millard*: 1216.

Murray, Joseph. *Gallipoli as I Saw It*: 754.

Ogle, Henry. *The Fateful Battle Line: The Great War Journals and Sketches of Captain Henry Ogle, MC*: 768.

Paton, Alexander Watson. *Occasional Gunfire: Private War Diary of a Siege Gunner*: 785.

Pedley, James H. *Only this: A War Retrospect, 1917–1918*: 252.

Plowman, Max [pseud. Mark VII]. *A Subaltern on the Somme in 1916*: 790.

Potter, R. C. *Not Theirs the Shame Who Fight: Edited Selections from the World War I Diaries, Poems and Letters of 6080 Private R. C. (Cleve) Potter, A Company 21st Battalion A.I.F.*: 136.

Read, I. L. *Of Those We Loved*: 801.

Renn, Ludwig. *War*: 329.

Richards, Frank. *Old Soldiers Never Die*: 806.

Roosevelt, Kermit. *War in the Garden of Eden*: 1296.

Rosenhainer, Ernst. *Forward March! Memoirs of a German Officer*: 335.

Sassoon, Siegfried. *The Complete Memoirs of George Sherston*: 828.

Shephard, Ernest. *A Sergeant-Major's War: from Hill 60 to the Somme*: 837.

Triplet, William S. *A Youth in the Meuse-Argonne: A Memoir, 1917–1918*: 1358.

Subject Index

(References are to entry numbers)

About the Author

Edward Lengel holds a Ph.D. in European History from the University of Virginia, where he currently is an Associate Professor and editor on the staff of the Papers of George Washington documentary editing project. He is the author of several books and articles on European and military history.